THE HUMOR OF
KIERKEGAARD

AN ANTHOLOGY

Søren Kierkegaard

Edited and Introduced by
Thomas C. Oden

PRINCETON UNIVERSITY PRESS

PRINCETON AND OXFORD

Published by Princeton University Press, 41 William Street, Princeton, New Jersey 08540
In the United Kingdom: Princeton University Press, 3 Market Place, Woodstock,
Oxfordshire OX20 1SY

Library of Congress Cataloging-in-Publication Data

Kierkegaard, Søren, 1813–1855.
[Selections. English. 2004]
The humor of Kierkegaard : an anthology / Søren Kierkegaard ; edited and introduced by
Thomas C. Oden.
p.   cm.
Includes bibliographical references and index.
ISBN 0-691-07406-2 (alk. paper) — ISBN 0-691-02085-X (pbk. : alk. paper)
1. Wit and humor. 2. Kierkegaard, Søren, 1813–1855—Humor. I. Oden Thomas C.
II. Title.

B4372.E5 2004
198'.9—dc22   2003064125

British Library Cataloging-in-Publication Data is available

This book has been composed in Goudy Old Style Typeface
Printed on acid-free paper. ∞
www.pupress.princeton.edu
Printed in the United States of America

10 9 8 7 6 5 4 3 2 1

C O N T E N T S

ACKNOWLEDGMENTS

EXCERPTS from the following titles in the series Kierkegaard's Writings are used and amended by permission of Princeton University Press. Except where noted, all works in this series were edited and translated by Howard V. Hong and Edna H. Hong.

The Book on Adler, © 1998 by Postscript, Inc.

Christian Discourses (with *The Crisis and a Crisis in the Life of an Actress*), © 1997 by Postscript, Inc.

The Concept of Anxiety, edited and translated by Reidar Thomte and Albert B. Anderson © 1980 by Princeton University Press.

The Concept of Irony, with Continual Reference to Socrates, © 1989 by Howard V. Hong.

Concluding Unscientific Postscript to Philosophical Fragments, © 1992 by Howard V. Hong.

The Corsair *Affair and Articles Related to the Writings*, © 1982 by Howard V. Hong.

Early Polemical Writings, edited and translated by Julia Watkin © 1990 by Julia Watkin.

Eighteen Upbuilding Discourses, © 1990 by Howard V. Hong.

Either/Or, © 1987 by Howard V. Hong.

For Self-Examination (with *Judge for Yourself!*), © 1990 by Howard V. Hong.

Judge for Yourself! (with *For Self-Examination*), © 1990 by Howard V. Hong.

The Moment *and Late Writings*, © 1998 by Postscript, Inc.

Philosophical Fragments (with *Johannes Climacus*), © 1985 by Howard V. Hong.

THE HUMOR OF KIERKEGAARD

INTRODUCTION

KIERKEGAARD WROTE: "I consider the power in the comic a vitally necessary legitimation for anyone who is to be regarded as authorized in the world of spirit in our day" (*Concluding Unscientific Postscript to* Philosophical Fragments, ed. and trans. Howard V. Hong and Edna H. Hong [Princeton: Princeton University Press, 1992]—hereafter *CUPPF*—1:281).

Søren Kierkegaard (1813–1855; often SK hereafter) explored comic perception to its depths. He also practiced the art of comedy as astutely as any writer of his time. This collection shows how his theory of comedy is integrated into his practice of comic perception, and how both his theory and practice of comedy are integral to his entire authorship.

THE COMIC SIDE OF A
BRILLIANT MIND

What's So Funny?

In these pages you will meet a host who offers his guests a menu rather than a meal and the wife of an author who burned her husband's manuscript. You will learn of a book whose typesetting occurred through a misunderstanding. You will encounter a businessman who, even with an abundance of calling cards, forgot his own name. You will hear of an interminable vacillator whom archeologists found still pacing thousands of years later, trying to come to a decision. Then there is the emperor who became a barkeeper in order to stay in the know.

Kierkegaard's humor ranges from the droll to the rollicking, from farce to intricate, subtle analysis, from nimble stories to amusing aphorisms. Some of these selections are merely a brief fantastic flight of imagination or an amusing word picture. Think of them as flying glimpses into an outrageous comic premise. In some extracts we do not have a fully developed comic plot at all but merely a droll analogy, witty reasoning, or a ridiculous metaphor. All these levels of musings, from wild fancy to cerebral philosophical humor, are a part of the always dialectical and sometimes preposterous buffoonery that we find in SK. Still, he bears, unjustly, a reputation for deadly sobriety and unremitting melancholy.

Cautions

It is not fair to judge Kierkegaard by the standards of a modern stand-up comedian. Laughter as such is not his major objective but rather the understanding of laughter within the stages of development of the human spirit. Nonetheless, while writing intricately dialectical philosophy, he is often not only funny, but keenly aware of just why something is funny.

I implore the reader not to impose contemporary standards of humor on a nineteenth-century writer. Comic perception is often subtly geared to its own distinctive culture and language, hence difficult to transpose and not always easily translatable. This doubles the challenge of putting together a collection of this sort, which aims to reveal Kierkegaard's best comic moments without explaining them ad nauseum. If two hundred years from now someone read a collection of the best comic moments of Lewis Carroll, G. B. Shaw, P. J. O'Rouarch, or Woody Allen, they would miss some nuances that would be understandable only in our own particular cultural context. But there would still be a lot that would be amusing. So with SK.

In making these selections I have not sought to sustain any particular level of comic intensity throughout. This is not a Marx brothers movie. Do not expect every line to be hilarious, but do anticipate in each episode some level of comic incongruity. Consider this an unhurried venture into the leisurely writings of a brilliant author who is enjoying himself immensely as he pushes and challenges and seduces his reader.

My primary criterion in evaluating a particular passage has been single-minded and simple: Is it funny to me? I am asking not how important it is to world history or to the vast corpus of Kierkegaardian literature nor whether it contains deep philosophical insight or enriches self-awareness—only whether it is amusing. I admit to enjoying the privileged and highly subjective position of editor; I have tried not to exploit it. If you see something in this collection that you think is not so funny, be gentle, and at least be assured that someone else thinks it is. And remember: it is possible that you might have missed something.

For Whom?

This collection is for anyone ready to be amused by human follies. Even if you have never read a page of Kierkegaard, you may well find him to be a dazzling mind worth meeting. He is determined to entertain you.

This collection can be used like a crowbar, wedging open a treasure chest containing the literary craftsmanship of an otherwise complex and difficult philosophical figure.

Some may have read Kierkegaard intensively without having ever really noticed his comic side. Here they will find what they have been missing. Others will come to this collection already having read SK extensively, already aware of his comedic style, yet wanting to see it set forth and illustrated more fully. Here they will find the best of it. Some academic readers may even already be somewhat familiar with his theory of comedy but would like to see it concisely set forth and adequately exemplified. I welcome all these readers with the caveat that they will not find in this book a labored discussion of Kierkegaard's theory of comedy (aside from this spare introduction). It is primarily a modest collection of some instances of it. But I hope these few examples will do it at least partial justice. The selections that follow include both his thoughts on humor and examples of his humor.

Kierkegaard is addressing "that single individual" whom he affectionately called "my reader"—as if to say my one and only reader, one who has elected to risk entering into Kierkegaard's own special world of reflection on human existence, his unique authorship. The collection is not designed primarily to serve a small coterie of veteran Kierkegaard aficionados but rather "my reader." As I made my selections (from a vast supply of possibilities), I tried to keep these hawk-eyed veteran Kierkegaard specialists out of my mind. I know these experts are out there, and some may be ready to pounce upon my choices, for sins of either commission or omission. Nonetheless, even to seasoned readers, this collection may help identify stories or episodes they have read at sometime but cannot recall precisely where in the vast sea of Kierkegaard's sentences. The indices, topical arrangement, and editorial apparatus are especially designed to help readers, old and new, to locate themes, aphorisms, raucous images, and amusing ideas quickly.

The erudite are those, in Kierkegaard's view, most prone to ignore or misinterpret the comic dimension. It is to the "assistant professor" that Kierkegaard assigns the role of being the most "devoid of comic power," and the least likely to grasp his or her own comic contradictions. "A ludicrous sullenness and paragraph-pomposity that give an assistant professor a remarkable likeness to a Holberg bookkeeper are called earnestness by assistant professors" (*CUPPF* 1:281).

The Gauntlet

This prompts a more serious question: Who might reasonably be nominated as the funniest philosopher of all time? I want to throw down this gauntlet: Bundle together any other ten philosophers who have made a major impact in the history of philosophy. I challenge any reader to assemble a selection of humor from all of them put together that is funnier than what you find in this volume of Kierkegaard.

Until this challenge is answered successfully, I provisionally declare Søren Aabye Kierkegaard (despite his enduring stereotype as the melancholy, despairing Dane) as, among philosophers, the most amusing. Just think of the frail, awkward, crippled Magister Kierkegaard actually being entered into Guinness' *World Book of Records*! He might also be the world's funniest psychologist and the world's funniest theologian, but I do not wish to exaggerate.

Whether There Is Any Scholarly Legitimation for Such a Project

I do not pretend to enter this batch of stories into some solemn arena in which it was never intended to compete. Such an entry would be, as Kierkegaard quips, "as welcome as a dog in a game of bowls" (*Kierkegaard's Concluding Unscientific Postscript*, trans. David Swenson, [ed.] Walter Lowrie [Princeton: Princeton University Press, © 1941]— hereafter *CUPPF-L*—p. 29). Nor can it be my purpose to justify why a particular narrative is funny; the secondary corpus is already too heavily weighted with tedious footnotes to burden it with more. Readers who want help with SK's many allusions are referred to the Princeton University Press series Kierkegaard's Writings (hereafter KW).

Think of this collection simply as entertainment with no noble purpose. Any learning or edification or wisdom derived is wholly incidental and inadvertent. Furthermost from my mind is a work of moral counsel or religious instruction. Let these pages serve as a deserved break from heavy chores. After having committed the sin of writing thousands of scholarly footnotes in my previous books on ethics, theology, and patristic studies, I have been told that my pedantry dues are fully paid up. I can now break free from such expectations, and the reader can break free from insisting upon them.

Admittedly, it is true that I could not have accomplished this task without having taught repeatedly, for a quarter-century, a graduate seminar on Kierkegaard at Drew University and directed weighty dissertations on his work. But my purpose here is not to add to an already ponderous burden of bibliographies on Kierkegaard.

SK teaches us how to revel in the comedy of the contradictions inherent to human existence. I want to dispel the dreary myth that SK is full of despair, would never be caught laughing, and that waves of his despair flood like the surf into the reader's consciousness. In addition, this volume, I suppose, might serve some function at the lectern, in the pulpit, and on the after-dinner dais, with its topics and indices so conveniently arranged for easy access.

The Editorial Apparatus

Following Howard and Edna Hong's protocol in *Søren Kierkegaard's Journals and Papers* (ed. and trans. Howard V. Hong and Edna H. Hong, 4 vols. [Bloomington: Indiana University Press, 1967–75]— hereafter *JP*), a series of five periods (. . . . .) indicates an ellipsis found in the Danish text and English translation, whereas a three-dot ellipsis (. . .), sometimes following a period, indicates an omission I have made to eliminate extraneous material. To facilitate smooth reading, I have begun all excerpts with a capital letter whether or not there was a capital at that point in the original.

This volume is intended to serve as a sequel to one I previously assembled, *Parables of Kierkegaard*, published in 1978 by Princeton University Press, which has remained in print with a steady readership for almost a quarter-century. Untold numbers of readers have treasured his narrative genius as exhibited in that collection. When asked about a sequel, I thought the next obvious step would be a long-awaited collection of his humorous stories. Following basically the pattern of *Parables of Kierkegaard*, each selection begins with a *topical heading* in the upper left corner, followed by a *centered title* and a *lead question*. The lead question frames the situation in which the passage appears; the topical heading gives it focus; the title names it. None of this editorial bridging is supplied by Kierkegaard; it is derived from the context and suggests something of the argument surrounding the selection without intruding on the reader's discovery. All this is to save the reader's time and avoid the necessity of writing a dreary essay about each comic episode. The format also assists the reader in locating quickly the issue or concern central to the selection.

Since I have chosen to arrange these selections by theme rather than voice, after each selection the voice speaking (if other than SK's) has been noted in brackets. Where no pseudonymous voice is indicated, it is Kierkegaard's own voice. A dash (—) before the title indicates that a single title is being referenced in a multititled volume.

Wherever the concept of "Christendom" appears, I have ordinarily enclosed it in quotation marks, to remind the reader that what is meant is not Christianity as such but so-called Christianity, especially of the sort that prevailed in nineteenth-century Denmark.

An asterisk indicates that a translation has been amended. I have sometimes divided long sentences with semicolons into shorter sentences, reduced archaisms, and shifted punctuation for easier reading. Where more than one translation of a selection was available, I carefully examined the differences. The literary quality of some of the earlier translations of Kierkegaard into English in my view equals or exceeds the later translation. I have made a meticulous case-by-case decision, in most cases preferring the rendition of Howard and Edna Hong, but in some cases that of Walter Lowrie or David F. Swenson or some other translator. The titles of Kierkegaard's works may appear differently in various translations, and where they do, the book title used indicates by inference the translator, as in the case of *Attack on "Christendom"* (Lowrie) or *The Moment* (Hong and Hong). KW (Kierkegaard's Writings) is always a clue that the current Princeton critical edition is being used. (If KW does not appear in the reference, the extract has been taken from some other source.) Thus the bibliography of primary sources contains both older and newer translations.

Text and Context

Is this or any other anthology justified in lifting texts out of their contexts? Some texts have some measure of narrative detachability. These are the ones I have tended to select, the ones that can transfer as independent narratives (anecdotes or comic metaphors) out of the larger text without too much deadly explanatory background. The reader may explore the context further as desired.

Literary purists may complain. What a shame to cut the text up into little pieces! How negligent to miss the context! (Implicitly: How offensive to contextuality to assemble any anthology whatever!) With the purists I agree, so far as purity goes. Those who want the text rather than an anthology will surely be happier putting this book down immediately and reading the full, uncut text rather than any editor's short selections. But purists may forget that there are others not so pure who need a map to travel the countryside.

It is the editor's task to set parameters that serve the reader. This I have done by deciding not to weight this book heavily with clarifications of Kierkegaard's probable intent. That, though possible to do, and tempting for any scholar, would hardly have served the ordinary reader's interest.

I have gleaned these selections from SK's published authorship, leaving aside his journals and papers to be explored by another scholar. I have deliberately avoided selections that appeared in my previous anthology on Kierkegaard and have largely tried not to repeat selections that have appeared in other anthologies. To Kierkegaard experts who can't find their favorite story in this collection, I would commend *The Laughter Is on My Side* (ed. Roger Poole and Henrik Stangerup [Princeton: Princeton University Press, 1989]).

Søren as a One-Man Performance

As I have assembled this collection, I have often fantasized of a one-man show in which an actor portraying Kierkegaard might narrate some of this material in his own name, and then assume different masks or hats to represent Kierkegaard's various fictional personae. Others intrigued by such a fantasy could use this book as a resource, selecting from it the episodes suited to their particular thematic interests.

So I invite you to think of all these many pseudonymous voices as a one-man comic performance, expressing the contradictions of life through a series of outrageous and often disreputable characters, not all of whom speak in Kierkegaard's own personal voice. Pseudonyms like John the Seducer and Judge William do not self-evidently or directly represent SK's views any more than Falstaff or Iago represent Shakespeare's. But through all of these voices Kierkegaard describes alternative modes of consciousness and relationship. A clarification of the pseudonyms does not belong in this inquiry but is readily available in the secondary literature.

THE THEORY OF COMEDY

Most of the major themes of Kierkegaard's authorship can be observed, and even studied, through the window of his humor. His theory of humor stands up well against others in the history of ideas: those of Aristotle, Schopenhauer, Bergson, Freud, and Suzanne Langer, among others. This study could be an undergraduate's first look at the intellectual life and language games of modern academia. But no doubt SK would forewarn us that this would diminish the seriousness of the university curriculum.

Despite my resistances, I have supplied the following brief account of Kierkegaard's intriguing theory of humor. Although it makes the overture a little long and delays the performance, I have conceded this. I say "resistances" and "conceded" because when this manuscript was first produced in 1993, the publisher requested a more scholarly introduction, and I resisted and parried for almost ten years. Why did I resist? As an editor, I thought this would be the dullest part of an otherwise stimulating book. I may have been wrong all along. In any case I urge the impatient reader to skip over this theoretical section if not intensely dedicated. I refer really serious readers to the last two hundred pages of *Concluding Unscientific Postscript to Philosophical Fragments*, and to *The Concept of Irony* for SK's own extensive thoughts on ironic and comic analysis. To those wishing to see a useful analysis of Kierkegaard's theory of comedy, I commend Lloyd Ellison Parrill's ("The Concept of Humor in the Pseudonymous Works of Søren Kierkegaard" diss., Drew University, 1975—hereafter CH) written under my direction. Long before that the seeds of this volume were planted in conversations with H. Richard Niebuhr, Joseph Mathews, and W.B.J. Martin.

Contradiction as the Defining Category of the Comic

"The category of the comic is essentially contradiction" (*JP* 2:266 [1737]). "If a king disguised himself as a butcher and a butcher happened to resemble the king in a striking way, people would laugh at both of them, but for opposite reasons—at the butcher because he was not the king, and at the king because he was not the butcher" (*JP* 2:267 [1744]). The comic incongruities hinge on the fact that we expect a king to be a king and a butcher to be a butcher, so far apart are they in social location and prestige. That social distance makes funny the very thought that each might be disguised to look like the other.

Kierkegaard tells the story of a horsefly that "sat on a man's nose the very moment he made his last running leap to throw himself into the Thames" (*JP* 2:257 [1697]). The extreme seriousness of suicide is here utterly incongruous with the entirely accidental landing of the fly.

Among SK's earliest writings is the outline of a play called "The Battle between the Old and the New Soap-Cellars." The name comes from a fierce competition between rival soap dealers near the University of Copenhagen, one of whom had a sign that read "Here is the genuine old soap-cellar where the genuine old soap-cellar people live." His rival's sign: "Here is the new soap-cellar; the old soap-cellar people moved in on May 1, 1808" (*Early Polemical Writings*, ed. and trans. Julia Watkin [Princeton: Princeton University Press, 1990], 260n). In this play, Kierkegaard includes as one of his characters "A Fly, who has wisely wintered for many years with the late Hegel and who has been so fortunate as to have sat on his immortal nose several times during the composition of his work: *Phaenomenologie des Geistes*" (*Early Polemical Writings* 106).

Comic perception is drawn to incongruity, especially when the incongruity is unexpected or accidental: "Just as a shriek wrung from pain could very well appear to be laughable to someone at a great distance who had no intimation of the situation of the person from whom it came, just as the twitch of a smile on the face of a deaf-mute or a taciturn person could appear to someone to be laughable" (*JP* 2:260 [1706]). Kierkegaard does not hesitate to push his comic analogies to gross extremes: he imagines a man who pretends to let "himself be skinned alive in order to show how the humorous smile is produced by the contraction of a particular muscle—and thereupon follows this with a lecture on humor" (*JP* 2:262 [1718]). The comic incongruity lies in the contrast between the safe setting of the lecture hall and a man presumably being skinned alive in order to demonstrate that an involuntary contraction of a tiny muscle appears to be a smile.

Kierkegaard tells the story of the "man who, standing two miles away from the windmill, makes it go by laying his finger on one nostril and blowing through the other" (*JP* 2:257 [1695]). The comic incongruity (here I am explaining what I promise not to explain in the performance itself) is that one nostril could never affect a windmill two miles away. The nose itself is that part of the face that most easily yields to comic caricature. If the man blew through his mouth or if the windmill were only two feet away, there would be proportionally less incongruity, and hence less comedy.

"A drunken man can have such a comic effect because he expresses a contradiction of motion. The eye insists upon evenness in walking; the more there is some reason to insist upon it, the more comic is the effect of the contradiction (thus a stone-drunk person is less comic). If a superior, for example, comes along and the drunken man, aware of him, wants to pull himself together and walk straight, the comic becomes more obvious because the contradiction becomes more obvious. He succeeds for a few steps, until the spirit of contradiction once again carries him away. If he succeeds completely while passing by his superior, the contradiction becomes a different one, that we know he is drunk and yet this is not visible. In the one case, we laugh at him when he staggers because the eye insists upon evenness; in the other case, we laugh at him because he is holding himself straight when our knowing that he is drunk insists upon seeing him stagger" (*CUPPF* 1:516–17n).

Locating Comic Contradiction within the Human Contradiction

Understanding comic consciousness requires understanding human nature in its three existential stages: aesthetic, ethical, and religious. It is fairly easy to locate the stage in which one is currently operating if one understands comic sensibilities. And it is easy to see where a person stands in the "stages on life's way" by looking toward how that person experiences and understands the comic.

The dynamic between existing and suffering is the heart of comic perception. That dynamic reveals a person's grasp of the contradiction which the human self *is*. "On the whole, the comic is present everywhere, and every existence can at once be defined and assigned to its particular sphere by knowing how it is related to the comic"

(*CUPPF* 1:462). To run short of a comic sense is to lack an essential aspect of matured self-awareness.

Here is the theoretical part of this book, about which readers have already been forewarned. Take a deep breath for a thousand-fathom plunge.

Extreme Opposites Constitute the Human Self

Human existence is a synthesis of extreme opposites that make for ironic-comic awareness:

- body/soul
- temporality/eternity
- possibility/necessity
- finitude/freedom

These contradictories give comedy plenty to play off of: I exist as a body here and now, yet I also remain, through reason and fantasy, capable of imagining infinite possibilities worlds away. I am a finite body in time while also being a self in relation to eternity. The human situation is by these very polarities enmeshed in ongoing contradictions "of the extremest opposites," caught in persistent discrepancies, hence fraught with pathos and existential suffering, characterized by the uneasiness of freedom with itself. *The very arena in which the comic appears is a juxtaposition of these opposites—internally conflicted passion—which is the most basic feature of being human.* It is in this unremitting interplay, of finitude and freedom, temporality and eternity, that human life is daily lived out. Hence *incommensurability, polarity, and contradiction are the always-available makings of comedy.* Incongruity is the feast on which comedy feeds.

Thesis: This incommensurability is seen at its apogee in the religious consciousness, in which *the temporality/eternity incongruities are heightened to the utmost in suffering, but finally transmuted in Christianity, which views the human situation in the light of the Incarnation. This event is the most humorous and unexpected reversal: God is born into time to save humanity, whereby the comic is resolved in praise.*

12

How the Comic Appears in the Stages on Life's Way

Comic consciousness is viewed in relation to a distinct sequence of modes of existence:

immediacy,
  immediacy with reflection, ⟩
    aesthetic existence,
      irony,
        ethical existence,
          comic perception,
            suffering and guilt,
              immanent forms of religious consciousness, and
              Christianity.

Comic forms of self-deception and self-recognition are seen in all of these stages, viewed in relation to the mutations of passion and pathos that accompany this sequence or journey of stages.

Simply put, the comic can best be analyzed, as can the rest of human existence, in terms of esthetic, ethical, and religious stages along life's way.

The comic is always based on an experienced contradiction or incongruity. Christianity is blessed with many such incongruities: God in time, joy amid suffering, sin forgiven. Hence Christianity is the most humorous of all forms of religion (JP 2:252–53 [1682]; JP 2:255 [1689]).

Stages or Spheres of Relationship to Existence as Platform for the Comic

Comic episodes may appear at any of these stages:

the unreflective immediacy of the *aesthetic* stage,
  its movement into immediacy with reflection,
    its recognition of the necessity of *ethical* decision,
      its despair over the necessity of decision,
        its recognition of suffering and guilt,
          its relating to the *religious* ground of its existence

in faith, and finally

> the joy of living with suffering amid time as
> viewed in relation to eternity.

The more one enters into a relation with oneself, an active recognition of who one is as body/soul, temporal/eternal incongruence, the more one becomes a self, owns one's personhood and personal freedom, the more one is welcomed into comic consciousness.

The comic appears at each stage along life's way (aesthetic, ethical, and religious), but has a essential relation with the religious, and especially with Christianity, where the self is understood decisively in relation to the Incarnation and the Atonement.

HOW THE COMIC APPEARS IN AESTHETIC CONSCIOUSNESS

What Kierkegaard means by the aesthetic is very close to what Augustine meant by the natural human condition and what Luther meant by natural man prior to the law. The three stages which Augustine described as human existence under *nature*, under *law*, and under *grace*, Luther delineated as natural, legal, and evangelical existence. Kierkegaard is appropriating this familiar sequence in his description of aesthetic, ethical, and religious existence.

His early pseudonyms are replete with comic forms of aesthetic strife. The comic appears in aesthetic consciousness in the voices of Kierkegaard's pseudonymous masks: John the Seducer, Hilarius Bookbinder, the Fashion Designer, Nicolaus Notabene, etcetera. The prototype of the first stage, aesthetic existence, is a Young Man who is known in *Either/Or* only as "A." There is much that is amusing about "A," which Judge William, the prototype of ethical criticism, is constantly pointing out.

Despairing over their human limitations or possibilities or both, the aesthetic non-deciders and can't-deciders such as "A" elicit comic occasions in abundance. These incongruities are viewed by "A" as misfortunes, not as essential, ongoing expressions of the human contradiction; to him they are accidental, not intrinsic, to the human situation. These comic contradictions are so built into human existence that they keep presenting the aesthetic way of life with challenges to grow beyond its despair and frustration. Typically the aesthete responds to each of them by fleeing from himself (= despair), grieving over the sorry and irrevocable nature of finite human freedom. That is, he does not want this freedom (but cannot get rid of it), and at the same time wishes it were infinite.

Kierkegaard tells the story of "One who walked along contemplating suicide—at that very moment a stone fell down and killed him, and he ended with the words: Praise the Lord!" (JP 2:249 [1672]). The incongruity of this situation is that suicide is a violent act of freedom against oneself, whereas the entirely coincidental falling of the stone, which kills him without involving his intention, is briefly glimpsed by the dying man as an unexpected gift or blessing, hence a reason for praise. He no longer has the burden of ending his own life, since it is happily ended by an absurd, unexpected falling stone. This is an example of contradiction, and it appears within the sphere of the aesthetic because it is focused on pain avoidance.

There is a keen awareness of finite limitation in the earliest (aesthetic, immediate) stage. The aesthetic character constantly fantasizes infinite possibilities within these limitations. He gasps for possibility. His motto: Give me air! Yet in gasping for possibility, one remains here and now always enmeshed in finitude. Aesthetic existence wants desperately to escape into possibility, but that is never accessible to a person who dwells in time.

The aesthete fixates upon the self's keen awareness of its vulnerabilities, whether in the direction of an inordinate assertion of freedom or an inordinate compliance with destiny. The aesthete wishes despairingly to go back to the fantasized situation of total non-risk. He seeks to be eternally happy in time, but that is not possible without meeting and dealing with suffering and guilt. This is precisely what constitutes the chronic frustration of the aesthete (or "esthete" as the translation requires).

The Resolve to Marry as the Prototype of Decision Making

The transition from aesthetic to ethical consciousness appears in the correspondence between the two major figures of *Either/Or*: the Young Man or "A" (aesthetic archetype) and Judge William (ethical archetype). They are presumably good friends, one young and unestablished, the other older and established, who differ in viewpoint, especially toward marriage. Their interaction constitutes the dynamic

drama of Kierkegaard's first masterpiece, *Either/Or* (ed. and trans. Howard V. Hong and Edna H. Hong [Princeton: Princeton University Press, 1987]—hereafter *E/O*), *Either* being the papers of "A," col‑
× lected by William Afham, and *Or* the observations of Judge William.

The key to the transition from aesthetic to ethical existence is seen in the decision to marry. In this presumably irrevocable decision, one transmutes erotic love into covenant fidelity. The ethical relation to existence is expressed prototypically in the marriage vows and their fulfillment, whereby eroticism is constrained and nurtured by enduring commitment and fidelity. The erotic in marriage stands under moral and social requirement, and does so in relation to eternity. The aesthetic consciousness views the erotic as a spontaneous pursuit of pleasure, while the ethical consciousness views the erotic as a commitment between two persons with the welfare of children in mind. One who lives in ethical consciousness has already learned how to bind time. But aesthete's awareness of time is focused more primitively on immediacy, on avoiding pain and seeking gratification now. The ethical relation with time is always placed in a durable time-frame, a decisive commitment that binds time. This decision is what the aesthete studiously (and comically) avoids.

In the commitment to marriage, the erotic is seen not only in relation to the whole of one's life but also in relation to eternity. Time is bound in relation to eternity. That is what is freely agreed in the wedding vows. Marriage binds time in the context of one's accountability to eternity, in an irrevocable commitment of one's erotic energies in relation to the whole of time, and beyond time. That is what makes marriage so frightening to the aesthete and so comforting in the ethical sphere.

How does the comic find its way into this transition? Both ironic and comic perception are always acutely attentive to present incongruities and contradictions, wherever they emerge. Endless situational incongruities arise as one moves from indecision to decision, from singleness to marriage, from "Either/Or" (deciding) to "Or" (having decided). These indecisions are narrated in the aesthetic pseudonyms, and the need for decision is invoked in ethical pseudonyms. There is much comic potential embedded in this solemn event of marriage and its consequences.

16

Binding Time in the Transition from Aesthetic to Ethical Consciousness

Any decision binding time challenges the self to move beyond the esthetic into the ethical sphere of existence. Ethical existence is not understood just in terms of the decision to marry but in relation to any decision to bind time in durable commitment. Yet marriage is undoubtedly its most solemn and obvious example. The ethical binds eroticism within time in the presence of eternity.

What incongruities appear at this juncture, the moment of deciding to marry? This, in fact, is the moment the young male aesthetes of SK's "Banquet" face and debate and bungle and try fitfully to work through. The aesthetic life does not want to give up the free possibilities that abound prior to decision making. It accentuates the real or pretended pleasures of the moment and seeks to avoid its limitations. This is precisely how aesthetic consciousness is focused: maximize pleasure now, avoid suffering. Yet suffering is the doorway to becoming more fully human, more aware, more fully oneself.

Irony

The way to comic perceptions is always being signaled by irony. What is irony? SK illustrates: "In the case of Swift, it was an irony of fate that in his old age he entered the insane asylum he himself had erected in his early years" (*JP* 2:264 [1727]; cf. *E/O* 1:21, *Stages on Life's Way*, ed. and trans. Howard V. Hong and Edna H. Hong [Princeton: Princeton University Press, 1988], 99–200).

Irony is at work throughout aesthetic existence to reveal its incongruities and to prepare the way for the comic. Irony is not merely a literary genre but "a mode of existence, and there is nothing more absurd than to suppose that it is a manner of speech, or for an author to congratulate himself on having here and there expressed himself ironically. Whoever essentially possesses irony possesses it as long as the day lasts, and it is fettered to no form because it is the expression in him, of infinity" (*Søren Kierkegaards Samlede Værker*, ed. A. B. Drachmann et al., 14 vols. [Copenhagen: Gyldendals, 1901–6]— hereafter SV—7:438; cf. Hermann Diem, "The Dialectician's Irony and Humour," *Kierkegaard's Dialectic of Existence*, trans. Harold Knight [Edinburgh: Oliver and Boyd, 1959]—hereafter KDE—44).

Socrates was the supreme master of irony. He worked by pretending ignorance and asking questions. His maieutic (birth-assisting) method helped the learner walk through human incongruities first by recognizing them and then by seeking the truth, immanent already within oneself, that will to resolve or transcend them. By presuming ignorance in the questioner and asking questions about the truth as if already embedded in the learner, Socrates was constantly moving the learner through this indirect communication toward a greater recognition of the truth and of selfhood.

The movement of irony at its early stages proceeds by indirect communication. This is a necessary process of revealing the truth to the self-deceived, which is not otherwise possible because of self-deception. SK does this brilliantly by means of pseudonymous voices describing episodes of consciousness and decision during these stages and substages. A consciousness aware of irony every moment will draw the learner toward recognition of the incongruities and deceptions that pervade aesthetic consciousness. Ironic awareness moves the self from an immature pure immediacy, eroticism, despair, and finite freedom toward a maturing awareness of the ongoing human contradiction. This contradiction is constantly revealing one's own finite freedom, amid the time-eternity and soul-body relationship.

The contradiction which *is* human existence is manifested prototypically in the decision to be married, or to back out of a decision to marry, which "binds time" erotically—or any other decision that binds time. Kierkegaard's own personal history was full of these ambivalences. Any vocational decision to which one is committing oneself over time is prone to expose the human contradiction. The more the aesthete is frustrated by the constraints of finitude, the more he glimpses the unremitting incongruence in which the body-soul relationship (which is the self) constantly exists.

The incognito of irony and the potentiality of humor accompany any decision requiring time-binding choice. The person who is deciding to bind time, hence moving from the aesthetic to the ethical, is caught in various moments of incongruity that irony reveals and comedy transmutes into jest. The ironic-comic dynamics of the aesthetic stages are only adequately grasped from the viewpoint of the subsequent stages of ethical and religious consciousness.

Ironic consciousness beholds and reveals the contradiction between who one is and how one misconstrues who one is. The pose of the clergy, the gossip with a forbearing smile, etcetera—the ironist sees through these, searching for the truth of how they reveal one's relation to one's existence. The ironist is always keenly aware of the extraordinary difficulty of being human. His spyglass is focused on the arena between ideal self-image and actual behavior. Imagine an actor who says on stage: "It is I who speak, these are my words—and then has not a single word to say the second the prompter is silent" (JP 2:225 [1616]). The incongruity lies in his claiming ownership of words he does not own.

Repetition and recollection play into a comic perception of aesthetic consciousness. In recollection one hopes to recapture a moment of pleasure, or repeat it, or sustain it in time. Meanwhile time continues to spin away to another moment, always fleeting, constantly pursued.

Locating Irony within the Stages

Although the ironic mode of existence may appear in any stage, it lurks especially in the transitions and interfaces between aesthetic and ethical existence. It grasps and reveals by indirect communication the incongruence between the universal ethical requirement and the uncertainties of finitude. When the demands of absolute truth telling collide with the demands and special finite conditions of the moment, the critique of the ironist hovers over that collision, ready to leap into action.

"A pastor who uses a manuscript in the pulpit and steals a look at it. Just at the moment when, with a bold, sweeping, upward motion, he says the words, 'The soul rises upward,' [with feeling], he discovers he has not looked at the manuscript long enough to make such an expansive gesture—and he must now look at the paper" (JP 2:269 [1750]). The contradiction in this case lies in the pretentious motion contrasted with the humbling necessity of having to look at the paper to see where his sweeping gesture was supposed to lead. Thus he himself made his gesture comic by shifting abruptly from imagined infinitude to the lowliness of the finite.

Again: "A man knows that God exists—and he says: I know it, damn it all!" (JP 2:268 [1747]). The comic incongruity here lies in the avowed certainty that God exists contrasted with the ambiguity implied in the frustration.

Irony reveals the problem, not its resolution. Its expertise lies in revealing that hidden part of esthetic existence in which the self is afraid to disclose itself to itself. It sees the incongruent side of both singleness and marriage, of both indecision and decision. The incongruent side is already anticipatively the funny side.

HOW THE COMIC APPEARS IN THE TRANSITIONS FROM AESTHETIC TO ETHICAL EXISTENCE

Judge William has a very different perspective on eroticism than does the aesthetic Young Man, "A." The judge is settled, happy, erotically fulfilled through commitment, at home in the ethical world, binding time through his longstanding marital and vocational decisions. There are many flashes of comic perception in Judge William, as we see in volume 2 (*Or*) of *Either/Or*, where he comments upon the aesthetic characters.

Although the Young Man is brilliantly filled with despair, there are many scintillating comic moments in his self-perception. They are largely an expression of his frustration with the limits of his finitude or the unboundedness of his freedom. The aesthetic pseudonyms rehearse Kierkegaard's own struggle first to decide to marry and then to decide not to marry, his own tendency to be attracted to a vocation and then to back away from it. The pathos of the aesthete is that he cannot choose between "either" and "or," which leaves him despairing over his freedom and destiny. The aesthete is aware of the self's contradictions but despairs of finding any way out of them (CH 48). Seeing no way out, the aesthetic author of the *Diapsalmata* laughs the laughter of despair (CH 51). The aesthete is always making the comic assumption that the contradiction which constitutes selfhood can be thought, but with each thought finds he cannot live it out. He conceives of something good immediately and individualistically (for me, right now, rather than for all in the long run).

The ethical consciousness, on the other hand, conceives of good socially and historically and for the whole, not for the individual or the present moment only. Ethical awareness views the individual's good in relation to some universal conception of the good. One is placed within a system of human organization, within an economic process, not immediately as a here-and-now individual, but in relation to a larger flow of shared historic values and social goods. Ethical consciousness is a movement toward the law, toward the universal good, toward living with choice and guilt.

Sampling Moments of Comic Contradiction

"The comic is always based upon contradiction. If a man tries to establish himself as a tavern keeper and fails, this is not comic. However, if a girl tries to get permission to establish herself as a prostitute and fails, which sometimes happens, this is comic—very comic, inasmuch as it contains many contradictions" (JP 2:266 [1741]). The contrast lies in the illegitimacy which tries to legitimize itself—that is funny—but even more so in that it fails! That brings together a double valence of contradictions. The tavern keeper is only trying to be a tavern keeper, not a part of the establishment. "If the tavern keeper was debarred because there were so many of them, it would not be comical, but if he were debarred because there were so few, it would be a laughing matter, just as when a baker upon being asked for something by a poor person answered: No, Mother, you cannot get anything; we cannot give to everybody; there was another one here recently, and he didn't get anything either" (JP 2:267 [1742]).

SK loves to force incongruities into extremes for comic effect, as in the story of the child baptized as a Hegelian: "All that was lacking was for Hegelian philosophy to have also a visible custom such as baptism, an act which could be performed with small children. Thus one could bring it to the point where babies fourteen days old would be everything, Hegelians as well. And if a person baptized at fourteen days as a Hegelian were to announce himself as a Hegelian, if a watchman, for example, had his child baptized as a Hegelian and then brought the child up to the best of his humble abilities and the child had no special aptitudes and grew up to become a watchman too—but also a Hegelian—would this not be ridiculous?" (JP 2:221 [1609]). The unpretentious child becomes a baptized Hegelian watchman, doing an ordinary job but with pretensions.

SK spies out these moments avidly: "I wish I could see through the crowns of hats when people hold their hats in front of their eyes to pray; I dare say faces would be caught there which physiognomists have not yet described" (*JP* 2:213 [1586]). The presumed solemnity of prayer conflicts with the contorted body language of unconscious facial expressions.

"Insofar as money is a something, the relativity between richer and poorer is not comic, but if it is token money, it is comic that it is a relativity" (*CUPPF* 1:555). Money is supposed to be reliable, but not token money. To think that token money has clout is funny, and funnier the more clout it is thought to have.

"Caricature is comic. By what means? By means of the contradiction between likeness and unlikeness. The caricature must resemble a person, indeed, an actual, specific person. If it resembles no one at all, it is not comic but a direct attempt at meaningless fantasy. The shadow of a man on a wall while you are sitting and talking with him can have a comic effect because it is the shadow of the man with whom one is speaking (the contradiction: that one at the same time sees that it is not he). If one sees the same shadow on the wall but there is no man or if one sees the shadow and does not see the man, that is not comic. The more the man's actuality is accentuated, the more comic the shadow becomes" (*CUPPF* 1:517n).

Suppose a ship is sinking, and passengers and crew are frenetically running around in circles. What is comic in the freneticism is the contradiction that "despite all this movement" no one is moving any closer to being safe (*CUPPF* 1:555).

When one has an idealized self-conception, he may come to fear whatever might undermine his idealization. "It is something like watching a man write with hands which tremble so much that one fears the pen will run away from him any moment into some grotesque stroke" (*JP* 2:251 [1679]). The zany incongruence here is that the imagination is awakened at the thought that the pen will itself take charge of the penman and move into the unexpected.

How Persistently the Ironic-Comic Accompanies the Spheres of Existence (Aesthetic, Ethical, Religious)

"The comic is present in every stage of life (*except that the position is different*), because where there is life there is contradiction, and wherever there is contradiction, the comic is present" (*CUPPF* 1: 513–14).

"There are three existence-spheres: the esthetic, the ethical, the religious. To these there is a respectively corresponding *confinium* [border territory]: irony is the *confinium* between the esthetic and the ethical; humor is the *confinium* between the ethical and the religious" (*CUPPF* 1:501–2).

Within the aesthetic relation to existence we stand on the rungs of immediacy, the pleasure principle, and finite common sense. Irony recognizes the possibility of an ethical relation to existence that transcends and challenges the aesthetic consciousness to bind time with decision.

As we ascend the ladder of John Climacus, about which we will speak later, we are moving inwardly toward intensified self-recognition. A superb map of the ladder is hidden by Kierkegaard in a footnote: "The spheres are related as follows: *immediacy; finite common sense; irony; ethics with irony as its incognito; humor; religiousness with humor as its incognito—and then, finally, the essentially Christian, distinguished by the paradoxical accentuation of existence, by the paradox, by the break with immanence, and by the absurd*" (*CUPPF* 1:531–532n, italics added). No sentence better encapsulates our study, yet it is adroitly concealed in an annotation.

Commenting on this sequence, we can visualize its transitions in the following way:

Aesthetic immediacy
  Finite common sense
    Irony
      Ethics with irony as its incognito
        Humor
          Religiousness with humor as its incognito
          Immanental (Socratic) religiousness
            Paradox, the break with immanence, and
            Christianity

Note the location of humor in the sequence: "*Humor is the last stage in existence-inwardness before faith*" (*CUPPF* 1:291, italics added). To have faith is to trust the Giver and ground of these polarities of human existence which tend toward self-contradiction. "Humor is not faith but is before faith, is not after faith or a development of faith" (*CUPPF* 1:291). Like Moses glimpsing the Promised Land from a distance, humor glimpses the arena of faith from afar but does not enter it. "Even when humor wants to try its hand at the paradoxes, it is not faith. Humor does not take in the suffering aspect of the paradox or the ethical aspect of faith but only the amusing aspect" (*CUPPF* 1:291).

One who has proceeded further and deeper into the existence-spheres is better able to recognize the comedy implicit in a previous sphere (*CUPPF* 1:449–50). "The comic is always a sign of maturity, and then the essential thing is only that a new shoot emerges in this maturity, that the *vis comica* [comic force] does not suffocate pathos but merely indicates that a new pathos is beginning" (*CUPPF* 1:281). While in the aesthetic phase "immediacy has the comic outside itself," the humorist discovers "the comic *within itself*" (*CUPPF* 1:521).

Aesthetic existence fails to grasp the very nature of the self in relation to eternity. Ethical existence grasps the problem but not its resolution beyond guilt. The ethical life has its terminus in guilt, which is overcome by faith in the Incarnate God who suffers for sinners.

Honing the Precise Distinction between Irony and Humor

A key point difficult to grasp: While irony is present in the transition from aesthetic to ethical consciousness, comedy is present in the transition points between the ethical and the religious. Irony reveals the pathos that characterizes the human situation. Comedy objectifies it temporarily through jest. Irony stops short of a full recognition of the implications of sin, suffering, and guilt. Comedy unveils this painful recognition. There is a deeper pathos at work in humor than in irony. For in humor it is not merely finitude or misfortune but freely willed sinfulness upon which everything turns.

In ironic consciousness, reality is first revealed by being camouflaged. There reality is presented to the self in the form of a disguise. When one reveals truth by disguising its appearance, the ironic is in play.

Irony unveils the hidden contradictions of aesthetic and ethical

24

existence. Comedy discovers something different: their permanence as intrinsic to human existence.

Socrates is the master of irony (CH 56), but not necessarily of humor. He constantly insisted on his own ignorance. Socrates, by ignorance, sought as an individual in time to be related to eternal truth. Ignorance is the most remote relation one can have, amid time, to eternal truth, but even the most remote relationship embodies a relationship to the truth (CH 65).

Humor, in Kierkegaard's view, embraces a more intense and decisive relation to suffering than does irony. Humor does not move merely within this-worldly premises and humanistic assumptions. Rather it points implicitly but constantly toward the incarnational premise that humanity is being enabled by grace to partake of the divine nature and has the image of God stamped precisely upon its very creaturely existence (*The Concept of Irony, with Constant Reference to Socrates*, trans. Lee M. Capel [Bloomington: Indiana University Press, 1968, © 1965]—hereafter CI—341–42). Some aspect of comedy always hints gently of the Incarnation, the most exceptional of all events, the "offense" of God entering time.

The ironist grasps the contradiction between the ethical, with its infinite requirement, and everything finite. The humorist evokes the deeper contradiction between the God-idea and everything else, between the incomparably Existent One, the holy, and all that falls short of that One (*CUPPF* 1:507–18; cf. CH 137).

The last paragraph of *The Concept of Irony* brilliantly describes this transition: "Finally, insofar as there may be a question concerning irony's 'eternal validity,' this question can be answered only by entering into the realm of humor. Humor has a far more profound skepticism than irony, because here the focus is on sinfulness, not on finitude. The skepticism of humor is related to the skepticism of irony as ignorance is related to the old thesis: *credo quia absurdum* [I believe that which is absurd], but it also has a far deeper positivity, since it moves not in human but in theanthropological categories; it finds rest not by making man man but by making man God-man" (*The Concept of Irony, with Continual Reference to Socrates*, ed. and trans. Howard V. Hong and Edna H. Hong [Princeton: Princeton University Press, 1989]—hereafter CI-KW—329*). This paragraph already

25

glimpses and anticipates the profound discussion of humor that would finally unfold in *Concluding Unscientific Postscript to* Philosophical Fragments.

Humor points beyond itself to that which creates, enables, and embraces the self as soul/body contradiction. In this way "the humorist himself has come alive to the incommensurable which the philosopher can never figure out and therefore must despise" (*JP* 2:259 [1702]; cf. CH 137). "Humor is irony carried through to its maximum oscillations" (*JP* 2:258 [1699]).

The humorist is aware that comic consciousness may be tempted toward the demonic. He knows that when the self has lost the equilibrium of finitude and freedom, it may move in the direction of the demonic. At that point humor tends to go either one way or another: "religious or demonic" (*JP* 2:263 [1721]). At this juncture humor will be directed either to the truth of its own subjectivity or to that madness which consists in having an absolute relation to the relative. Don Quixote is the prototype of a subjective madness which is comic in its extreme contradiction (*CUPPF-L*, 175). In this way Kierkegaard marks the boundary between ironic and comic forms of consciousness.

Existential Material for the Comic

There is more potential for irony than comedy at the more primitive (aesthetic) stages of self-relation, and more potential for comedy as one risks moving into the more profound and subtle (ethical and religious) stages. The comic is more distinctly visible in the religious stage than before, because it is freer from idolatry and freer for eternity. But it is potentially present in all stages. The ironic and comic perceptions play out through all the incongruities of human existence, but with different valences, moving from irony toward comedy as one penetrates further into the human condition.

On the ladder of awareness, each step of comic consciousness is offered the possibility of seeing the previous step a bit more clearly. "The lower can never make the higher comic, that is, cannot legitimately interpret the higher as comic and does not have the power to make it comic." Kierkegaard illustrates: "Thus a horse can be the occasion for a man to look ludicrous, but the horse does not have the power to make him ludicrous" (*CUPPF* 1:519–20). The more attentive one is to one's own finite freedom, the more material becomes available for comic treatment, and the more comic consciousness comes into view. The more essentially one exists, the more material is procured for the comic (*CUPPF* 1:461–65).

Comic possibilities appear wherever any incongruence emerges. Incongruence or contradiction is endemic to the human condition, because the self is an embodied synthesis of the temporal/eternal, body/soul, finitude/freedom predicament. Hence the most deeply self-aware person becomes most intensively enmeshed in comic consciousness.

While Hegel sought to soften and intellectually mediate all contradiction into rational unity, SK delighted in accentuating the contradictory tension between irreconcilable poles of the dialectic which the self is: possibility struggling with necessity; freedom facing its own finitude; soul and body in one person—how funny.

So in what sense a synthesis?

The utter dissimilarity between soul and body is the key fact of human existence upon which comic awareness is based. The continuing disparity between human finitude and the infinite reach of freedom's possibilities is the seedbed from which comic situations blossom. The arena of comic consciousness is the matrix of incommensurability between freedom and finitude. Suppose I were confiding a secret to someone under the pledge of strict silence, and he answers eagerly: "You may absolutely rely on me; one can unconditionally confide a secret to me, because I forget it the moment it is said" (*CUPPF* 1:552n). Nothing makes this funny except the contradiction that if he forgets it, there is no point to confiding in him. The contradiction is freedom in the mode of promising, clashing with finitude in the mode of forgetting its promise.

Passion is intensified as one moves step by step toward increased awareness of the polarities which constitute the self. With increased self-awareness, the multiplying incongruities of human freedom accelerate the intensity of that passion and its comedy. The most decisive polarity is the absolute disparity between finitude and infinite possibility, which together constitute finite freedom. That disparity vexes human consciousness, since human existence in fact is precisely that contradiction.

27

The Clash of Philosophy and Comedy

Philosophy, which is prone to comedy because of its pretensions, may be at any time confronted with its own finitude: "If a man like Kant, standing on the pinnacle of scientific scholarship, were to say in reference to demonstrations of the existence of God: well, *I do not know anything more about that than that my father told me it was so*— this is humorous and actually says more than a whole book about demonstrations, if the book forgets this" (*CUPPF* 1:552–53, italics added). Hegel, who did forget it, having dodged immediate existence in favor of thought, serves as the prototype for one devoid of a sensitivity for the comic (*CUPPF* 1:303).

SK relates the story of a man who warned Socrates that "people were slandering him in his absence." Socrates replied: "Is that anything to care about? It makes so little difference to me what people do with me in my absence that they are even quite welcome to beat me up in my absence" (*CUPPF* 1:552n*). The best place to be thrashed is "in one's absence." By saying less, Socrates says more. There is something funny in Diogenes' saying that where you have a poor marksman, stand close to the target. But that is made existentially more funny when a poor marksman is found standing close to the target (*JP* 2:259 [1793]).

HOW THE COMIC FLOWERS AMID RELIGIOUS CONSCIOUSNESS

Now we come to the most demanding part of the analysis. One will not understand Kierkegaard's theory of comedy without thinking seriously about religion.

Johannes Climacus, the Humorist

Johannes Climacus is SK's "most personal pseudonym" (*CUPPF-L* xvi). He is a character who regularly designates himself as a humorist. Kierkegaard employs Johannes' voice to speak of himself as one who is "essentially a humorist" but, having lived his life in the Socratic search for truth within himself, is now "seeking the Christian-religious" (*CUPPF* 1:451). Johannes always lives on the "border territory of the religious" (*CUPPF* 1:451).

The historical and actual John Climacus (John of the Ladder) was a sixth-century monk of the Sinai desert. He wrote a famous ascetic work about a "ladder of spiritual perfection" for the Byzantine monastery of St. Catherine's in Sinai. Some of Byzantium's greatest icons were created during his lifetime. John of the Ladder caught Kierkegaard's eye early as a rigorous patristic model of the movement through decisive stages of spiritual self-examination. The monk, John of the Ladder, and the humorist Kierkegaard, under the pseudonym of Johannes Climacus, appear to be very much alike. They both view the struggle to become a person before God as an inward wrestling, a series of stages or steps on a ladder of deepening awareness that leads inexorably toward faith in the Incarnation, which Kierkegaard calls the "Absolute Paradox" of God entering time.

Following his own abortive relation with Regina Olson, Kierkegaard in fact lived a decidedly monastic-ascetic life. In this respect he came to think of himself as resembling the historic monk of Sinai. In his theological studies he became intrigued by this great Church Father. He viewed his own vocation, his struggle for resignation and new birth, as analogous to that of a monk in the desert.

But why did he regard his key pseudonym, Johannes Climacus, as a "humorist"? His special symbolic form of monasticism after the end of the engagement with Regina was to give up all worldly passions, all erotic joys, all pleasures, and devote himself wholly to the ascesis of probing each and every aspect of human self-awareness. Only then did he find the comic, flowering in the desert of penitence and self-control.

In Johannes he found a pseudonym that would function for him on the boundary between the historical and the eternal and between humor and religious consciousness. Kierkegaard's whole pseudonymous authorship "must be characterized as being within the sphere of humor . . . Kierkegaard chooses Climacus to be the one who, with the aid of humor, is to exercise control over his poetic productions, because Climacus has a comprehensive view of the existential spheres" (Gregor Malantschuk, *Kierkegaard's Thought*, ed. and trans. Howard V. Hong and Edna H. Hong [Princeton: Princeton University Press, 1968], 212).

The humorist Johannes fantasizes: "If I could live to see the day when my landlord had a new bell pull installed in the courtyard of the place where I live so that one could clearly and swiftly know for whom the bell is being rung in the evening, then I would consider myself extremely fortunate" (*CUPPF* 1:448). The comic incongruity here is that it is upon something so inconsequential as a bell pull that one's entire life happiness appears to depend. In this way the distinction between fortune and misfortune is canceled "in a higher lunacy" (*CUPPF* 1:448). The humorist makes a jest out of what the esthete views as a misfortune.

How Does the Comic Reveal the Religious?

The relation between humor and religious consciousness is deeply interwoven and extremely subtle. Wherever as the religious life fails to understand humor, the religious itself is prone to becoming comic. When one bases eternal happiness (which is the highest form of desire or pathos) upon that which is finite, yet purports to guarantee eternal certainty, he is swimming in the comic.

Suppose a man conceives of a great plan for the benefit of the world but is found babbling interminably about it. He himself thereby becomes comic. Why comic? Because of the incongruity of the greatness of the plan with his inability to keep silent about it, which seems to contradicting its greatness. "But the resolution of the religious person is the highest of all, infinitely higher than all plans to transform the world and to create systems and works of art—therefore of all people the religious person must discover the comic, if he actually is religious, because otherwise he himself becomes comic" (*CUPPF* 1:463).

Guilt longs for a salve. Humor offers that salve even while aware that there is no way out of the inexorable contradiction which constitutes selfhood. The way beyond despair over selfhood, as we learn in Kierkegaard's own non-pseudonymous authorship, is faith—trusting in the Giver of the contradiction which is the self.

Tragic consciousness remains fixated on the pain. But comic consciousness focuses on the contradiction, the absurdity, and the incongruity to which pain points. In this way it transmutes pain into jest. But comedy does not itself take the leap of faith. It only peers into the abyss and recognizes its possibility. Religious consciousness is able to grasp the comic everywhere because the contradictions exist everywhere.

Suffering and guilt are "the decisive and essential expression" of the struggle of freedom to fully actualize itself. Religion comes to celebrate suffering and guilt as taken up and made understandable in relation to God's own suffering for us. "The religious person is one who has discovered the comic on the greatest scale," namely, the Incarnation (CUPPF 1:462).

What's So Funny about Suffering?

Nothing, of course, seen from within the suffering subject. Nothing, aesthetically, from the viewpoint of immanence. But comic consciousness looks from the outside to turn the internal suffering itself into a new configuration by contradiction.

Comedy thus becomes the reverse side of suffering. It objectifies and transmutes inward discord by a reversal of perspective. It views pain in relation to eternity. Humor is directly attuned to the pathos of pain, but with an attitude.

Hence, wherever suffering exists, precisely there the seeds of comedy are planted. The parry of jest always springs from pain. With every quip goes a little piece of the humorist's guts (JP 2:260 [1706]).

Religiously speaking, comic perception is being freed from idolatry to see beyond it, but toward what? Eternity and eternal happiness. The eternal transcends the despair of freedom.

To those who live aesthetically, suffering is merely an occasional misfortune to be avoided. But for religious consciousness, suffering accompanies every step of human freedom. It is not merely accidental. Suffering is the essential trigger of religious perception. But if viewed merely in aesthetic (pleasure/pain) terms, suffering is not intrinsic to human existence but the least essential of all things.

Comedy detaches itself from absolute seriousness about human incongruities. It maintains distance (absolutely and precisely) through the perspective of eternity. Comic consciousness provides a greater detachment than does the ethical, because it can grasp the relativity of creaturely human values in relation to eternity. This demystifies the surfeit of gods the self manufactures.

Suffering is the essential feature of religious consciousness. The reality of the suffering secures its "persistence as essential to the religious life." But "esthetically viewed, suffering stands in an accidental relation to existence" (*CUPPF-L*, 400). There is no plausible explanation of comedy without suffering and guilt, the essential and decisive stages of self-recognition.

To exist is to suffer by standing freely within the incongruities that define body-soul existence. These incongruities are a part of the territory of freedom; they constitute suffering and make the self ever vulnerable to suffering. But what does humor do with suffering? "The humorist makes the deceptive turn and revokes the suffering in the form of jest" (*CUPPF* 1:447).

Aesthetic existence, focusing on pleasure and pain, has a finite frame of reference which regards misfortune as accidental within finitude. The humorist, however, works out of a relation to the infinite which grasps the intrinsic connection between existing and suffering. But at the crucial moment comic perception transcends suffering in the form of jest.

Meanwhile, "immediacy cannot comprehend suffering" (*CUPPF* 1:449), but humor grasps and transmutes it to a different form of consciousness. This is especially so of humor within religious consciousness. To locate the human quandary before God is to take away its despair.

What Is Comic about Tragedy?

Humor is never without traces of tragic consciousness. It is forever storming the walls of the infinite recollection of guilt. Yet humor deflects these tragic aspects by means of jest. "The tragic and the comic are the same inasmuch as both are contradiction, but *the tragic is suffering contradiction, and the comic is painless contradiction*" (*CUPPF* 1:514). Comic perception frees me to transcend my tragic seriousness by beholding it as finite, hence not absolute (CH 156). "Finite common sense wants to interpret immediacy as comic but in doing that becomes comic itself, because what presumably is supposed to justify its comic effects is that it easily knows the way out, but the way out that it knows is even more comic" (*CUPPF* 1:520). "The

comic interpretation produces the contradiction or allows it to become apparent by having *in mente* [in mind] the way out; therefore
the contradiction is painless. The tragic interpretation sees the contradiction and despairs over the way out" (*CUPPF* 1:516).

Despair in its despairing "knows no way out, does not know the
contradiction canceled" (*CUPPF* 1:520). Hence, despair interprets
the contradiction as tragic. Frater Taciturnus in *Stages* is one of
Kierkegaard's voices who grasps the unity of the comic and tragic.
Quidam by contrast sees himself as having chosen only the tragic
(CH 172). Love is tragic when its passion is thwarted by external
circumstances. Love is comic when it feigns fidelity yet remains devoid of passion (CH 167–68).

*But Q is
said to be
higher!*

Living on the Boundaries of Comic and Religious Awareness

Religious consciousness is "protected by the comic against the
comic" (*CUPPF* 1:522). In uncovering the seriousness of finitude,
comic awareness points beyond finitude (*CH* 160). Hence "It does
the comic an injustice to regard it as an enemy of the religious"
(*CUPPF* 1:522).

The relation of comedy and religious consciousness is of central
interest to Kierkegaard. "The religiousness that has humor as its incognito is able to turn to see the humorous as comic, but it has
legitimation to see it only by continually keeping itself in religious
passion oriented to the relationship with God, and thus perceives it
only as continually disappearing" (*CUPPF* 1:521–22).

Stages on Life's Way is a series of reflections that take place on the
border between humor and religious consciousness. There it is clear
that humor is the boundary zone of the religious stage. Humor is the
terminus a quo requisite for entry into "religiousness B," which is
Climacus' term for Christianity (CH 78).

Comic perception can never be possessed as a durable mode of
consciousness. In religious consciousness one "discovers the comic,
but since in eternal recollecting he is continually relating himself to
an eternal happiness, the comic is a continually vanishing element"
(*CUPPF* 1:555).

33

How Quickly the Religious Awareness May Turn
into Comic Contradiction

Religious awareness that insists upon being serious stands in a contradiction that itself is comic. He illustrates: "The religious person
who could not bear, if it so happened, that everyone laughed at what
absolutely occupies him lacks inwardness and therefore wants to be
consoled by illusion, that many people are of the same opinion, indeed, with the same facial expression, as he has, and wants to be built
up by adding the world-historical to his little fragment of actuality"
(*CUPPF* 1:522).

Suppose two people are interacting, and one becomes aware that
each wants to be "more religious than the other"—in that case the
situation is comic. The contradiction is characterized as "simultaneously wanting to be visible and invisible" (*CUPPF* 1:523). "May I
have the honor of asking with whom I have the honor of speaking,
whether it is a human being, etc.?" (*CUPPF* 1:523). Suppose someone seeks to embody the holy life. Another wants to seek the holy
life as if it were like an athletic competition. In this latter the contradiction is intensified, and it becomes comedy. "The law for the comic
is very simple: the comic is wherever there is contradiction and
where the contradiction is painless by being regarded as canceled,
since the comic certainly does not cancel the contradiction (on the
contrary, it makes it apparent). But the legitimate comic is able to do
it; otherwise it is not legitimate" (*CUPPF* 1:523).

Comedy illuminates the contradiction which always is lurking in
the human situation. Its gift is to embrace the human contradiction
while transcending it in jest. "But childishness and impudence are
very different from humor. The humorist possesses the childlike but is
not possessed by it, continually keeps it from expressing itself directly
but allows it only to shine through a consummate culture. If, therefore, a fully cultured person is placed together with a child, they
always jointly discover the humorous: the child says it and does not
know it; the humorist knows that it was said" (*CUPPF* 1:551).

Humor, according to Climacus, recognizes guilt as pervasive of all
human interactions. "The humorist seldom speaks of this or that
guilt, because he comprehends the total" (*CUPPF* 1:550). There is
something funny about the awareness that guilt lurks in the vicinity

of every human interaction: "Humor reflects upon the consciousness of guilt totally and therefore is truer than all comparative measuring and rejecting" (*CUPPF* 1:553).

HUMOR IN CHRISTIANITY

Nowhere in the literature on theories of humor is there a closer connection between Christianity and humor than in Kierkegaard. "Humor [is] intrinsic to Christianity" (*JP* 2:251 [1681]*), he says. It is "even present throughout Christianity," because "truth is hidden in . . . mystery . . . no matter how much Christian knowledge increases, it will still always remember its origin and there know everything ἐν μυστηρίω" (Col. 1.26; *JP* 2:252 [1682]).

The Incarnational Reversal

The incarnation of God in time is the prototypical event of divine humor. Here the contradictories that make up humor clash and dance in the highest form. Here the paradox is absolute. Cross and resurrection constitute an absolute reversal of all human expectations.

In Christianity contradiction becomes normative and paradigmatic; it becomes the perspective through which all else is interpreted. It is easier for a camel to go through the eye of a needle than for a rich man to enter the kingdom of heaven (Mt. 19:24). It is the blind who recognizes the Messiah (Mt. 9:27). It is children who know more than the wise. The lilies of the field exceed in finery the clothing of Solomon. All this refracts and pictures the humor of the Incarnation. In Kierkegaard's view, "humor appears in Christ's own utterances" (*JP* 2:254 [1686]), constantly.

Just as Socrates pled ignorance in seeking to reveal the truth, so does Christianity seek the lowliest position (slave, servant) to point to that which is infinitely high. It is precisely from the cave in Bethlehem that it points to the Incarnation of God in a particular person. It is from the cross that it points to the atonement. God uses the lowliest things to soar and transcend: Water is changed into wine. It is the child in whom the Messiah comes. It is the thief who is admitted immediately to Paradise. It is the ass who is transformed into a prophet. In the Kingdom of God, everything is (comically) upside down.

Christianity is nowhere more intensely comic to Kierkegaard than in the Christmas story. There we meet the Absolute Paradox, the Incarnation itself, and there we find the decisive expression of the comic—God's coming to humanity in the least expected way, with the greatest depth of contradiction. The nativity demonstrates God's own unexpected and seemingly incongruent way of breaking into time. Only God could have thought of meeting us this way. It is as if the miracle is performed "only to disconcert the professors of physics" (JP 2:253 [1682]) Here biblical comedy comes to its apex.

SK sees humor even in Calvin, especially in his love of the contradiction that one's weakness constitutes precisely one's glory. One who is already disgraced has no need to dread disgrace (JP 2:587). That Christ bore divine life precisely in the form of his human debasement is indeed "genuinely humorous" (JP 2:260 [1704]).

Johannes, the almost religious humorist, writes: "What is the meaning of life? Yes, tell me. How should I know? We were born yesterday and know nothing. But this I do know, that the greatest pleasure is to trudge through life unknown, unknown to His Majesty the King, to Her Majesty the Queen, to Her Majesty the Queen Dowager, to his Royal Highness Prince Ferdinand, because such aristocratic acquaintanceship only makes life burdensome and awkward, just as it must be for a prince living in poverty in a rural village to be known by his royal family. Similarly, it also seems to me that to be known *in time by God* makes life enormously strenuous. Wherever he is present every half hour is of infinite importance. But to live in that way cannot be endured for sixty years; one can hardly endure three years of strenuous study for an examination, which still is not as strenuous as a half hour like that. . . . So one commences, puts forward the best foot of the infinite, and plunges in with the most precipitous speed of passion. No man in the bombing attack could hurry faster; the Jew who fell down from the gallery could not fall headlong more precipitously. What happens? Then we hear: The auction is postponed. There will be no stroke of the hammer today, but perhaps in sixty years" (CUPPF 1:449–50). Normally the auction begins clearly and instantly with a fall of the hammer, with no further waiting. The

36

comic incongruity lies in having to wait sixty years for the auction hammer to fall, analogous to having to wait until the Last Day for final judgment. So one does not want to be known even by the king, and certainly not by the holy and just God, because that would put his entire life under minute examination. Being a king's son, known as such by everybody but living as a poor man in a rural village, is nothing like the awkwardness and intensity of living before God.

What Christianity Did for Humor

Kierkegaard has a profoundly religious conception of comedy and a profoundly comic conception of religion, especially Christian religion. Laughter has its native pasture not in heaven but on the way to heaven: "Granted that eternity is too earnest a place for laughter (something I have always been convinced of), it seems that there must be an intermediary state where a person is permitted to laugh outright. The person who with extreme effort and much self-sacrifice discovers the comic really has no opportunity to laugh himself out; he is too tense and concerned for that. . . . Socrates would be found in this intermediary state" (JP 2:272 [1756]). We find Socrates not in heaven but somewhere on the road to heaven, where one is permitted to laugh outright, where it is fitting to behold the contradictions in jest, contradictions resolved in endless praise in the celestial city.

Even while the world is retrogressing, there is ever more opportunity for laughter, ever increasing materials for comedy. "It is also noteworthy that the world manifestly tends toward the comic, to the greater and greater development of laughter, all of which hangs together with the world's retrogression. Nowhere do we pause with pathos; we shudder at nothing—but say: Knock it off and see the comical side; human corruption is comical, and we try to express it comically . . . All is phony—so let us laugh" (JP 2:272 [1757]).

Kierkegaard then undertakes the most surprising and radical turn of argument that *"All humor [is] developed from Christianity itself"* (JP 2:229 [1622]*)! Humor, in this definition, is implicitly and intrinsically grounded in the Absolute Paradox, rightly understood, which hinges finally on the incongruity and offense of God becoming human. The play with incongruity is heightened to its utmost in the Incarnation. Out of that flows the highest perception of the human contradiction. If so, the history of humor awaited the Incarnation to become fully catalyzed.

J. G. Hamann the Humorist and A. E. Scribe the Pretended Humorist

While Socrates is the greatest ironist, he was not strictly speaking a humorist. Rather, Kierkegaard opines: "Hamann is the greatest humorist in Christianity" (JP 2:252 [1681]). Johann Georg Hamann (1730–1788), the eccentric philologist of Koenigsberg, "preferred exceptions to rules, imagination to understanding, poetry to prose, the particular to the general" (W. Scherer, *History of German Literature* [New York: Scribner's, 1888], 86). Hamann's answer to Hegel was a roar of laughter. Hamann "enabled Kierkegaard to find, not another system, but—himself" (T. H. Croxall, *Kierkegaard Studies* [New York: Roy, 1956], 63).

With exceptional generosity Kierkegaard describes Hamann as of all time "still the greatest and most authentic humorist" (JP 2:258 [1699]). Why? Hamann "would rather hear wisdom from Balaam's ass or from a philosopher against his will than from an angel or an apostle" (JP 2:257 [1693]; cf. JP 2:201 [1542]). As Socrates is the master of irony, Hamann is the master of comedy: "Just as Socrates left no books, Hamann left only as much as the modern period's rage for writing made relatively necessary, and furthermore only occasional pieces" (JP 2:258 [1700]).

The then popular author Augustin Eugene Scribe was a contemporary of Kierkegaard's who styled himself as a comic writer. What Scribe called comedy, Kierkegaard thought nauseating. Scribe is "relished by the age," yet "Scribe himself is absolutely just as sordid as the world he depicts" (JP 2:273 [1761]). The best proof of the demoralization to which the present age has sunk is the fact that what once was called repentance now is reduced to "an assignment for subtle ingenuity which wittily and interestingly entertains the age—with the sins of the age" (JP 2:273–4 [1761]).

When our sins have become little more than an object of entertainment, what might have been humor has deteriorated to cynicism. So we say: "Let's not only be miserable scoundrels but refine it with witty and clever knowledge and virtuosity in depicting it dramatically." "Done for, they say, we are all done for; nobody should complain about anybody—let's all laugh!" (*JP* 2:274 [1761]).

Humor and Suffering

The fullest measure of humor is "the joy which has overcome the world" (*JP* 2:262 [1716]). After the apostles were flogged by the Jerusalem authorities and warned not to witness anymore, they went away from the jail "thanking God that it was granted them to suffer something for the sake of Christ" (*CUPPF* 1:452)! The humor embedded in Christianity stands valiantly against the world.

To be glad for the privilege of suffering is the heart of the New Testament view of humor, where suffering is transmuted into joy by its relation with eternal happiness. Thus "the essential relation to an eternal happiness is not suffering but joy . . . joy in the consciousness that the suffering signifies the [redeemed God-human] relation" (*CUPPF* 1:452*). Hence, in the case of martyrdom, the martyr no doubt is experiencing suffering, but more profoundly experiences "joy over the significance of this suffering as [redeemed] relationship" (*CUPPF* 1:453*).

Release from dread in *The Concept of Anxiety* and from despair in *The Sickness unto Death* comes only when one grounds one's very self in the Giver, Source, and Ground of existence, which is only finally possible when freed by the incarnate One who actually shares this existence in all its comic dimensions, transmutes it, and enables it to be lived out freely toward eternity. The illusion of aesthetic and ethical (proto-religious) existence is that this grounding is unnecessary, even bothersome.

"It is just impossible to keep from laughing when I think of Hegel's conception of Christianity—it is utterly inconceivable . . . . The time will . . . come when the idea of 'professor' will be equated with a comical person. One thinks of Christianity! Alas, how changed since the time when it had unwavering confessors, and now when it has professors who accommodate in all *casibus*" (*JP* 2:225 [1615]). The professors have learned by evasion to accommodate any idea to any other idea. The confessors, by their willingness to lay down their lives for the truth, were unwilling to be even the slightest bit evasive.

Hence Kierkegaard lamented the decline of heresy, not because he wished for erroneous teaching as such, but because he viewed the concept of heresy as an inevitable accompaniment to true Christianity which he found entirely absent in "Christendom." Nowadays we do not even have as much as a heresy. There is not even enough character for that—for a heresy presupposes (a) honesty enough to let Christianity pass for what it is and (b) passion to think differently" (JP 2:226 [1619]).

What happens when Christianity becomes wedded to some particular philosophy? "Just as in domestic life there is a type of person who, as it is excellently phrased, peddles gossip among families, so there are a goodly number of men who with regard to the question of the union of Christianity with philosophy, really gossip, since, without knowing either party very well, they have gotten to know in a second- or third-hand way someone with a master's degree who during his foreign travels has drunk tea with this or that great scholar, etc." (JP 2:209 [1570]).

The speculative thinker "has finished on paper and mistakes this for existence" (CUPPF 1:454), missing the joy the believer knows in relating all of his contingencies to eternal happiness. Kierkegaard contrasts the drabness of medieval speculation with the vitality of the "humor in Clement of Alexandria's praise of writing allegories so that the heathen could not understand" (JP 2:263 [1724]). "There no doubt are men in whom genius manifests itself just as inconveniently as genius in stampeding cows" (JP 2:81 [1287]). "Even though, in view of the importance of his discovery, we forgive Archimedes for running split-naked through the streets of Syracuse, it by no means follows as a matter of course that we are obliged to tolerate these modern versions of return-to-nature" (JP 2:57 [1235]).

The comic, from a Christian perspective, is a mode of consciousness that has already matured through the aesthetic and ethical stages, is decisively shaped through suffering, and stands at the threshold of faith itself. Faith takes the leap beyond the contradictions by beholding happiness in time in relation to eternal happiness. The comic sense is always penultimate, but a penultimate to the deepest relationality of the self, viz., as grounded in the Giver of the self.

In bracing for critics of my editorial extracts, I conclude with two of SK's acid comments on "the relation between the daily press and authors" (*JP* 2:479 [2149]): "The relation between the daily press and authors is as follows. An author writes a coherent and consistently clear presentation of some idea—perhaps even the fruit of many years of labor. No one reads it. But a journalist, in reviewing the book takes the occasion to slap together some rubbish which he presents as representing the author's book—this everyone reads. We see the author's significance in existence—he exists so that a journalist can have the occasion to write some rubbish which everyone reads" (*JP* 2:479–80 [2149]). Just remember his motto for the press: "In fact, if the daily press, like some other occupational groups, had a coat of arms, the inscription ought to be: Here men are demoralized in the shortest possible time, on the largest possible scale, at the cheapest possible price" (*JP* 2:489 [2171]).

THE HUMAN CONDITION

The Absurd

WHERE AM I?   How Did I Get Here and Why
               Was I Not Asked if I Wanted
               to Come?

Isn't it outrageous that the self is not asked whether it wants to be born?

One sticks a finger into the ground to smell what country one is in. I stick my finger into the world—it has no smell. Where am I? What does it mean to say: the world? What is the meaning of that word? Who tricked me into this whole thing and leaves me standing here? Who am I? How did I get into the world? Why was I not asked about it, why was I not informed of the rules and regulations but just thrust into the ranks as if I had been bought from a peddling shanghaier of human beings? How did I get involved in this big enterprise called actuality? Why should I be involved? Isn't it a matter of choice? And if I am compelled to be involved, where is the manager—I have something to say about this. Is there no manager? To whom shall I make my complaint?

—Repetition
Fear and Trembling; Repetition 200
(KW 6) [Voice: The Young Man]

THE UNEXPECTED   The Roof Tile

Can present decision be based on predicting future contingencies?

It would sound like jesting if a person in receiving an invitation replied: I will come, definitely, believe me,

45

except in case a roof tile falls down and kills me, because then I cannot come. And yet this may also be the highest earnestness.

Concluding Unscientific Postscript to
Philosophical Fragments 1:88 (KW 12)
[Voice: Johannes Climacus]

SAVING COPENHAGEN   THE CURE FOR DENMARK'S
DEBT CRISIS

What might be done about the national debt?

Now and then we hear that someone is a genius and does not pay his debts; why should a nation not do the same, provided there is agreement? Borrow fifteen million; use it not to pay off our debts but for public entertainment. Let us celebrate the millennium with fun and games. Just as there currently are boxes everywhere for contributions of money, there should be bowls everywhere filled with money. Everything would be free: the theater would be free, prostitutes would be free, rides to Deer Park would be free, funerals would be free, one's funeral eulogy would be free. I say "free," for if money is always available, everything is free in a way.

No one would be allowed to own any property. An exception should be made only for me. I shall set aside for myself one hundred rix-dollars a day deposited in a London bank, partly because I cannot manage on less, partly because I am the one who provided the idea, and finally because no one knows if I will not be able to think up a new idea when the fifteen million is exhausted.

What would be the result of this prosperity? All the great would stream to Copenhagen: the greatest artists, actors, and dancers. Copenhagen would become another Athens. What would be the result? All the wealthy would settle in this city. Among others, the emperor of Persia and the king of England would undoubtedly also come here. Here is my second idea: kidnap the emperor. Someone may say that then there would be a revolution in Persia, a new emperor placed on the throne—it has frequently happened before—and the price of the old emperor would slump. In that case, my idea is that we should sell him to the Turks. They will undoubtedly know how to make money out of him.

In addition, there is yet another circumstance that our politicians seem to ignore entirely. Denmark holds the balance of power in Europe. A more propitious position is inconceivable. This I know from my own experience. I once held the balance of power in a family. I could do as I wished. I never suffered, but the others always did.

O may my words penetrate your ears, you who are in high places to counsel and control, you king's men and men of the people, you wise and sensible citizens of all classes! You just watch out! Old Denmark is foundering—it is a matter of life and death; it is foundering on boredom, which is the most fatal of all [conditions]. In olden days, whoever eulogized the deceased most handsomely became the king. In our age, the king ought to be the one who delivers the best witticism and the crown prince the one who provides the occasion for the best witticism.

—*Either:* "The Rotation of Crops"
Either/Or 1:287–88 (KW 3)
[Voice: "A"]*

THE ACCIDENTAL AS HUMAN CLASSIFICATION SYSTEM
A New Taxonomy for Human Behavioral Types

Is an accidental classification an improvement over an incomplete one?

A wit has said that mankind can be divided into officers, servant girls, and chimney sweeps. In my opinion, this remark is not only witty but also profound, and it would take great speculative talent to make a better classification. If a classification does not ideally exhaust its object, the accidental is preferable in every way, because it sets the imagination in motion.

—*Repetition*
Fear and Trembling; Repetition 162
(KW 6) [Voice: Constantin
Constantius]

47

STUPIDITY   THE GROUND FOR
                   PHILOSOPHICAL RENEWAL

How is a new stupidity the hope of philosophy?

My purpose, then, is to serve philoso-
phy, my qualification for that, that I am stupid enough not to understand it, indeed stupider still—stupid enough to show it. And yet my
undertaking can only benefit philosophy, for it surely cannot be
harmed by even the stupidest person making it out. It wins its most
complete victory precisely by that, and demonstrates the correctness
of making everyone into philosophers. . . .

In relation to this purpose of mine I have examined myself seriously, and by this self-examination found myself to be in possession of
the necessary qualities. I venture to say this without violating modest
and decency. The qualities are: stupidity and resignation. That I am
in possession of the former, no one, presumably, will be so polite as to
talk me out of. As far as the latter is concerned then, I prove by
making a confession of the former that I am in possession of the
latter. . . . When all is said and done, who then, for want of something better, would not with pleasure be the absurd question that
gave occasion for a young girl to blush more beautifully than ever?
the almost infantile simplemindedness that brought the wise man to
smile more significantly than ever? the stupidity that gave occasion
for a witticism to be said? the misunderstanding that gave wisdom
occasion to explain itself more comprehensively than ever! . . . I am
not one of the mighty who live on intimate terms with philosophy
and treat it as their equal. I am like a humble thrall in the princely
palace who sees the royal majesty every day, though a yawning abyss
separates me from him. Yet, like the thrall in *Palnatoke*, I have only
one wish, to be able to see it in all its pomp. . . .

There is one thing I know with tolerable certainty, that is, what I
do not understand. There is one thing I crave of my contemporaries,
that is, an explanation. So I do not deny that Hegel has explained
everything—I leave that to the stronger minds, who also explain
what is lacking. I remain down-to-earth and say: I have not understood Hegel's explanation. . . .

Yet of course something else can also happen: I can be declared to be so stupid that philosophy cannot so much as associate with me. "If that is the case, everything has surely been lost. The periodical must be discontinued." By no means! No matter how stupid I am, I can still see that it is impossible for philosophy to answer so unphilosophically. . . . I am so stupid that philosophy cannot be intelligible to me. The antithesis of this is that philosophy is so clever that it cannot grasp my stupidity. These antitheses are mediated in a higher unity, i.e., in a joint stupidity. Oddly enough, I still slip in.

Prefaces: Light Reading for Certain Classes as the Occasion May Require 82–83, 87, 89 [Voice: Nicolaus Notabene]*

THE NOBLER ANIMALS THE POSSIBLE CHRISTIANIZATION OF DOMESTIC ANIMALS

What could the phrase possibly mean, that one is "to a certain degree 'Christian'"?
I ask the experts, the professionals, whether among domestic animals, the nobler ones, the horse, the dog, and the cow, there would appear a sign of something Christian? It is not improbable. Consider what it means to live in a Christian state. . . . It is not improbable that this is bound to have an influence upon the nobler domestic animals. . . . It is not improbable that eventually it will turn out that domestic animals in "Christendom" bring Christian offspring into the world. I become almost dizzy at the thought.

—*The Moment*
The Moment *and Late Writings* [115]–16 (KW 23)*

Vacillation

COMMITMENT Pledging Fidelity to the Flag Astride a Hobbyhorse

Should one be prepared to pledge allegiance to an officially Christian country such as Denmark?

Rather than take part in official Christianity with the thousandth part of my little-finger nail, I would rather engage in the following display of seriousness. A flag is purchased at a hardware store, it is unfurled; with great reverence I approach it, lift up three fingers and swear fidelity to the flag. Thereupon, rigged out in a cocked hat, a cartridge-belt and sword (all from the hardware store), I mount a hobbyhorse, proposing in union with others to make an attack upon the enemy, with contempt for the mortal danger into which I am evidently casting myself, with the seriousness of one who knows what it signifies to have sworn fidelity to the flag.

Kierkegaard's "Attack upon 'Christendom'" [277–78]

DECISION The Ease of the Guillotine

Why does taking the leap of faith look so easy?

Although, as frequently noted, the leap is the decision, Jacobi nevertheless wants to fashion a little transition to it. He, the eloquent speaker, wants to entice Lessing. "It does not amount to much," he says, "it is not such a difficult matter.

Just step on this elastic spot—then the leap will come by itself." This is a very good example of the pious fraud of eloquence; it is as if someone were to recommend execution by guillotine and say, "This whole business is an easy matter. You just lie down on a board, a string is pulled, then the ax falls down—and you have been executed."

> *Concluding Unscientific Postscript to*
> *Philosophical Fragments* 1:102–3
> (KW 12) [Voice: Johannes Climacus]

THE INTERMINABLE VACILLATOR
FOUND BY ARCHEOLOGISTS
STILL PACING

With what might we compare the unpredictability of life's meaning?

Long live the stagecoach horn! It is the instrument for me for many reasons, and chiefly because one can never be certain of wheedling the same notes from this horn. A coach horn has infinite possibilities, and the person who puts it to his mouth and puts his wisdom into it can never be guilty of a repetition, and he who instead of giving an answer gives his friend a coach horn to use as he pleases says nothing but explains everything. Praised be the coach horn! It is my symbol. Just as the ancient ascetics placed a skull on the table, the contemplation of which constituted their view of life, so the coach horn on my table always reminds me of the meaning of life. . . . Travel on, you fugitive river! You are the only one who really knows what you want, for you want only to flow along and lose yourself in the sea, which is never filled! Move on, you drama of life—let no one call it a comedy, no one a tragedy, for no one saw the end! Move on, you drama of existence, where life is not given again any more than money is! . . .

In the excavation of Herculaneum and Pompeii, everything was found in its place just as the respective owners left it. If I had lived at that time, the archeologists, perhaps to their amazement, would have

come upon a man who walked with measured pace up and down the
floor.

> —*Repetition*
> *Fear and Trembling; Repetition* 175–76,
> [179] (KW 6) [Voice: Constantin
> Constantius]

INDECISION   AVOIDING THE LEAP

To what may courtship be compared?

I must confess that I have never
cared very much for all that infatuated billing and cooing of the
engagement, and the more that is made of this period, the more it
seems to me to resemble the time it takes many people to dive into
the water when they go swimming, time in which they walk up and
down the dock, thrusting now a hand, now a foot, into the water,
think that it is now too cold, now too warm.

> —*Or*
> *Either/Or* 2:33 (KW 4) [Voice: Judge
> William]

SUDDENNESS   THE LEAP OF THE HARE

What effect does abruptness have on human interactions?

The disproportion of my body is that
my forelegs are too short. Like the hare from New Holland, I have
very short forelegs but extremely long hind legs. Ordinarily, I sit very
still; if I make a move, it is a tremendous leap, to the horror of all
those to whom I am bound by the tender ties of kinship and
friendship.

> —*Either*: "Diapsalmata"
> *Either/Or* 1:38 (KW 3) [Voice: "A"]

Beginning and Risking

RISK AVERSION THE HIGH DIVER'S CHALLENGE

Does high-risk behavior encourage risk taking by others?

When a swimmer, practiced in diving from the ship's mast and in turning somersaults before touching water, invites another person to follow his example, and this one climbs down the ladder instead, sticking out one foot and then the other, and finally flops in—then, well, then I do not need to find out what the first one does.

—*Repetition*
Fear and Trembling; Repetition 193
(KW 6) [Voice: The Young Man]

REGRET HOW TO STOP PHILOSOPHIZING

Is there any beginning point that does not end in regret?

Marry and you will regret it. Do not marry, and you will also regret it. Marry or do not marry, you will regret it either way. . . . Laugh at the stupidities of the world, and you will regret it; weep over them, and you will also regret it. . . . Whether you trust a girl or do not trust her, you will regret it either way. Hang yourself, and you will regret it. Do not hang yourself, and you will also regret it. . . . This, gentlemen, is the quintessence of all the wisdom of life. . . . My wisdom is easy to grasp, for I have only one maxim, and even that is not a point of departure for me. . . . My maxim is not a point of departure for me, because if I made it a point of departure, I would regret it, and if I did not make it a point of departure, I would also regret it. If one or another of my esteemed listeners thinks there is anything to what I have said, he merely demonstrates that he has no head for philosophy. . . . Experience shows that it is not at all difficult for philosophy to begin. Far from it. It begins, in fact, with nothing and therefore can always begin. But it is always difficult for philosophy and philosophers to stop. This difficulty, too, I have avoided, for if anyone thinks that I, in stopping now, actually stop, he demonstrates that he does not have speculative comprehension. The point is that I do not stop now, but I stopped when I began. My philosophy, therefore, has the advantageous characteristic of being brief and of being irrefutable.

—*Either:* "Diapsalmata"
Either/Or 1:38–40 (KW 3) [Voice: "A"]

COMMENCEMENT   AN AVERSION TO BEGINNING

Can one who never begins ever be described as "farther along"?

If a man says, "I am now further along in this and that work than when I began," it makes sense and there is a determination of time; he has one point of time with the aid of which it is firmly established that he has begun, and he measures the distance from the beginning to see where he is now. But if this man had never begun this work, well, then his talk makes no sense; it is meaningless to say that one is closer *now* than *when* one began if one did not begin at all. . . .

Can one say that one person is larger than another who simply does not exist? . . . Just as someone on board a ship never leaves the ship no matter how many hours he walks the deck and how many miles he covers, so also the person who never began the course that takes one closer and closer does not come closer to something.

—*Christian Discourses*
*Christian Discourses; The Crisis and a
Crisis in the Life of an Actress* 216, 219
(KW 17)

54

How does venturing everything differ from pretending to do so?

The serious man continues: If he can have certainty that such a good is in store, he will venture everything for it; otherwise it would indeed be lunacy to venture everything. The serious man speaks almost like a jester. It is quite clear that he wants to poke fun at us, just like the militiaman when he makes a run in order to leap and does indeed make the run—but says goodbye to the leap. If it is certain, then he will venture everything. But what is it to venture? To venture is the correlative of uncertainty; as soon as there is certainty, venturing stops. . . . It is not venturing for me to give away all my possessions for a pearl if in the moment of trading I hold the pearl in my hand. If it is perhaps an imitation pearl, I have been tricked and thus have made a bad trade, but I have not ventured anything. But if that pearl is perhaps far away in Africa in a secret place difficult to reach, if I have never had the pearl in my hand, and I then leave house and home, give up everything, make that long and arduous journey without certainty that my undertaking will succeed—well, then I am venturing—and then some evening at the club one will hear what the serious man said: that it is lunacy. . . . It is always lunacy to venture, but to venture everything for an expected eternal happiness is general lunacy.

Concluding Unscientific Postscript to
Philosophical Fragments 1:424–26
(KW 12) [Voice: Johannes Climacus]

STAGES IN BECOMING ONESELF

Aesthetic Existence

ARBITRARINESS   Schnur

Into what meaningful epochs of development does random pleasure-seeking fall?

My life is utterly meaningless. When I consider its various epochs, my life is like the word *Schnur* in the dictionary, which first of all means a string, and second a daughter-in-law. All that is lacking is that in the third place the word *Schnur* means a camel, in the fourth a whisk broom.

—*Either*: "Diapsalmata"
Either/Or 1:36 (KW 3) [Voice: "A"]

ENTERTAINMENTS   An Impeccable Banquet

How does aesthetic imagination fantasize a perfect moment?

To banquet on matches or, like the Dutch, on a sugar lump of which everybody takes a lick, no, thanks. But my demand is difficult to satisfy, because the meal itself must be calculated to awaken and incite that unmentionable craving that every worthy member brings with him. I insist that the earth's fruitfulness be at our service, as if everything sprouted the very instant desire craves it. I insist on a more lavish abundance of wine than Mephistopheles had just by boring a hole in the table. I insist on more voluptuous lighting than the trolls' when they lift the mountain up onto pillars and dance in an ocean of fire. I insist on what arouses the senses most of all, I insist on that delicious refreshment of scents more glorious than those found in the *Arabian Nights' Entertainments*. I insist on a coolness that voluptuously inflames desire and cools the satisfied desire. I insist on the ceaseless exhilaration of a fountain. If Maecenas could not sleep without hearing the splashing of a fountain, then I cannot dine without it. Do not misunderstand me; I can eat dried fish without it, but I cannot eat at a banquet without it; I can drink water without it, but I cannot drink wine at a banquet without it. I insist on a staff of servants, select and handsome, as if I were sitting at the table of the gods. I insist on dinner music, intense and subdued, and I insist that it be my accompaniment at all times. And with regard to you, my friends, I make incredible demands. You see, on the basis of all these demands, which are just as many reasons against it, I think that a banquet is a *pium desiderium* [pious wish], and in this respect I am so far from wanting to talk about a repetition that I assume that it cannot be done even once.

Stages on Life's Way 25 (KW 11)
[Voice: Victor Eremita]

THE VANISHING OF A PEAK EXPERIENCE
THE SPECK OF DUST THAT ENDED
AN ECSTATIC EXPERIENCE

To what extent is complete satisfaction sustainable over time?

At one time I was very close to complete satisfaction. I got up feeling unusually well one morning. My sense of well-being increased incomparably until noon; at precisely one o'clock, I was at the peak and had a presentiment of the dizzy maximum found on no gauge of well-being, not even on a poetic thermometer. My body had lost its terrestrial gravity; it was as if I had no body simply because every function enjoyed total satisfaction, every nerve delighted in itself and in the whole, while every heartbeat, the restlessness of the living being, only memorialized and declared the pleasure of the moment. My walk was a floating, not like the flight of the bird that cuts through the air and leaves the earth behind, but like the undulating of the wind over a field of grain, like the longing rocking of the sea, like the dreaming drifting of clouds. My being was transparent, like the depths of the sea, like the self-satisfied silence of the night, like the soliloquizing stillness of midday.

Every mood rested in my soul with melodic resonance. Every thought volunteered itself, and every thought volunteered itself jubilantly, the most foolish whim as well as the richest idea. I had a presentiment of every impression before it arrived and awakened within me. All existence seemed to have fallen in love with me, and everything quivered in fateful rapport with my being. Everything was prescient in me, and everything was enigmatically transfigured in my microcosmic bliss, which transfigured everything in itself, even the most disagreeable: the most boring remark, the most disgusting sight, the most calamitous conflict. As stated, it was one o'clock on the dot when I was at the peak and had presentiments of the highest of all; when suddenly something began to irritate one of my eyes, whether it was an eyelash, a speck of something, a bit of dust, I do not know, but this I do know—that in the same instant I was plunged down almost into the abyss of despair, something everyone will readily understand who has been as high up as I was and while at that point has also pondered the theoretical question of whether absolute satisfaction is attainable at all.

—*Repetition*
Fear and Trembling; Repetition 173–74
(KW 6) [Voice: Constantin
Constantius]

ENDURANCE   THE EPHEMERAL ENDURANCE
                             OF THE AESTHETE

How long does it take to become a person?

Once there were two Englishmen who journeyed to Arabia to purchase horses. They even brought along some English race horses and wanted to test their excellence against the Arabs' horses. They proposed a race, and the Arabs were willing and let the Englishmen choose the horse they wanted from among the Arabian horses. This [race] they did not want to [happen] right away, for they explained that they would first take forty days for training. They waited the forty days, the prize was determined, the horses saddled, and now the Arabs asked how long they were to ride?

61

"One hour," was the answer. This amazed the Arabs, and they answered quite tersely: "We thought we were going to ride for three days."

You see, so it is with you. If one wants to run a race with you for one hour, then "the devil himself cannot keep up with you." Three days and you get the worst of it. I recall that I told you this story once, and I also recall your answer—that it was a dubious matter to run a race for three days; one took the risk of working up such momentum that one could never stop.

—Or
Either/Or 2:198–99 (KW 4) [Voice:
Judge William]*

DESPAIR   PROCURE POSSIBILITY

What therapy is required for despair?

When someone faints, we call for water, eau de Cologne, smelling salts; but when someone wants to despair, then the word is: Get possibility, get possibility, possibility is the only salvation. A possibility—then the person in despair breathes again, he revives again, for without possibility a person seems unable to breathe.

The Sickness unto Death 38–39 (KW 19)
[Voice: Anti-Climacus]

ADDICTION   THE HERMIT WHO LIVED ON DEW

How long can one live on the nothing of possibility without becoming inebriated?

It is told of one Indian hermit who for two years lived on dew that he once came to the city, tasted wine, and became addicted to drink.

The Concept of Anxiety 158 (KW 8)
[Voice: Vigilius Haufniensis]

Ethical Existence

THE ETHICAL AS LIFELONG TASK
ON FINISHING TOO SOON

When the task of learning is lifelong, is there any merit in a quick finish?

Since almost everyone in our age is a tremendous fellow on paper, one sometimes has groundless worries to deal with. An example of this is the danger in which people are today, that they finish everything so fast that they are in the awkward situation of finding something to fill their time. One writes on paper, "Doubt everything"—then one has doubted everything. If a person is only thirty years old, he is in the awkward situation of finding something to fill up his time, especially if one has only poorly taken care of one's old age by not having learned to play cards. . . . Just as it must be tedious for the teacher (and just as the mediocre pupil in a school is usually recognized by his running up with his paper scarcely ten minutes after the task has been assigned and saying, "I have finished," so also in life the mediocrities promptly come running and have finished, and the greater task the more quickly they have finished), so also it must be wearisome for the power who governs existence to have to deal with a generation like this. Holy Scripture speaks of God's patience with sinners as being incomprehensible, which it is indeed, but what angelic patience it takes to deal with human beings like that—who are promptly finished.

Concluding Unscientific Postscript to
Philosophical Fragments 1:405–6
(KW 12) [Voice: Johannes Climacus]

What about those who too readily offer pious advice without practicing it?

If a bowlegged man wants to act as a dancing master but is unable to execute a single step, he is comical. So it is also with the religious. Sometimes one may hear such a pious person beating time, as it were, exactly like one who cannot dance but nevertheless knows enough to beat time, although he is never fortunate enough to get in step.

The Concept of Anxiety 141 (KW 8)
[Voice: Vigilius Haufniensis]

ETHICAL EXPERTISE THE PERSON AS THREE-EIGHTHS
OF A PARAGRAPH

Can we discern the personal meaning of the ethical by looking at the logic of world history?

That is a rare, ingeniously comic invention. O fortunate nineteenth century! If no such prophet arises, we can all call it a day, for then no one knows what the ethical is. It is indeed odd enough that the ethical is in such low esteem that instruction in it is preferably left to normal-school graduates and parish clerks; it would indeed be ludicrous if someone were to say that the ethical has not yet been discovered but is still to be discovered. And yet, it would not be insane if he meant that it was to be discovered by the individual's becoming immersed in himself and in his relationship with God. But that it takes a prophet, not a judge, no, but a seer, a world-historical brawler, who, aided by one dark and one blue eye, aided by familiarity with world history, perhaps aided also by coffee grounds and fortune-telling cards, believes he discovers the ethical, that is, what the times demand (for this is the modern slogan of the demoralizing ethics)—now that is confusion-producing . . . something for which a person who likes to laugh must always feel indebted to the wise men! . . .

What the most obtuse person, confirmed in a house of correction, is able to understand is improved by cathedral wisdom and made into that genuine speculative profundity. Alas, while the speculating, honorable Herr Professor is explaining all existence, he has in sheer absentmindedness forgotten what he himself is called, namely, that he is a human being, a human being pure and simple, and not a fantastical three-eighths of a paragraph.

Concluding Unscientific Postscript to
Philosophical Fragments 1:144–45
(KW 12) [Voice: Johannes Climacus]*

WORK   THE HUMILIATION OF LIVING
                              ON NOTHING

How is "living within one's means" viewed differently by people with very different assumptions (aesthetic vs. ethical) about immediate pleasure and long-range responsibility?

I have in mind, then, a specific individual who in a certain sense is just like everyone else and in another sense is concrete in himself. Let us be utterly prosaic. This person must live, must clothe himself—in short must be able to exist. Perhaps he turned to an esthete for advice on how he should order his life. He would not be short of information either. The esthete will perhaps say to him, "If one is single, one spends three thousand rixdollars a year to live comfortably; if one has four thousand, one spends that too; if one wants to marry, then one needs at least six thousand. Money is and remains the *nervus rerum gerendarum* [moving force in accomplishing something], the true *conditio sine qua non* [necessary condition]. To be sure, it is beautiful to read about rustic contentment, about idyllic simplicity, and I like to read poetry of that sort; but one would soon become bored with that way of life, and the people who live that way do not enjoy that life half as much as the person who has money and then in all tranquillity and leisure reads the poets' songs . . ."

But obviously this explanation would not help our hero; all the worldly wisdom of the other would leave him cold, and he must have

65

felt just about as uncomfortable as a sparrow in a dance of cranes. If he said to the esthete, "That is all very fine, but I have neither three thousand nor six thousand a year. I have nothing at all either in capital or in interest; I own nothing at all, scarcely a hat," the esthete would shrug his shoulders and say, "Well, that's another matter; then there is nothing else to be done. Then you'll have to be satisfied with going to the workhouse." If the esthete is good-natured, he perhaps would motion to the poor wretch and say, "I don't want to bring you to despair before I have made a supreme effort. There are a couple of temporary expedients one ought not to leave unexplored before one says goodbye forever to joy and makes the pledge and puts on the straitjacket. Marry a rich girl, play the lottery, travel to the colonies, spend a few years scraping money together, insinuate yourself into the good graces of an old bachelor so that he will make you his heir. Just now our paths part; get some money, and you will always find in me a friend who can forget that there was a time when you did not have money." . . .

Listen now to what an ethicist would respond to him. His answer would be as follows: "It is every person's duty to work for a living." If he had no more to say, you would presumably answer, "There we have again that old stuff and nonsense about [this] duty and [that] duty; it is duty everywhere. Is there anything more boring than this straitlaced conformity that suppresses everything and clips its wings?" Please recall that our hero had no money, that the callous esthete had none to give him . . . If a person looks at the matter ethically he will look upon having money as a humiliation, for every preferential favor is a humiliation. If he looks at it this way, he will not become hypnotized by any preferential treatment. He will humble himself under it, and, having done that, he will be uplifted by the thought that the preferential treatment is a sign that a greater demand is made upon him.

—Or

Either/Or 2:277–78, 280–81 (KW 4)
[Voice: Judge William]*

MELDING VIRTUE AND PLEASURE

Are pleasure and virtue two paths or one?

The pastor says that there are two paths, and it is certainly a pious wish that the pastor might say this with proper emphasis. So there are two paths, says the pastor, and when he begins this discourse we know very well what he means, but we can gladly hear it again, because this is no anecdote or witticism that can be heard only once. There are two paths: the one, smiling and carefree, easy to travel, beckoning, strewn with flowers, meanders through lovely regions, and walking on it is as light as dancing in the meadow. The other path is narrow, stony, difficult in the beginning, but little by little . . . . . It is the path of pleasure and the path of virtue. At times the pastor speaks this way, but what happens? Just as the path of virtue changes little by little, so the pastor's discourse also changes, and little by little the two paths begin to resemble each other quite closely. In order to entice the listener to virtue, the description of the path of virtue becomes almost seductive. . . .

Just as there is a committee in Copenhagen that works to beautify the city, so there seems to be a modern pastoral wisdom at work to beautify the path of virtue with esthetic decorations.

> *Concluding Unscientific Postscript to*
> Philosophical Fragments 1:403, 403n
> (KW 12) [Voice: Johannes Climacus]

CHANGING ONESELF   Changing Places

What is it that changes in the movement of the spirit through the stages?

In the world of spirit, the different stages are not like cities on a journey, about which it is quite all right for the traveler to say directly, for example: We left Peking and came to Canton, and were in Canton on the fourteenth. A traveler like that changes place, not himself; and thus it is all right for him to mention and to *recount* the change in a direct, unchanged form. But in the world of spirit to change place is to be changed oneself.

Concluding Unscientific Postscript to
Philosophical Fragments 1:281–82
(KW 12) [Voice: Johannes Climacus]

Religious Existence

WRITING AS RELIGIOUS VOCATION
The Winged Pen

Does the advocate of truth-telling debase his own calling by resorting to pseudonyms?

This God-relationship of mine is the "happy love" in a life which has been in many ways troubled and unhappy. And although the story of this love affair (if I dare call it such) has the essential marks of a true love story, in the fact that only one can completely understand it, and there is no absolute joy but in relating it to one only, namely, the beloved, who in this instance is the Person by whom one is loved, yet there is a joy also in talking about it to others. . . .

Now that I am to talk about my God-relationship, about what every day is repeated in my prayer of thanksgiving for the indescribable things He has done for me, so infinitely much more than ever I could have expected, about the experience which has taught me to be amazed, amazed at God, at His love and at what a man's impotence is capable of with His aid, about what has taught me to long for eternity and not to fear that I might find it tiresome, since it is exactly the situation I need so as to have nothing else to do but to give thanks. Now that I am to talk about this there awakens in my soul a poetic impatience. . . . And lo! it presents itself—thoughts as enchanting as the fruits in the garden of a fairy-tale, so rich and warm and heartfelt; expressions so soothing to the urge of gratitude within me, so cooling to my hot longing—it seems to me as if, had I a winged pen, yes, ten of them, I still could not follow fast enough to keep pace with the wealth which presents itself. But no sooner have I taken pen in hand, at that very instant I am incapable of moving it, as we say of one that he cannot move hand or foot. In that situation not a line concerning this relationship gets put down on paper. It seems to me as if I heard a voice saying to me: Silly fellow, what does he imagine? Does he not know that obedience is dearer to God than the fat of rams? Then I become perfectly quiet, then there is time enough to write each letter with my slow pen almost painfully. And if that poetic impatience awakes in me again for an instant, it seems as though I heard a voice speaking to me as a teacher speaks to a boy when he says: Now hold the pen right, and form each letter with equal precision. And then I can do it, then I dare not do otherwise, then I write every word, every line, almost without knowing what the next word or the next line is to be. And afterwards when I read it over it satisfies me in quite a different way. For though it may be that one or another glowing expression escapes me, yet the production is quite a different one: it is the outcome, not of the poet's or the thinker's passion, but of godly fear, and for me it is a divine worship. . . .

It is said of the "poet" that he invokes the muse to supply him with thoughts. This indeed has never been my case, my individuality pro-hibits me even from understanding it; but on the contrary I have needed God every day to shield me from too great a wealth of thoughts. . . . When I learn obedience, as I have described above, when I do the work as if it were a sternly prescribed task, hold the pen as I ought, write each letter with pains, then I can do it. And thus, many and many a time, I have had more joy in the relation of obedience to God than in thoughts that I produced. This, it can readily be perceived, is the expression of the fact that I can lay no claim to an immediate relationship with God, that I cannot and dare not say that it is He who immediately inserts the thoughts in me, but that my relationship to God is a reflection-relationship, is inwardness in reflection, as in general the distinguishing trait of my individuality is reflection, so that even in prayer my *forte* is thanksgiving. . . .

Nothing is less like my procedure than the stormy entrance of genius upon the scene, and then its tumultuous *finale*. Substantially I have lived like a clerk in his *comptoir*. From the very beginning I have been as it were under arrest and every instant have sensed the fact that it was not I that played the part of master, but that another was Master. . . .

The whole productivity has had in a certain sense an uninterrupt-edly even course, as if I had had nothing else to do but to copy daily a definite portion of a printed book. . . .

What I cannot understand is that now I can understand it and yet cannot by any means say that at the instant of commencing it I understood it so precisely . . .

The movement is, *Back!* And although it is all done without "au-thority," there is, nevertheless, something in the accent which recalls a policeman when he faces a riot and says, Back! Hence also more than one of the pseudonyms applies this expression to himself, saying that he is a policeman, a member of the detective force.

—*The Point of View for My Work as an Author*
The Point of View for My Work as an Author: A Report to History, and Related Writings 64–69, 72, 75

INDICTMENT   THE RICOCHETING ACCUSATION

How carefully does God listen to our accusations about others' irresponsibilities?

There was once a criminal who had stolen some money, including a hundred-rix-dollar bill. He wanted to change this bill and turned to another criminal at the latter's house. The second criminal took the bill, went into the next room as if to change it, came out again, acted as if nothing had happened, and greeted the waiting visitor as if they were seeing each other for the first time—in short, he defrauded him out of the hundred-rix-dollar bill. The first criminal became so furious over this that in his resent-ment he notified the authorities of the matter, how shamefully he had been defrauded. The second criminal was of course imprisoned and charged with fraud—but alas, the first question the authorities raised in this case was: How did the plaintiff get the money? Thus there were two cases. The first criminal understood quite correctly that he was in the right in the case of the fraud; now he wanted to be the honest man, the good citizen who appeals to the authorities to obtain his rights. Ah, but the authorities do not function privately or take up any isolated matter it pleases someone to lay before them, nor do they always give the case the turn the plaintiff and the informer give it—the authorities look more deeply into the circumstances. So it is also with the relation to God. If you accuse another person before God, two actions are instituted immediately; precisely when you come and inform on the other person, God begins to think about how you are involved.

Works of Love 381–82 (KW 16)

THE LIMITS OF WORDS   THE DANGER OF ATTRACTING FOLLOWERS

Is religion prone to overestimate how profoundly words can change behavior?

It is quite easy to jump on an omnibus and ride around and say a few admonitory words. There may also be something beautiful in wanting to do it. But it is stupid to be able to teach that a person is capable of nothing whatsoever and then to be able to ascribe such enormous influence to a few admonitory words. . . .

Sallying forth into the world must be left to knights-errant. True earnestness is aware of every danger, and especially of this one—that someone might *bona fide* become a thoughtless follower . . . So let the history books tell of kings who introduced Christianity—I am of the opinion that a king can introduce an improved breed of sheep and railroads etc., but not Christianity.

Stages on Life's Way 343–45 (KW 11)
[Voice: Quidam]*

READINESS TO DIE   MARTYR FOR TEN DOLLARS

Can a dollar value be placed on courage?

When the pastor gesticulates most vehemently where the category is from a lower sphere, it is comic. It is as if someone, calm and indifferent, were to say, "I would give my life for my fatherland," and then with highest pathos, with gestures and facial expression, were to add, "Indeed, I would do it for ten rix-dollars." But when this happens in church, I must not laugh at it.

Concluding Unscientific Postscript to
Philosophical Fragments 1:515n
(KW 12) [Voice: Johannes Climacus]

INWARDNESS

Incongruities

ELICITING PASSION IN PHILOSOPHY

THE HEGELIAN IN THE

CONFESSIONAL BOOTH

Can one simultaneously understand a philosophical system yet fail to understand oneself?

Socrates has rather ironically said that he did not know for sure whether he was a human being or something else, but in the confessional a Hegelian can say with all solemnity: I do not know whether I am a human being—but I have understood the system. I prefer to say: I know that I am a human being, and I know that I have not understood the system. . . .

I have often thought about how one might bring a person into passion. So I have considered the possibility of getting him astride a horse and then frightening the horse into the wildest gallop. Or even better, in order to draw out the passion properly, the possibility of getting a man who wants to go somewhere as quickly as possible (and therefore was already in something of a passion) astride a horse that can hardly walk—and yet existing is like that if one is conscious of it.

Concluding Unscientific Postscript to

Philosophical Fragments 1:311 (KW 12)

[Voice: Johannes Climacus]

SINGLEMINDEDNESS   THE DAZZLING CONVERSATIONALIST

Who has more to recollect, the quiet soul or the talkative activist?

One person talks day in and day out to general assemblies and always about what the times demand, yet not repetitiously in a Cato-like, tedious way, but always interestingly and intriguingly he follows the moment and never says the same thing; at parties, too, he imposes himself and doles out his fund of eloquence, at times with full even measure, at times heaped up, and always to applause; at least once a week there is something about him in the newspaper; also at night he bestows his favors, on his wife, that is, by talking even in his sleep about the demands of the times as if he were at a general assembly. Another person is silent before he speaks and goes so far that he does not speak at all. They live the same length of time—and here the question of the result is raised: Who has more to recollect? One person pursues one idea, one single idea, is preoccupied only with it; another is an author in seven branches of scholarship and "is interrupted in this significant work" (it is a journalist who is speaking) "just as he was about to transform veterinary science." They live the same length of time—and here the question of the result is raised: Who has more to recollect?

Stages on Life's Way 11–12 (KW 11)
[Voice: William Afham]

LISTENING TO MYSELF   MUST I GO TO LONDON TO FIND OUT WHAT IS IMPORTANT?

Does one learn more by traveling or intently listening to oneself?

About this I could write a whole book, although I have not been, according to the custom and the established convention among the observers of our day, in Paris and London, as if by such visits one could learn something great, more than chatter and the wisdom of traveling salesmen. If an observer will only pay attention to himself, he will have enough with five men, five women, and ten children for the discovery of all possible states of the human soul.

The Concept of Anxiety 126 (KW 8)
[Voice: Vigilius Haufniensis]

Do outward advantages help when the inward self is insecure?

Of what good is an armchair of velvet when the rest of the environment does not match? It is like a man going around naked and wearing a three-cornered hat.

—*Repetition*
Fear and Trembling; Repetition 169
(KW 6) [Voice: Constantin
Constantius]*

Suffering

MODERN MARTYRDOM   The Perfumed Martyr

What distinguishes a martyr nowadays from one in ancient times?

Nowadays a martyr, a reformer, is a man who smells of perfume, a man who sits at table with garlands in his hair, and perhaps with guests, a man who has all his goods in gilt-edged securities, a man who really never risks anything and yet wins all, even the title of reformer, his glorious title.

> *On Authority and Revelation: The Book on Adler, or a Cycle of Ethico-Religious Essays 33*

THE PHANTOM REVERSAL OF A REAL CALAMITY
The Cargo in Peril

When the anticipated loss is drastic, does the sufferer want to hear vague news that it might be recoverable?

My soul is oppressed, my mind troubled, and my hope is like an overcrowded lifeboat on a troubled sea. . . .

When the merchant stands at the furthest tip of the harbor and watches his ship and its rich cargo in distress and, concentrating his mind on the loss, goes away saying to himself: It is your own fault that you did not insure it—I wonder if he would really be happy if a sailor came running after him and said, "We can see the ship again; it has not gone down!"—and the merchant turned around, and the sailor took the telescope to look out there and said, "Why, now it is gone again!"

Stages on Life's Way 328–29 (KW 11)
[Voice: Quidam]

DISSATISFACTION — The Vague Hankering for a Divining Rod

Is human longing ever satisfiable?

That in which you find your satisfaction is absolute dissatisfaction. To see all the glories of the world is no concern of yours, for in thought you are beyond them, and if they were offered to you, you would very likely say, as always: Well, maybe one could spend a day on that. You do not care that you have not become a millionaire, and if the chance were offered to you, you would very likely answer: Well, it could really be interesting to have been a millionaire, and one could probable spend a month on it. If you could be offered the love of the most beautiful of girls, you would nevertheless answer: Yes, it would be all right for half a year. . . . You crave nothing, wish [ønske] for nothing, because the only thing you could wish for would be a divining rod [Ønskeqvist, wishing twig] that could provide you with everything, and you would then use it for cleaning out your pipe.

—*Or*

Either/Or 2:202–3 (KW 4) [Voice: Judge William]

IMMOBILITY — The Impatient Chessman

How does chronic despair feel?

I feel as a chessman must feel when the opponent says of it: That piece cannot be moved. . . . I feel like a letter printed backward in the line, and yet as uncontrollable as a pasha with three horse tails, as solicitous for myself and my thoughts as a bank for its banknotes, indeed, as reflected into myself as any *pronomen reflexivum* [reflexive pronoun]. . . . On the whole, I lack the patience to live. I cannot see the grass grow, and if I cannot do that, I do not care to look at it at all. My views are the superficial observations of a *"fahrender Scholastiker* [traveling scholastic]" who dashes through life in the greatest haste. . . . I examine myself; when I am tired of that, I smoke a cigar for diversion and think: God knows what our Lord actually intended with me or what he wants to make of me.

No woman in maternity confinement can have stranger and more impatient wishes than I have.

—*Either:* "Diapsalmata"
Either/Or 1:22, 25–26 (KW 3)
[Voice: "A"]

HOPE RECRUITED BY AFFLICTION
Wings Used Only in
Extreme Need

Can there be any spiritual formation for eternity without a villain, any good without evil, any growth without affliction?

The Joy Of It—That Affliction Does Not Bereave Of Hope, But Recruits Hope. What a strange business proposition—to acquire hope in a way like that! Is it not as strange as though a merchant were to become rich by having nobody enter his shop, or that a traveler reached his destination because somebody showed him the wrong way? Ah, people often complain that life is so unimportant, so meaningless, so totally lacking in entertainment—it seems to me that in this one thought there is entertainment enough for an eternity! . . .

Imagine a creeping creature which nevertheless has wings which it can use when it is reduced to extremities, but for daily use thinks it not worthwhile to employ them—such likewise is the hope of eternity in man's bosom; he has wings, but he must be reduced to ex-

82

tremities before he discovers them, or before he obtains them, or before he employs them!

—*Christian Discourses*
Christian Discourses; and the Lilies of the Field and the Birds of the Air, and Three Discourses at the Communion on Fridays
111, 116–17

MENTORS   THE BEST SENSE

To whom do we turn to learn the best sense of comedy, opulence, morality, and religion?

The melancholy have the best sense of the comic, the opulent often the best sense of the rustic, the dissolute often the best sense of the moral, and the doubter often the best sense of the religious.

—*Either:* "Diapsalmata"
Either/Or 1:20 (KW 3) [Voice: "A"]

Finding and Losing Oneself

SELF-LOSS   THE QUIET HAZARD

Can one entirely lose oneself without ever noticing it?

> The greatest hazard of all, losing the self, can occur very quietly in the world, as if it were nothing at all. No other loss can occur so quietly; any other loss—an arm, a leg, five dollars, a wife, etc.—is sure to be noticed.

> *The Sickness unto Death* 32–33 (KW 19)
> [Voice: Anti-Climacus]

BECOMING A PERSON   ON CLUTCHING THE SEAT TO TRY
                           TO SLOW THE TRAIN DOWN

Is the task of becoming oneself ever complete?

> Becoming subjective [becoming a self] should give a person plenty to do as long as he lives; . . . to finish too quickly is the greatest danger of all.

> I do not have time to try to exercise restraint directly upon the age in which I live, and furthermore I think that trying to restrain the age directly is as futile as for a passenger on a train to try to stop it by clutching the seat ahead of him—he identifies himself directly with the age and yet he wants to restrain it. No, the only thing to do is to get off the train and restrain oneself.

> If one gets off the train (and especially in our day, when one is keeping up with the age, one is continually *auf der Eisenbahn* [on the railway]), [one] never forgets that the task is to exercise restraint.

84

The temptation is to finish too quickly. [In life,] nothing is more certain than that the task is enough for a lifetime.

Concluding Unscientific Postscript to
Philosophical Fragments 1:163–65
(KW 12) [Voice: Johannes Climacus]*

INSTANTLY TRANSFORMING ONESELF
How to Become a Jellyfish

How does the self acquire its own selfhood if it is merely a receptacle for absorbing external values?

There is a creature about which I fall into reverie rather often—it is the jellyfish. Have you noticed how this gelatinous mass can flatten itself into a plate and then slowly sink, then rise, so still and firm that one would think one could step on it. Now it notices its prey approaching; then it funnels into itself, becomes a pouch, and sinks with prodigious speed, deeper and deeper, with this speed snatching in its prey—not into its pouch, for it does not have a pouch, but into itself, for it is itself a pouch and nothing else. It is so able to contract itself that one cannot imagine how it could possibly extend itself. It is just about the same with you, and you must forgive me that I have not had a more beautiful creature with which to compare you and also that you perhaps can hardly keep from smiling at the thought of yourself as nothing but pouch.

—Or
Either/Or 2:38–39 (KW 4) [Voice: Judge William]

A NAME FOR SALE   Just Call Me Number Fourteen

Why not sell your name and start being a different self?

My own name is enough to remind me of everything, and all life seems to contain only allusions to this past. The day before I left, I read in *Adresseavisen* "that sixteen yards of heavy black silk cloth are for sale because of a change in plan." I wonder what the first plan could have been, perhaps a bridal dress! Would that I, too, could sell my name in the newspaper because of a change in plan. If a powerful spirit were to take away my name and offer it back to me resplendent with immortal honors, I would hurl it away, far away, and would beg for the most insignificant, the most commonplace name, to be called no. 14 like a blue boy [whose uniform is furnished by an orphan asylum]. Of what avail to me is a glorious name, even if it were mine:

> For what is the flattering voice of fame
> To the sigh of love from a maiden's breast?

What am I doing at present? I am walking in my sleep during the day and lying awake at night, I am busy and working hard, a model of domesticity and home industry. I moisten my finger, I press my foot on the treadle, I stop the wheel, I set the spindle in motion—I spin. But when I come to put the spinning wheel away in the evening, nothing is there and what has happened to what I have spun only my cat knows.

—*Repetition*
Fear and Trembling; Repetition 194–95
(KW 6) [Voice: The Young Man]*

NEW BIRTH   THE COMPLICATION OF DISCOVERING
                             THAT ONE DOES NOT EXIST

Can one unborn imagine birth?

This matter of being born—is it thinkable? Well, why not? But who is supposed to be thinking it— one who is born or one who is not born? The latter supposition, of course, is an absurdity which never could have entered anyone's head. For one who is born could scarcely have conceived the notion. When one who is born thinks of himself as born, he of course is thinking of this transition from "not to be" to "to be." The situation must be the same with the new birth. . . . It would indeed be unreasonable to require a person to find out all by himself that he does not exist.

—*Philosophical Fragments*
Philosophical Fragments; Johannes
Climacus 20, 22 (KW 7) [Voice:
Johannes Climacus]*

Death

FITNESS   HALE WHEN HE DIED

Is it wise for one to live for his health?

The man who lived for his health was, to use one of your expressions, just as hale and hearty as ever when he died.

—*Or*
Either/Or 2:191 (KW 4)
[Voice: Judge William]

THE LABOR THEORY OF IMMORTALITY

THE DEATH THAT ACCIDENTALLY
DEMONSTRATED IMMORTALITY

Is there a whiff of imagined immortality embedded in the work ethic?

I was genuinely moved some time ago when I read in the newspaper an announcement in which a wife reported her husband's death. Instead of copiously lamenting the pain of losing the best of husbands and the fondest of fathers, she was very brief: this death was so very grievous because just recently her husband had found such a good job. There is much more to this than the grieving widow or a casual newspaper reader sees in it.

This comment can be developed into a proof of human immortality. This demonstration could be stated as follows: It is the destiny of every human being to make a good living. If he dies before he does that, he has not fulfilled his destiny, and everyone is free to surmise

88

whether in another world he will fulfill his destiny. But if he makes a good living, then he has achieved his destiny, but the destiny of making a good living cannot be that he is supposed to die but, on the contrary, that he is supposed to live well on his good living—*ergo*, man is immortal. This demonstration could be called the popular demonstration or the making-a-living demonstration. If this demonstration is added to . . . [other] demonstrations, then every reasonable doubt about immortality must be regarded as conquered. This demonstration lends itself splendidly to being placed in conjunction with the other demonstrations—indeed, it shows up here in its full glory since as a conclusion it implies the others and substantiates them. The other demonstrations presuppose that man is a rational creature. Now insofar as anyone should doubt that, the making-a-living demonstration steps up and demonstrates this presupposition by means of the following syllogism: God gives understanding to the person to whom he gives a living; God gives a good understanding to the person to whom he gives a good living—*ergo*. That grieving widow had an intimation of this.

—*Or*

Either/Or 2:279–80 (KW 4) [Voice: "A," quoted by Judge William]*

IMPERSONAL THOUGHTS ON PERSONAL IMMORTALITY
The Doctor Who by Ending the Patient's Life Drove out the Fever

To what extent can abstract thinking, by explaining immortality through rational argument, assist one in entering personally into a relation with eternity?

Abstract thinking helps me with my immortality by killing me as a particular existing individual and then making me immortal and therefore helps somewhat as in Holberg—the doctor took the patient's life with his medicine—but also drove out the fever. . . . When reading the biography of such a thinker (for his books may very well be excellent), one sometimes shudders at the thought of what it means to be a human being. Even if a lace-maker made lace ever so lovely, it is still sad to think of this poor stunted creature. Thus it is comic to see a thinker who, despite all his bravura, personally exists as a fussbudget, who personally did marry but was scarcely acquainted with or moved by the power of love, whose marriage therefore was presumably as impersonal as his thinking, whose personal life was without pathos and without passionate struggles and was philistinely concerned only about which university provided the best job.

> Concluding Unscientific Postscript to
> Philosophical Fragments 1:302–3
> (KW 12) [Voice: Johannes Climacus]

EQUALITY IN DEATH   AFTER THE CURTAIN FALLS

Is equality in eternity after death something like the bizarre sense of equality felt by actors immediately after the curtain falls?

It is like a play. But when the curtain falls, the one who played the king, and the one who played the beggar, and all the others—they are all quite alike, all one and the same: actors. And when in death the curtain falls on the stage of actuality (for it is a confused use of language if one speaks about the curtain being rolled up on the stage of the eternal at the time of death, because the eternal is no stage—it is truth), then they also are all one; they are human beings. All are that which they essentially were, something we did not see because of the difference we see. They are all human beings. The stage of art is like an enchanted world. But just suppose that some evening a common absent-mindedness confused all the actors so they thought they really were what they were representing. Would this not be, in contrast to the enchantment of art, what one might call the enchantment of an evil spirit, a bewitchment? And likewise suppose that in the enchantment of actuality (for we are, indeed, all enchanted, each one bewitched by his own

90

distinctions) our fundamental ideas became confused so that we thought ourselves essentially to be the roles we play. Alas, but is this not the case? It seems to be forgotten that the distinctions of earthly existence are only like an actor's costume.

Works of Love: Some Christian Reflections in the Form of Discourses 95

MOURNING A LOST RELATIONSHIP
The Deceased First Love

When an infatuated lover "dies of love," is there a need for a burial?

A dead person is one of the most amusing figures to be met in life. Strange that this is not used on the stage more frequently—now and then in real life we can meet such a one. Even one feigning death has an essentially comic oddity about him, but a person who is actually dead furnishes all the amusement one can reasonably require of a contribution to amusement. Just keep on the alert; I myself actually became aware of this one day while walking along the street with an acquaintance. We met a passing couple. My companion's demeanor led me to assume that he knew the couple, and I asked him about them. "Oh," he answered, "I know them very well and very intimately, especially the lady, for she was my late departed." "What late departed?" I asked. "Oh, my late departed first love; yes, it was a strange story. 'I am dying,' she said, and at the same moment departed, as is natural with death—otherwise one could have invested in the widows' pension fund. It was too late; dead she was and dead she remained, and now I am wandering about, as the poet says, 'looking in vain for my beloved's grave so that I can offer her a tear.'"

So it was with that dejected man who was left alone in the world, notwithstanding that it comforted him to find the late beloved already so far along, if not because of someone else nevertheless with

91

someone else. How fine it is for the girls, I thought, that they do not have to be buried every time they die.

Stages on Life's Way 54–55 (KW 11)
[Voice: Constantin Constantius, quoted by William Afham]

THE HOPE OF REASON   Hilarius the Executioner

What did the gravestone of the executioner's son say?

When, out in the cemetery, one reads on a gravestone the effusions in verse of a man who, mourning in three lines the loss of his little son, at the end bursts forth in the line, "Take comfort, reason, he lives!" and this effusion is signed: Hilarius, Executioner—this certainly will produce a comic effect on everyone. First, the name itself (Hilarius) in this connection produces a comic effect; one involuntarily thinks: Well, if a man is named Hilarius, no wonder he knows how to comfort himself! Then comes his position as executioner. It is true that every human being can have feelings, but there still are certain occupations that cannot be perceived as standing in a close relation to feeling. Finally the outburst, "Take comfort, reason!" It is thinkable that it could occur to a philosophy professor to confuse himself with reason, but an executioner will be less successful in this.

Concluding Unscientific Postscript to
Philosophical Fragments 1:518n
(KW 12) [Voice: Johannes Climacus]

CHRISTIANITY

Becoming a Christian

CHRISTIANITY   JUST CHECK THE GEOGRAPHY BOOK

Why is it no longer perilous to profess oneself as a Christian?

At one time it was perilous to profess being a Christian; now it is precarious to doubt that one is. . . . If someone were to say, plainly and simply, that he was concerned about himself, that it was not quite right for him to call himself a Christian, he would not be persecuted or executed, but people would give him an angry look and say, "It is really boring of this fellow to make so much ado about nothing; why can't he be like the rest of us, who are all Christians. He is just like F. F., who does not want to wear a hat, as the rest of us do, but has to be eccentric." If he were married, his wife would tell him, "Hubby, darling, where did you ever pick up such a notion? How can you not be a Christian? You are Danish, aren't you? Doesn't the geography book say that the predominant religion in Denmark is Lutheran-Christian? You aren't a Jew, are you, or a Mohammedan? What else would you be, then? It is a thousand years since paganism was superseded; so I know you aren't a pagan. Don't you tend to work in the office as a good civil servant; aren't you a good subject in a Christian nation, in a Lutheran-Christian state? So of course you are a Christian." . . .

When it is a matter of something that presupposes proficiency and the like, it is easier to make an admission. But the less significant the object, that is, less significant because everyone possesses it, the more embarrassing is the admission.

Concluding Unscientific Postscript to
Philosophical Fragments 1:50–51
(KW 12) [Voice: Johannes Climacus]

THE PRICE OF DYING   The Price Is Ten Dollars

Dying—what is the price?

Christianity cannot be introduced without this existential qualification. It is: to *die to*. Just try it. Someone comes along proclaiming Christianity—and it is his livelihood, his career—he says to a man, "You must die to—the price is ten dollars." "What? Ten dollars? For whom?" "For me, since it is my livelihood, my career, to proclaim that one must die to." Between God (who requires "You must die to") and me, the single individual, the poor fellow who has to bite the sour apple and die to, there is introduced as a middle term (of the proclamation) a livelihood, a lucrative, good livelihood for a man with a family, the rank of a councilor, and advancement—this is impossible; the proclamation contradicts itself.

—*Judge for Yourself!*
For Self-Examination; Judge for Yourself!
131 (KW 21)*

SMOKING OUT ILLUSIONS The Incendiary Nature of
Truth-Telling

Is it more fitting now to stop ringing the fire alarm on modernity or set some new fires?

It would, indeed, be indefensible to stop ringing the alarm as long as the fire is burning. But, strictly speaking, I am not the one who is ringing the alarm; I am the one who, in order to smoke out illusions and skullduggery, is starting the fire, a police operation, and a Christian police operation, since according to the New Testament Christianity is incendiarism—Christ himself says, "I came to cast fire upon the earth." . . .

Christianity, which came into the world as the truth for which one dies, has now become the truth on which one . . . lives.

—"Newspaper Articles, 1854–1855"
The Moment *and Late Writings* [51]–52
(KW 23)

To what extent has the price of being Christian within modernity become grossly discounted?

The history of Christendom, from generation to generation, became a story of steadily scaling down the price of what it is to be a Christian. At last it came to be such a ridiculously low price that it soon had the opposite effect that people scarcely wanted to have anything to do with Christianity, because through this false leniency it had become so sickly and cloying that it was disgusting. To be a Christian—well, if only one does not literally steal, does not literally make stealing one's occupation, since to be a thief in one's occupation can very well be combined with being an earnest Christian who goes to communion once a year or to church a few times a year, at least on New Year's Day for sure. To be a Christian—well, if in committing adultery one does not overdo or, forsaking the golden mean, carry it to extremes, since observing—decorum!—that is, secretly, with good taste and culture, it can still be combined with being an earnest Christian who listens to a sermon at least once for every fourteen times he reads comedies and novels. . . . This is a *wohlfeil* [cheap] edition of what it is to be a Christian. Yet this is the actual state of affairs, because preachers' declaiming about the lofty virtues, etc. during a quiet hour on Sunday does not alter the actual state of affairs on Monday.

> —*Judge for Yourself!*
> *For Self-Examination; Judge for Yourself!*
> 188–89 (KW 21)

THE NATURALIZATION OF CHRISTIANITY
THE LOSS OF BITE

To what extent has the language of primitive Christianity lost its power to evoke meaning?

To dispute about loose words and to be in agreement on loose words are indeed always ludicrous, but when even the firmest words have become loose—what then? Just as an old man who has lost his teeth now munches with the help of the stumps [of the teeth], so the modern Christian language about Christianity has lost the power of the energetic terminology to bite. . . .

In short: *it is easier to become a Christian if I am not a Christian than to become a Christian if I am one.* . . .

Everyone is a Christian as a matter of course by being baptized when he was a fortnight old. . . . An attempt has been made to naturalize Christianity, so that in the end to be a Christian and to be a human being are identical, and one is born a Christian just as one is born a human being, or at least birth and rebirth are moved together in the space of a fortnight.

Concluding Unscientific Postscript to
Philosophical Fragments 1:363, 366–67,
367n (KW 12) [Voice: Johannes
Climacus]*

Incarnation and Atonement

AVOIDING AN OPINION   IGNORING HIS MAJESTY'S VISIT

Suppose God became a human in time—could that be something about which a reasonable person could choose not to have an opinion?

When God lets himself be born and become man, this is not an idle caprice, some fancy he hits upon just to be doing something, perhaps to put an end to the boredom that has brashly been said must be involved in being God—it is not in order to have an adventure. No, when God does this, then this fact is the earnestness of existence. And, in turn, the earnestness in this earnestness is: that everyone shall have an opinion about it. When a king visits a town in the provinces, he regards it as an insult if a public official fails, without sufficient cause, to pay his respects to him; but I wonder what he would think if someone were to ignore completely the fact that the king was in town and played the private citizen who says: "The devil take His Majesty and the Royal Law." And so also when it pleases God to become man—and then it pleases someone (and what the public official is before the king every person is before God) to say: Well, this is something I do not care to form any opinion about.

The Sickness unto Death 130 (KW 19)
[Voice: Anti-Climacus]

INCARNATION WHETHER GOD COULD HAVE
BECOME INCARNATE AS A LARGE
GREEN BIRD

**Why did not God in the Incarnation become something a bit more
spectacular than simply an ordinary human being?**

If God had taken the form, for exam-
ple, of a rare, enormously large green bird, with a red beak, that
perched in a tree on the embankment and perhaps even whistled in
an unprecedented manner—then our partygoing man would surely
have had his eyes opened. . . .

If God [*Gud*] wants to reveal himself in human form and provide a
direct relation by taking, for example, the form of a man who is
twelve feet tall, then that imaginatively constructed partygoer and
captain of the popinjay shooting club will surely become aware. But
since God is unwilling to deceive, the spiritual relation in truth spe-
cifically requires that there be nothing at all remarkable about his
form; then the partygoer must say: There is nothing to see, not the
slightest.

Concluding Unscientific Postscript to
Philosophical Fragments 1:245–46
(KW 12) [Voice: Johannes Climacus]

CONTEMPORANEITY WITH CHRIST

A MUSICAL INTERLUDE OF PRECISELY
1,843 YEARS

**Is the 1,843-year interlude between the Christian salvation event
and the present an obstacle to becoming contemporary with the
Incarnation?**

My dear reader! We assume, then,
that this teacher [the God] has appeared, that he is dead and buried,
and that an interval of time has elapsed. . . . Also in a comedy there
may be an interval of several years between two acts. To suggest this
passage of time, the orchestra sometimes plays a symphony or some-

thing similar in order to shorten the time by filling it up. In a similar manner, I, too, have thought to fill the intervening time by pondering the question set forth. How long the intervening period should be is up to you, but if it pleases you, then for the sake of earnestness and jest we shall assume that precisely eighteen hundred and forty-three years have passed. You see, then, that for the sake of the illusion I ought to take plenty of time for eighteen hundred and forty-three years is an uncommon allowance of time, which will quickly place me in a predicament opposite to that in which our philosophers find themselves, whom time usually permits nothing more than to give a hint, a predicament opposite to that in which the historians find themselves, whom time, not the subject matter, leaves in the lurch.

—*Philosophical Fragments*
Philosophical Fragments; Johannes Climacus [72] (KW 7) [Voice: Johannes Climacus]

FLEEING THE PARADOX   PRETENDING TO BE CONTEMPORARY WITH THE INCARNATION WHILE RUNNING AWAY FROM IT

What is to be said of the pilgrim who announces his destination— the holy city—but at every opportunity runs away from it?

If someone coming later, someone who may even be carried away by his own infatuation, wishes to be a contemporary [of the Absolute Paradox, the Incarnation] (in the sense of immediacy), he demonstrates that he is an imposter, recognizable, like the false Smerdis, by his having no ears—namely, the ears of faith—even though he may have the long donkey ears with which one, although listening as a contemporary (in the sense of immediacy), does not become contemporary. If someone who comes later goes on talking extravagantly about the glory of being a contemporary (in the sense of immediacy) and is continually wanting to be away, then we must let him go, but if you watch him you will easily see by his walk and by the path he has turned onto that he is

101

not on the way to the terror of the paradox but is bounding away like a dancing teacher in order to reach that imperial wedding on time. And even though he gives his junket a holy name, and even though he preaches about community to others so that they join the pilgrimage in crowds, he will hardly discover the holy land (in the sense of immediacy), since it is to be found neither on the map nor on earth, but his journey is a spoof, like the game of escorting someone to grandmother's door. And even though he gives himself no rest, neither by night nor by day, and runs faster than a horse can run or than a man can tell lies, he still is only running on a wild-goose chase and misunderstands himself, like the birdcatcher, for if the bird does not come to him, running after it with a lime twig is futile.

—*Philosophical Fragments*
Philosophical Fragments; Johannes Climacus 70–71 (KW 7) [Voice: Johannes Climacus]*

Offense and Paradox

PARADOX   THE EXPONENTIAL INCREASE OF
ASSISTANT PROFESSORS

**At what future point in time will Christianity cease to be a
paradox?**

When Christianity entered into the
world, there were no professors or assistant professors whatever—
then it was a paradox for all. It can be assumed that in the present
generation every tenth person is an assistant professor; consequently
it is a paradox for only nine out of ten. And when the fullness of
time finally comes, that matchless future, when a generation of assistant professors, male and female, will live on the earth—then Christianity will have ceased to be a paradox.

Concluding Unscientific Postscript to
Philosophical Fragments 1:220–21
(KW 12) [Voice: Johannes Climacus]

THE SALE OF CHRISTIANITY
GETTING HURT BY A BOUQUET

Is Christianity to be commended without warning?

I wonder if a man handing another
man an extremely sharp, polished, two-edged instrument would hand
it over with the air, gestures, and expression of one delivering a bouquet of flowers? Would not this be madness? What does one do, then?
Convinced of the excellence of the dangerous instrument, one recommends it unreservedly, to be sure, but in such a way that in a
certain sense one warns against it. So it is with Christianity. . . .

Woe to the person who ingratiatingly, flirtatiously, commendingly, convincingly preached to mankind some dainty something which was supposed to be Christianity! Woe to the person who could make the miracles reasonable, or at least sketch and publicize the prospects of its being done soon! Woe to the person who betrayed and broke the mystery of faith, distorted it into public wisdom, because he took away the possibility of offence! Woe to the person who could comprehend the mystery of atonement without detecting anything of the possibility of offence; woe again to him because he thought thereby to make God and Christianity something for study and cultivation. Woe to all those unfaithful stewards who sat down and wrote false proofs, winning friends for themselves and Christianity by writing off the possibility of offence in Christianity and inserting foolishness by the hundreds! . . . Therefore take away from Christianity the possibility of offence or take away from the forgiveness of sin the battle of an anguished conscience (to which, nevertheless, according to Luther's excellent explanation, this whole doctrine leads), and then lock the churches, the sooner the better, or turn them into places of amusement.

Works of Love: Some Christian Reflections in the Form of Discourses 191–93*

INCOMPREHENSIBILITY THE EMPEROR'S GRACIOUS INVITATION TO THE DAY LABORER

How would a pure gift from one on high be received by one most lowly?

If I were to imagine a poor day laborer and the mightiest emperor who ever lived, and if this mightiest emperor suddenly seized on the idea of sending for the day laborer, who had never dreamed and "in whose heart it had never arisen" that the emperor knew he existed, who then would consider himself indescribably favored just to be permitted to see the emperor once, something he would relate to his children and grandchildren as the most important event in his life—if the emperor sent for him and told him that he wanted him for a son-in-law: what then?

104

Quite humanly, the day laborer would be more or less puzzled, self-conscious, and embarrassed by it; he would (and this is the humanness of it) humanly find it very strange and bizarre, something he would not dare tell to anyone, since he himself had already secretly concluded what his neighbors near and far would busily gossip about as soon as possible: that the emperor wanted to make a fool of him, make him a laughingstock of the whole city, that there would be cartoons of him in the newspapers, and that the story of his engagement to the emperor's daughter would be sold by the ballad peddlers.

The Sickness unto Death 84 (KW 19)
[Voice: Anti-Climacus]

INFINITE WEALTH   THE BANKNOTE SO LARGE IT
                         WAS UNNEGOTIABLE

Can the absolute worth of the Incarnation be quantified?

The illegitimate child, unacknowledged by any family, the concern of no family, an alien, outside society, who was born clandestinely at midnight behind a bush—this was how [the Lord] allowed himself to be born, for want of a room, just as he was indeed also crucified because the world had no room for him! In a stable (since the despised virgin had no family alliance ready with a layette), laid in a manger—if there was an alliance here, it had to be with the horses. . . .

When, for example, Christ sends out the disciples—well, he surely could have supplied them with the necessities, but no, they must own nothing. . . . Well, it is true that he has a check drawn on heaven, and properly viewed (therefore, unfortunately, not in this world), that is worth more than all the glories of this world, but he has no money and nothing of this earth (unfortunately it is in this world), where money, properly viewed!—surely has more worth than all the glories of heaven.

There is a story about a traveler who was short of money out in the country although he did indeed have a large denomination banknote—there was no one who could change it. So also with Christianity and the disciple.

—*Judge for Yourself!*
For Self-Examination; Judge for Yourself!
161–62 (KW 21)*

Eternal Happiness in Time

THE DANGER OF SUCCEEDING

Explain Eternal Happiness while I Shave

Can one learn easily and quickly about eternal happiness?

Esthetically one can very well wish for wealth, good fortune, the most beautiful girl—in short, everything that is esthetic-dialectical; but then to *wish* for eternal happiness *in addition* is double gibberish, partly because one does it *in addition* and thereby converts an eternal happiness into a prize on a Christmas tree, and partly because one *wishes.* . . .

But one of the gentlemen wishers, a "serious man" who really wants to do something for his eternal happiness, may say, "Is it not possible to find out for certain, clearly and briefly, what an eternal happiness is? Can't you describe it to me 'while I shave,' just as one describes the loveliness of a woman, the royal purple, or distant regions?" It is good that I cannot do it, good that I am not a poetic nature or a kindly clergyman, because then I would be capable of beginning to do it, and perhaps I might succeed.

Concluding Unscientific Postscript to
Philosophical Fragments 1:391–92
(KW 12) [Voice: Johannes Climacus]

CONQUERING CHANGE   ON RUNNING A FOOT RACE IN HEAVY ARMOR

Amid a sea of constant change, how are bearings gained?

It is certainly good for a person to be armed when he goes into combat, and even better to be appropriately armed for the specific combat. If a man who is going to compete in a race were to don heavy armor, he certainly would be well armed, but his armor would scarcely be of any advantage. Is it not the same with the weapon of one who is to struggle with the future, since experience is a double-tongued friend who says one thing now and something else later, and guessing is a deceitful guide who abandons one when he is needed most, and conjecture is a clouded eye that does not see very far, and inference is a snare that is more likely to snare oneself than someone else. Moreover, those weapons are difficult to use, because, inasmuch as the experiencing soul did not remain untouched during the experience, fear accompanies guessing, anxiety conjecture, and uneasiness inference. . . .

When the sailor is out on the ocean, when everything is changing all around him, when the waves are born and die, he does not stare down into the waves, because they are changing. He looks up at the stars. Why? Because they are faithful; they have the same location now that they had for our ancestors and will have for generations to come. By what means does he conquer the changeable? By the eternal.

Eighteen Upbuilding Discourses 18–19
(KW 5)

GOD'S TIME   SEVENTY YEARS

What is one hour, forty-six minutes, and three seconds so far as eternity goes?

For her God is very much like what one pictures as a kind elderly uncle who for a sweet word does everything the child wants, just as the child wants it. That is why one is so very fond of this uncle. . . . She swears by God, she beseeches in God's name, and yet with regard to the religious she is only romantic in the little multiplication table, and with regard to the religious she is, *valore intrinseco* [according to intrinsic value], only an ordinary dollar. . . .

But he is just the opposite, he is religiously constructed; his romanticism has the magnitude of infinity, in which God is a powerful God, and seventy years a stroke of the pen, and a whole life on earth a period of probation, and the loss of his one and only desire is something for which one must be prepared if one wishes to be involved with him, because as the eternal he has a round concept of time and says to the one who seeks him, "No, the moment hasn't come yet—wait just a bit." "How long?" "Well—seventy years." "My God, meanwhile a person could die ten times!" "That must certainly be left up to me, without whose will not one sparrow falls to the ground, so then—tomorrow, tomorrow very early." In other words, in seventy years, for since a thousand years for him is as one day, so seventy years is precisely one hour, forty-six minutes, and three seconds.

Stages on Life's Way 236–37 (KW 11)
[Voice: Quidam]

WEIGHING TEMPORAL SUFFERING AGAINST
ETERNAL HAPPINESS   WEIGHING GOLD VERSUS FEATHERS

Can the afflictions of temporality be measured against the blessedness of eternity?

The proverb says that a pound of gold and a pound of feathers weigh equally much, and this is indeed true. But then we add that in another and more important sense these two quantities cannot be weighed together. And why not? Because the scales cannot indicate that the one pound is gold and the other feathers, consequently because the gold has a special value which makes the direct weight of the gold and of the feathers in relation to one another meaningless. . . . The least portion of the eternal happiness weighs infinitely more than the most prolonged earthly suffering.

> —*The Gospel of Suffering*
> *The Gospel of Suffering and the Lilies of the Field* 134–35*

LIVING IN THE PAST   THE PHILOSOPHER'S COATTAILS

What remains in the present for a philosophy fixated upon the past?

Philosophy hastens so fast into the past that, as a poet says of an antiquarian, only his coattails remain in the present.

> —*Or*
> *Either/Or* 2:171 (KW 4) [Voice: Judge William]

THEOLOGY

God

"PROOF" OF GOD   The Vague Anxiety
                 of an Approximately
                 Absolute Monarch

**At what point does the demonstration of God's existence make
God uncertain of himself?**

                     Simon Tornacensis . . . thought that
God must be obliged to him for having furnished a proof of the Trin-
ity, because if he wanted, then—*profecto si malignando et adversando
vellem, fortioribus argumentis scirem illam infirmare et deprimendo im-
probare* [if out of malice and enmity I wished to do so, I could weaken
it with stronger arguments, and disprove it by reducing it]. . . . What
he lacked was not strenuous earnestness in dialectics and speculation
but an understanding of himself. This story has numerous analogies,
and in our time speculation has assumed such authority that it has
practically tried to make God feel uncertain of himself, like a monarch who is anxiously waiting to learn whether the general assembly
will make him an absolute or a limited monarch.

                         The Concept of Anxiety 151n (KW 8)
                         [Voice: Vigilius Haufniensis]

PROFANITY   Why Profanity Is at Home
                   in "Christendom"

What name is most frequently used in common speech?

                     Is it not epigrammatic enough that
cursing was not customary in paganism, whereas it really is right at
home in Christendom, that out of a kind of horror and fear of the

113

mysterious, paganism as a rule named the name God with tremendous solemnity, whereas in Christendom God's name is the word that most frequently appears in daily speech and is clearly the word that is given the least thought and used most carelessly, because the poor, revealed God (who instead of keeping himself hidden, as the upper class usually does, was careless and injudicious enough to become revealed) has become a personage far too familiar to the whole population, a personage for whom they then do the exceedingly great service of going to church every once in a while, for which they are also commended by the pastor, who on behalf of God thanks them for the honor of the visit, favors them with the title of pious, but is a little sarcastic about those who never show God the honor of going to church.

The Sickness unto Death 115–16
(KW 19) [Voice: Anti-Climacus]

ARGUMENT FOR THE EXISTENCE OF GOD
THE UNCOMMON DIFFICULTY OF
DEMONSTRATING THAT ANYTHING
AT ALL EXISTS

Is it a fool who says in his heart: "I shall demonstrate the existence of God"?

If . . . the god does not exist, then of course it is impossible to demonstrate it. But if he does exist, then it is foolishness to want to demonstrate it, since I, in the very moment the demonstration commences, would presuppose it not as doubtful—which a presupposition cannot be, inasmuch as it is a presupposition—but as certain (a presupposition is never doubtful for the very reason that it is a presupposition) because otherwise I would not begin, easily perceiving that the whole thing would be impossible if he did not exist. . . . It is generally a difficult matter to want to demonstrate that something exists—worse still, for the brave souls who venture to do it, the difficulty is of such a kind that fame by no means awaits those who are preoccupied with it. The whole process of demonstration continually becomes something entirely different from what it assumes to be, and becomes an additional development of what I conclude from having presupposed that the object of investigation exists. Therefore, whether I am moving in the world of sensate palpability or in the world of thought, I never reason in conclusion to existence, but I reason in conclusion from existence. For example, I do not demonstrate that a stone exists but that something which exists is a stone. The court of law does not demonstrate that a criminal exists but that the accused, who does indeed exist, is a criminal. . . .

And how does the existence of the god emerge from the demonstration? Does it happen straightway? Is it not here as it is with the Cartesian dolls? As soon as I let go of the doll, it stands on its head. As soon as I let go of it—consequently, I have to let go of it. So also with the demonstration—so long as I am holding on to the demonstration (that is, continue to be one who is demonstrating), the existence does not emerge, if for no other reason than that I am in the process of demonstrating it, but when I let go of the demonstration, the existence is there. . . . Trying to get rid of something by sleeping is just as useless as trying to obtain something by sleeping. . . .

For the fool says in his heart that there is no God, but he who says in his heart or to others: Just wait a little and I shall demonstrate it— ah, what a rare wise man he is! If, at the moment he is supposed to begin the demonstration, it is not totally undecided whether the god exists or not, then, of course, he does not demonstrate it, and if that is the situation in the beginning, then he never does make a beginning—partly for fear that he will not succeed because the god may not exist, and partly because he has nothing with which to begin.

—*Philosophical Fragments*
Philosophical Fragments; Johannes
Climacus 39–40, 42–44 (KW 7)
[Voice: Johannes Climacus]*

PROVING GOD'S EXISTENCE

Right Road, Wrong Direction

Does it represent a bold advance in the spirit to master arguments for the existence of God?

Any qualification that claims to render the god directly knowable is undoubtedly a milestone, bit a milestone on the way of approximation, registering retrogression rather than progress. It marks a movement away from the paradox, not toward it, missing the point of Socrates and Socratic ignorance. Close attention should be paid to this lest the same thing happen in the spiritual world that happened to the traveler who asked an Englishman if the road led to London and was told: Yes, it does—but he never did arrive in London, because the Englishman had omitted to mention that he needed to turn about, inasmuch as he was going away from London.

—*Philosophical Fragments*
Philosophical Fragments; Johannes
Climacus 64n (KW 7) [Voice: Johannes
Climacus]*

Explaining Hegel to God

ARGUMENTS ON JUDGMENT DAY

Explaining Hegel to God

With what arguments is the assistant professor armed for the final judgment?

Indeed, I do feel that I could make use of an unhappy love affair; it is appropriate to my existence. . . . What it depends upon is the positing of life's pathological elements absolutely, clearly, legibly, and powerfully, so that life does not come to be like the system, a peddler's cart where there is a little of everything, so that one does everything to a certain degree, even the most foolish thing of all, believing to a certain degree, so that one does not tell a lie but is ashamed of oneself, does not tell a lie and then, erotically speaking, romantically dies of love and is a hero, but does not stop at that or just lie there but gets up again and goes further and becomes a hero in novels of everyday life, and goes further yet and becomes frivolous, witty, a hero like those they laugh at in the comedies of A. E. Scribe. Imagine eternity in a confusion like that; imagine a man like that on Judgment Day; imagine hearing the voice of God, "Have you believed?" Imagine hearing the answer, "Faith is the immediate, one should not stop with the immediate as they did in the Middle Ages, but since Hegel one goes further; nevertheless one admits that it is the immediate and that the immediate exists but anticipates a new tome." My old schoolmaster was a hero, a man of iron. Woe, woe to the boy who could not answer yes or no to a direct question. And if on Judgment Day a person is no longer a boy, God in heaven can still pass for a schoolmaster. Just imagine that this paragraph-madness, this curriculum-craze, and this systematic sliding about have so taken over that eventually, to make a long story short, we want to brief our Lord on the most recent philosophy.—If God is unwilling, then I imagine the trumpet angel will take the trumpet and hit such an assistant professor on the head so that he is never more a man.

Stages on Life's Way 291–92 (KW 11)
[Voice: Quidam]*

APOSTOLICITY AS ACADEMIA
The Restless Renter Who
Pretended Ownership

To what extent has Christianity within modernity patterned itself after an academic society?

Suppose that the speculative thinker is the restless resident who, although it is obvious that he is a renter, yet in view of the abstract truth that, eternally and divinely perceived, all property is in common, wants to be the owner, so that there is nothing to do except to send for a police officer, who would presumably say, just as the subpoena servers say to Gert Westphaler: We are sorry to have to come on this errand. . . .

It is as if Christ—it is not my fault that I say it—as if Christ had been a professor and as if the apostles had formed a little professional society of scholars. Truly, if at one time it was difficult to become a Christian, I believe now it becomes more difficult year by year, because it has now become so easy to become one. There is a bit of competition only in becoming a speculative thinker.

Concluding Unscientific Postscript to
Philosophical Fragments 1:214–15
(KW 12) [Voice: Johannes Climacus]

118

FOLLOWING THE SPIRIT OF THESE TIMES

IS IT POSSIBLE TO SATISFY THE
DEMANDS OF THE TIME?

To what extent has philosophy conquered the imagination of the clergy?

Is it not, to take a single example, proclaimed again and again by philosophy's clergy, "that in our time it is a necessity for the theologian to be a philosopher, in order to be able to satisfy the demands of the time." But if it is a necessity, it must also be a possibility; for even I can see that it would be very unphilosophical of philosophy to regard as necessary that which is impossible. Every theologian, then, can become a philosopher. . . . This statement, so consoling for every theological graduate, gains in edifying power when one thinks of the following words: "in order to be able to satisfy the demand of the time." . . . See, philosophy is so good in these latter days, so different from that old, niggardly goddess who would only be loved and worshiped by some few, reveal herself to fewer. It makes every theologian a philosopher and does it in order to satisfy the demand of the time, which demand must then be philosophical, which again presupposes that the time—that is, the sum of individuals—is philosophical. What a noble hope for every theological graduate! If only the doubt did not remain about whether one really understood what one said and what was said.

What theology thus preaches, all the other branches of scholarship preach likewise, since they all gravitate toward philosophy. "Philosophy is the demand of the time!" sounds from all mouths like a tutti [full orchestra]. And philosophy, of course, acknowledges the time as reasonable, thus its demand as a reasonable demand. I readily think the best of my fellow humans and therefore readily believe of every individual who speaks that he understands what he says. But nevertheless for me there always remains a residuum of doubt. It is this remaining doubt I wanted extirpated.

Prefaces: Light Reading for Certain Classes
as the Occasion May Require 80–81
[Voice: Nicolaus Notabene]*

The Hazards of Regnant Theology

MIRACLE
                                    DR. HJORTESPRING'S
                                    HEGELIAN MIRACLE

What perils lurk in the appeal to miracles?

I have no miracle to appeal to. Ah, that was Dr. Hjortespring's happy fate! According to his own very well-written report, he became an adherent of Hegelian philosophy through a miracle at Hotel Streit in Hamburg on Easter morning (although none of the waiters noticed anything). He was an adherent of the philosophy that assumes that there are no miracles. . . . To be converted by a miracle to the teaching that accepts no miracles is rather topsy-turvy. The miracle occurred on Easter morning. . . . The whole thing remains exceedingly puzzling, even if it is assumed that Easter came very early that year, for example, on April first, so that in addition to becoming a Hegelian the doctor became an April fool.

Concluding Unscientific Postscript to
Philosophical Fragments 1:184 (KW 12)
[Voice: Johannes Climacus]

ASTRONOMY
                                    HOW HIRED WAITERS DISARMED
                                    A PROFESSOR

Has the hazard to theology been ended by Professor Heiberg's invasion of the field of astronomy?

Already it is glorious to picture the prof when he stands there and prophetically stares straight ahead until he glimpses the System and the realization of plans long contemplated. Or when, as recently, he fixes his eye on the celestial things, counts the stars, calculates their courses, watches for those distant orbs' celestial inhabitants, forgetting the earth and terrestrial life, states, empires, countries, societies, individuals, at the matchless discovery that in astronomical respects too, the earth occupies a highly respectable place in the heavens. Yet, let the outcome be whatever it will be, this latter is and remains of the utmost significance, that Prof. Heiberg has thrown himself into astronomy. Is this not a stroke of good fortune, if not for astronomy then for theology? A couple of years ago, when the prof unveiled in his apocalyptic poem the secret of the heavens, and an obliging critique and an officious public opinion let it be understood, not exactly obscurely, that Prof. Heiberg had now become Dante, I began privately to be afraid. The one who at that time paid attention to our situation a little more carefully will surely not deny that there sometimes appeared phenomena that seemed to suggest the horror that Prof. H., who in addition has always been a philosopher, should suddenly undergo a new metamorphosis and step forward as the one who had come into the world to solve theology's riddles. Now this would have been droll enough, but it was hardly desirable. Now the prof has chosen, and chosen astronomy. There is then no further danger, for it will be an easy matter in the future to keep him astronomically employed. The procedure is quite simple, like the one that Pernille uses against Vielgeschrey in Holberg's *Stundesløse* [The Restless One]. . . . One dresses up two hired waiters as envoys from a distant people versed in astronomy, who have come to compliment the prof and to put to him an astronomical riddle, by whose answer it will be shown that he is that people's awaited savior. To this end the hired waiters have been instructed as follows: as soon as the prof has answered, regardless of what, they will fall on their knees and worship him. In this position they announce the rest of their mission, that they have come to fetch him.

Prefaces: Light Reading for Certain Classes
as the Occasion May Require 47–49
[Voice: Nicolaus Notabene]

121

FORGETFULNESS · · · · · · · · · · The Lighthead Explaining the
· Source of His Wealth

**If one forgets how one has acquired one's wealth, does the civil
order demand an explanation?**

Look at him, that lucky one whom
good fortune delighted to indulge in everything. He does not work,
and yet he is a Solomon in magnificence; his life is a dance, his
thought is intoxicated with wishful dreaming, and every dream is
fulfilled; his eyes are satiated more swiftly than they crave, his heart
conceals no secret desire, his hankering has learned to recognize no
boundary. But if you were to ask him where it all comes from, he
would probably answer light-mindedly, "I myself do not know." Being
light-minded, he probably would even be amused by his answer as a
joke quite in keeping with everything else, but he would not comprehend or even suspect what he actually said and how he passed judgment on himself. The civil authorities see to it that everyone keeps
what legitimately belongs to him. When they find a person whose
abundance and wealth astonish everyone, they demand from him an
explanation of the source. But if he cannot explain it, he is suspected
of not having obtained it by honest means, of not being in legitimate
possession of it, of perhaps being a thief. Human justice is only a very
imperfect semblance of divine justice. It keeps a watchful eye on
every human being. If a person, in reply to its question as to the
source of it all, has no other answer than that he himself does not
know, then it judges him, then it turns out to cast suspicion on him
that he is not in *legitimate* possession of it. This suspicion is not a
servant of justice but is justice itself.

Eighteen Upbuilding Discourses 89
(KW 5)

GOD'S WORKING IN US   IF GOD IS WORKING, WHY
                       AM I SWEATING?

Does God work through our work?

Human beings spin and sew. "Yes, necessity teaches them that, all right; necessity teaches naked woman to spin." "Fie! How can you look down on your task that way—as if being human, as if God, as if existence—as if it all were a penitentiary! . . . You know that it is human beings who spin and sew; learn from the lilies and the birds to understand that when human beings spin and sew it is nevertheless really God who spins and sews. Do you believe that the seamstress, if she understands this, will therefore become less diligent in her work, that she will lay her hands in her lap and think: Well, if it is God who really spins and sews, then it is best that I be excused, excused from this unreal spinning and sewing? . . . Our own dear seamstress with the childlike piety, our lovable seamstress, she understands that only when she herself is sewing will God sew for her, and therefore she becomes all the more diligent in her work, so that by continually sewing she may continually understand that—what a gracious jest!—it is God who sews, every stitch, so that by continually sewing she may continually understand—what earnestness!—that it is God who sews, every stitch. And when, instructed by the lily and the bird, she has understood this, then she has grasped the meaning of life, and her life has in the highest sense become meaningful; and when she dies, at her graveside it can be said in truth with the greatest possible emphasis: She has lived; whether or not she was married is not crucial." . . .

"Is it perhaps actually God who is sweating; or if it is God who is harvesting, why should I be sweating this way? Your talk is pompous, impractical nonsense."

"Man, man . . . whether or not one sweats is not decisive; indeed, a dancer also sweats, and dancing is not therefore called work, toil, and trouble."

—*Judge for Yourself!*
For Self-Examination; Judge for Yourself!
182–85 (KW 21)

123

Immortality

KEEP SCHOOLBOY ESSAYS
ON IMMORTALITY

What might one do to benefit the human race?

In grammar school, when I was fif-
teen years old, I wrote very suavely on demonstrations for the existence of God and the immortality of the soul, on the concept of
faith, and on the meaning of miracles. For my *examen artium* [student
examination], I wrote a composition on the immortality of the soul,
for which I was awarded *præ ceteris* [distinction or first honors]; later I
won the prize for a composition on this subject. Who would believe
that in my twenty-fifth year, after such a solid and very promising
beginning, I would have come to the point of not being able to present a single demonstration for the immortality of the soul. . . . Alas,
alas, alas! I threw away this composition long ago. How unfortunate!
My doubting soul perhaps would have been captivated by it, by the
language as well as by the content. So this is my advice to parents,
superiors, and teachers—that they urge the children in their charge
to keep the Danish compositions written in the fifteenth year. To
give this advice is the only thing I can do for the benefit of the
human race.

—*Either:* "Diapsalmata"
Either/Or 1:34–35 (KW 3) [Voice: "A"]

124

THE APRIL FOOL ARGUMENT FOR IMMORTALITY
The Shifting Subject of the Danish History Exam

Might any objective argument for immortality have an effect on one's eternal destiny?

I have read Professor Heiberg's *Sjæl efter Døden* [Soul after Death]—indeed, I have read it with Dean Tryde's commentary. I wish I had not done so, because a poetic work gives aesthetic delight and does not require the ultimate dialectical exactitude commensurate with a learner who wants to organize his life according to such guidance. . . .

When in an oral examination on the history of Denmark, the teacher, aware that the pupil does not know anything about it, promptly turns the examination in another direction, for example, by asking about the relation of another country to Denmark and then asking about the history of that other country, can it then be said that the examination was on the history of Denmark? When school-children write a word in their books and add, "See also p. 101," and on p. 101, "See p. 216," and on p. 216, "See p. 314," and then finally, "April fool," can it be rightfully be said that one derives benefit from this guidance—in being made a fool? . . .

Objectively the question cannot be answered at all, because the question of immortality cannot be objectively asked, since immortality is precisely the intensification and highest development of the developed subjectivity.

Concluding Unscientific Postscript to
Philosophical Fragments 1:171–73
(KW 12) [Voice: Johannes Climacus]*

"PROOF" OF IMMORTALITY

Why does certitude decline amid ever more nuanced rational proofs of immortality?

What extraordinary metaphysical and logical efforts have been put forth in our time to produce a new, exhaustive, and absolutely correct proof, combining all earlier proofs, of the immortality of the soul; and strangely enough, while this is taking place, certitude declines. The thought of immortality possesses a power and weightiness in its consequences, a responsibility in the acceptance of it, which perhaps will recreate the whole of life in a way that is feared. And so one saves and soothes one's soul by straining one's mind to produce a new proof. . . . [One] who knows how to set forth the proof for the immortality of the soul but who is not himself convinced will always be anxious about every phenomenon that affects him in such a way that he is forced to seek a further understanding of what it means to say that a man is immortal. This will disturb him. He will be depressingly affected when a perfectly simple man talks quite simply of immortality. In the opposite direction, inwardness may be lacking. An adherent of the most rigid orthodoxy may be demonic. He knows it all. He genuflects before the holy. Truth is for him the aggregate of ceremonies. He talks of meeting before the throne of God and knows how many times one should bow. He knows everything, like the man who can prove a mathematical proposition when the letters are ABC, but not when the letters are DEF. So he becomes anxious whenever he hears something that is not literally the same. And yet, how he resembles a modern speculator who has discovered a new proof for the immortality of the soul and then, in peril of his life, cannot produce the proof because he does not have his notebooks with him!

The Concept of Anxiety 139–40 (KW 8)
[Voice: Vigilius Haufniensis]*

"CHRISTENDOM"

Sin

CONSTRUING THE FALL AS AN ACCOMPLISHMENT
Now Copy Me

What results when the fall of humanity is regarded as an achievement?

There is a story about a sailor who fell from the top of the mast without injuring himself, got up on his feet, and said: Now copy me—but most likely he himself refrained from doing it again.

> *Concluding Unscientific Postscript to*
> Philosophical Fragments 1:284 (KW 12)
> [Voice: Johannes Climacus]

A LOGICAL EXPLANATION OF SIN
The Calling Card Junkie Who Forgot His Own Name

Does the question "Why did sin come into the world?" yield to scientific investigation?

To want to give a logical explanation of the coming of sin into the world is a stupidity that can occur only to people who are comically worried about finding an explanation.

Were I allowed to make a wish, then I would wish that no reader would be so profound as to ask: What if Adam had not sinned? In the moment actuality is posited, possibility walks by its side as a nothing that entices every thoughtless man. If only science could make up its mind to keep men under discipline and to bridle itself! When someone asks a stupid question, care should be taken not to answer him, lest he who answers becomes just as stupid as the questioner. The foolishness of the above question consists not so much in the question itself as in the fact that it is directed to science. If one stays at home with it, and, like Clever Elsie with her projects, calls together like-minded friends, then he has tolerably understood his own stupidity. Science, on the contrary, cannot explain such things. Every science lies either in a logical immanence or in an immanence within a transcendence that it is unable to explain. Now sin is precisely that transcendence, that *discrimen rerum* [crisis] in which sin enters into the single individual as the single individual. Sin never enters into the world differently and has never entered differently. So when the single individual is stupid enough to inquire about sin as if it were something foreign to him, he only asks as a fool, for either he does not know at all what the question is about, and thus cannot come to know it, or he knows it and understands it, and also knows that no science can explain it to him. . . . That sin came into the world six thousand years ago is said in the same way that one should say about Nebuchadnezzar that it was four thousand years ago that he became an ox. When the case is understood in this way, it is no wonder that the explanation accords with it. What in one respect is the simplest thing in the world has been made the most difficult. What the most ordinary man understands in his own way, and quite correctly so—because he understands that it is not just six thousand years since sin came into the world—science with the art of speculators has announced as a prize subject that as yet has not been answered satisfactorily. How sin came into the world, each man understands solely by himself. If he would learn it from another, he would *eo ipso* misunderstand it. The only science that can help a little is psychology, yet it admits that it explains nothing, and also that it *cannot* and *will not* explain more. . . . Sin is no scientific problem, and thus no man of science has an obligation (and the project maker just as little) to forget how sin came into the world. If this is what he wants to do, if he magnanimously wants to forget himself in the zeal to explain all of humanity, he will become as comical as that privy councilor who was so conscientious about leaving his calling card with every Tom, Dick, and Harry that in so doing he at last forgot his own name. Or his philosophical enthusiasm will make him so absent-minded that he needs a good-natured, level-headed wife whom he

130

can ask, as Soldin asked Rebecca when in enthusiastic absent-mindedness he also lost himself in the objectivity of the chatter: "Rebecca, is it I who is speaking?"

The Concept of Anxiety 49–51 (KW 8)
[Voice: Vigilius Haufniensis]

TALENT AND VIRTUE   THE GROCER'S APPRENTICE

Does it take some special talent to be bad?

For everyone who wills it can be a good person, but to be bad always takes talent. This is why many a person prefers to be a philosopher, not a Christian, because to be a philosopher takes talent, to be a Christian, humility, and anyone who so wills can have that. . . . Therefore it is quite all right that in modern drama the bad is always represented by the most brilliantly gifted characters, whereas the good, the upright, is represented by the grocer's apprentice. The spectators find this entirely appropriate and learn from the play what they already knew, that it is far beneath their dignity to be classed with a grocer's apprentice.

—Or

Either/Or 2:227–28 (KW 4) [Voice:
Judge William]

THE SUDDENNESS OF SIN AS A SELF-DETERMINED LEAP
TENNIS BALLS

Does sin leap into existence by an instantaneous free act of will or accidentally and incrementally by degrees?

The Genesis story presents the only dialectically consistent view. Its whole content is really concentrated in one statement: *Sin came into the world by a sin.* Were this not so, sin would have come into the world as something accidental, which one would do well not to explain. The difficulty for the understand-

131

ing is precisely the triumph of the explanation and its profound consequence, namely, that sin presupposes itself, that sin comes into the world in such a way that by the fact that it is, it is presupposed. Thus sin comes into the world as the sudden, i.e., by a leap; but this leap also posits the quality, and since the quality is posited, the leap in that very moment is turned into the quality and is presupposed by the quality and quality by the leap. To the understanding, this is an offense; *ergo* it is a myth. As a compensation, the understanding invents its own myth, which denies the leap and explains the circle as a straight line, and now everything proceeds quite naturally. The understanding talks fantastically about man's state prior to the fall, and, in the course of the small talk, the projected innocence is changed little by little into sinfulness, and so there it is. The lecture of the understanding may on this occasion be compared with the counting rhyme in which children delight: One-nis-ball, two-nis-balls, three-nis-balls, etc., up to nine-nis-balls and tennis balls.

The Concept of Anxiety 32 (KW 8)
[Voice: Vigilius Haufniensis]

BONDAGE   TOY OR THE BOOK

Is the loss of freedom irreversible?

If a child who has received the gift of a little money—enough to be able to buy either a good book, for example, or one toy, for both cost the same—buys the toy, can he use the same money to buy the book? By no means, for now the money has been spent. But he may go to the bookseller and ask him if he will exchange the book for the toy. Suppose the bookseller answers: My dear child, your toy is worthless; it is certainly true that when you still had the money you could have bought the book just as well as the toy, but the awkward thing about a toy is that once it is purchased it has lost all value. Would not the child think: This is very strange indeed. And so it was also once, when man could buy freedom and unfreedom for the same price, and this price was the free choice of the soul and the surrender of the choice. He chose unfreedom, but if he then were to approach the god and ask whether he could make an exchange, the answer presumably would be: Undeniably there was a time when you could have bought what you wanted, but the curious thing about unfreedom is that once it is purchased it has no value whatsoever, even though one pays the same price for it.

—*Philosophical Fragments*
Philosophical Fragments; Johannes
Climacus 16n (KW 7) [Voice: Johannes
Climacus]

Prayer

SUPPLICATION   MAYBE IT'S BETTER NOT TO PRAY

Is prayer dangerous?

An elderly pagan, named and acclaimed in paganism as a sage, was sailing with an ungodly man on the same ship. When the ship was in distress at sea, the ungodly man lifted up his voice to pray, but the sage said to him, "Be quiet, dear fellow. If heaven discovers that you are on board, the ship will capsize."

Eighteen Upbuilding Discourses 65
(KW 5)

THE DIFFICULTY OF PRAYER

EASY AS BUTTONING
ONE'S TROUSERS

How hard is it to learn to pray?

To pray is, of course, a very simple matter; one would think it to be as easy as buttoning one's trousers, and if nothing else stood in the way, one could promptly tackle the world-historical. And yet how difficult! Intellectually, I must have an altogether clear conception of God, of myself, and of my relationship with him, and of the dialectic of the relationship of prayer—lest I confuse God with something else so that I do not pray to God, and lest I confuse myself with something else so that I do not pray—so that in the relationship of prayer I maintain the distinction and the relationship. Reasonable married people confess that they need months and years of daily life together in order to learn to know each

134

other, and yet God is much more difficult to know. God is not something external [to me], as is a wife, whom I can ask whether she is now satisfied with me. . . .

To pray is just as difficult as to play the role of Hamlet, of which the greatest actor is supposed to have said that only once had he been close to playing it well; nevertheless he would devote all his ability and his entire life to the continued study of this role. Should not praying be almost as important and significant?

> *Concluding Unscientific Postscript to*
> Philosophical Fragments 1:162–63
> (KW 12) [Voice: Johannes Climacus]*

THE TRIVIALIZATION OF THE GOD RELATION
Unlike Other Saloonkeepers

Is it prudent to address petty wishes to God?

Imagine an individual who is speaking with God in prayer and now it occurs to him to speak as follows: I fast three times a week, pay the tithe of mint and cumin. It is altogether comic, like the man who lay in the ditch and thought he was riding horseback. In other words, the Pharisee thinks he is speaking with God, whereas from what he says it is clear and distinct enough that he is speaking with himself or with another Pharisee. If, for example, a saloonkeeper were to stand in a church and talk this way with God in prayer, saying: I am not like the other saloonkeepers, who give only the prescribed measure; I give generous measure, and in addition that extra at the New Year—he is not thereby a hypocrite, but he is comic instead, since it is clear that he is not speaking with God but with himself *qua* saloonkeeper or with one of the other saloonkeepers. Therefore, one should never appeal to God for help with a wish, because one thereby binds oneself absolutely.

> *Stages on Life's Way* 238 (KW 11)
> [Voice: Quidam]

THANKSGIVING   AN APOLOGY FOR THANKING GOD

For what are we to thank God?

So I am to thank God, says the pastor, and for what? For the good that he gives me. Excellent! But for what good? Presumably for the good that I can discern is a good. Stop! If I thank God for the good I can discern to be a good, I am making a fool of God, because then my relationship with God means that I am transforming God in likeness to me instead of my being transformed in likeness to him. I thank him for the good that I know is a good, but what I know is the finite, and consequently I go ahead and thank God for complying with my notion. . . . What then? Shall I omit giving thanks to him when that which happens to me is a good according to my poor finite understanding, something I perhaps have ardently wished for and which, now that I have received it, makes me feel so overwhelmed that I must of necessity thank God? Not quite that, but I am to bear in mind that my having wished it so ardently is no merit and becomes no merit through receiving what I wished. Consequently, with my giving thanks I am to include an apology so as to be sure that it is God with whom I have the honor of speaking and not my friend and comrade [*Dusbroder*] Councilor Andersen. I must shamefacedly admit that it looks so good to me that I must pray for forgiveness for giving thanks for it, because I cannot help it. Consequently, I must pray for forgiveness for giving thanks. That is not what the pastor said.

Concluding Unscientific Postscript to
Philosophical Fragments 1:178 (KW 12)
[Voice: Johannes Climacus]

THE ABSENCE OF EXTERNAL EVIDENCE FOR PRAYER
DID SOCRATES PRAY WITH SILENCE?

Was there any external evidence that Socrates prayed?

Socrates is standing and gazing into space. Then two passers-by come along and the one says to the other: What is that man doing? The other replies: Nothing. Let us suppose that one of them has a little more of an idea of inwardness. He describes Socrates' action as a religious expression and says: He is absorbed in the divine, he is praying. Let us concentrate on the latter expression, "He is praying." But is he using words, perhaps ever so many words? No, Socrates understood his God-relationship in such a way that he did not dare to say anything at all for fear of talking a lot of nonsense and for fear of having a wrong desire fulfilled. Instances of the latter are said to have occurred, for example, when the oracle prophesied to a man that all his sons would become distinguished, and the troubled father went on to ask: And then will they all probably die a miserable death? The oracle replied: This, too. . . .

Praying is thus the highest pathos of the infinite, and yet it is comic, precisely because in its inwardness praying is incommensurate with every external expression.

Concluding Unscientific Postscript to
Philosophical Fragments 1:90n, 90
(KW 12) [Voice: Johannes Climacus]

The Status of Christianity within Modernity

BARBARITY IN MASQUERADE

The Establishment of a Christian Whorehouse

Have the original aims of Christianity faltered within modern "Christendom"?

The thought of Christianity was to want to change everything.

The result of the Christianity of "Christendom" is that everything, absolutely everything, has remained as it was, only everything has assumed the name of "Christian"—and so (musicians, strike up the tune) we live a life of paganism . . .

What Christianity wanted was chastity—to do away with the whorehouse. The change is this, that the whorehouse remains exactly what it was in paganism, lewdness in the same proportion, but it has become a "Christian" whorehouse. A whoremonger is a "Christian" whoremonger, he is a Christian exactly like all the rest of us; to exclude him from the means of grace—"Good God," the priest will say, "what would be the end of it if once we were to begin by excluding one contributing member!"

*Kierkegaard's "Attack upon
'Christendom' "* [164]

"CHRISTENDOM" AS AN INTOXICATING MELODY
THE MERRY CHRISTIAN
DRINKING SONG

To what tune is the song of modern Christianity set?

Christianity is sung to the tune of a drinking song, even more zestful than such songs, which are always accompanied by the sadness that it is soon over and in 100 years everything will be forgotten, whereas the zest-for-life Christian drinking song, the pastors assure us, "lasts an eternity." . . .

This whole business with Christendom is just like that inscription, "This must be Troy" instead of Troy, and like the title on the spine of an empty volume. . . .

Just as if one of the composers who compose variations had used one or two strains from a funeral march to compose with poetic license a vigorous gallop, just so has the official Christianity used some sentences in the New Testament (this doctrine about the cross and agony and terror and trembling before eternity, etc.) to compose with poetic license a lovely idyll with procreation and waltzing, where everything is so merry, so merry, so merry, where the pastor (a kind of pious municipal musician) for a fee has Christianity—this doctrine about dying to the world—provide music at weddings and christening parties.

—*The Moment*, no. 4, no. 5
The Moment *and Late Writings* 161–[62], 178 (KW 23)

IDENTITY DIFFUSION   THE EMPEROR WHO BECAME A
                            PART-TIME WAITER

Just how disoriented has Christianity become within the present age?

No human being has ever been in such hot water as Christianity has been of late. At times Christianity is explained speculatively and the result is paganism; at times it is not even known for sure what Christianity is. We merely have to read through a catalog of new books to see the times we are living in. In daily life, when we hear shrimp hawked on the street, we almost think that it is midsummer, when wreaths of woodruff are hawked that it is spring, when mussels are hawked that it is winter. But when, as happened last winter, one hears shrimp, wreathes of woodruff, and mussels hawked on the same day, one is tempted to assume that life has become confused and that the world will not last until Easter. . . .

It is appropriate for a king to be loved by his people, to be honored in his majesty, or, if things go badly, well, then let him be toppled from the throne in a revolt, let him fall in battle, let him languish in a prison far, far removed from everything that is reminiscent of him. But a king changed into a meddlesome part-time waiter who is extremely satisfied in his position—that is a more shocking change than murdering him.

> *Concluding Unscientific Postscript to*
> Philosophical Fragments 1:362, 364
> (KW 12) [Voice: Johannes Climacus]

BAPTISM THE DIGNITY OF A CERTIFICATE OF VACCINATION

In what way does "Christendom" faintly discern its own disgrace?

Christianity feels a sense of shame, like an old man who sees himself decked out in the latest fashion. It blushes when it sees this distorted figure that is supposed to be Christianity, a perfume-saturated and systematically accommodated and soirée-participating scholarliness, whose whole secret is half measures and then truth to a certain degree. Now a days it blushes when it sees a radical cure (and only as such is Christianity what it is) transformed merely into a vaccination. A person's relation to it is equivalent to having a certificate of vaccination.

Concluding Unscientific Postscript to
Philosophical Fragments 1:293–94
(KW 12) [Voice: Johannes Climacus]*

THE SINGLE THESIS ON "CHRISTENDOM"
WHY "CHRISTENDOM" REQUIRES A DETECTIVE

How many theses are needed to develop a critique of "Christendom"?

O Luther, you had 95 theses—terrible! And yet, in a deeper sense, the more theses, the less terrible. The matter is far more terrible—there is only one thesis:

The Christianity of the New Testament does not exist at all. . . .

As long as . . . one uses . . . tricks to maintain the appearance of being the Christianity of the New Testament—as long as the Christian crime continues, there can be no question of reforming, but of throwing light on this Christian criminal case.

As for myself, I am not what the times perhaps crave, a reformer, in no way; nor am I a profound speculative intellect, a seer, a prophet—no, I have, if you please, to a rare degree I have a definite detective talent.

—"Newspaper Articles, 1854–1855"
The Moment *and Late Writings* [39]–40
(KW 23)

PROCLAIMING CHRISTIANITY IN A "CHRISTIAN COUNTRY"
THE REVIVALIST AND THE SCOFFER

Why must inquirers resort to scoffers to hear Christianity creditably presented?

A man becomes reborn on New Year's Eve at precisely six o'clock. Now he is ready. Fantastically decked out with the fact of that revival, he must now run around and proclaim Christianity—in a Christian country. Of course, even if we are all baptized, each one perhaps needs to become a Christian in another sense. But here is the difference: in a Christian country it is not information that is lacking; something else is lacking, and one human being cannot directly communicate this something else to another. And in such fantastic categories a revivalist wants to work for Christianity, and yet he demonstrates—the busier he is propagating and propagating—that he himself is not Christian. Being a Christian is something so thoroughly reimagined that it does not allow the aesthetic dialectic that teleologically permits one person to be for another what he is not for himself.—On the other hand, a scoffer attacks Christianity and at the same time expounds it so creditably that it is a delight to read him, and the person who is really having a hard time getting it definitely presented almost has to resort to him.

Concluding Unscientific Postscript to
Philosophical Fragments 1:614 (KW 12)
[Voice: Johannes Climacus]*

The Bible

THE DIALECTICIAN'S EVALUATION OF SCRIPTURE
Welcome as a Dog in a Game of Bowls

What does the logician contribute to an argument on the inspiration of a sacred text?

He would be just like a dog in a bowling alley. Likewise it is not suitable for a stark-naked dialectician to enter into a scholarly dispute in which, despite all the talent and learning *pro et contra*, it is nevertheless, in the last resort, not dialectically decided what the dispute is about.

> *Concluding Unscientific Postscript to Philosophical Fragments* 1:27 (KW 12)
> [Voice: Johannes Climacus]

THE CAPTIVITY OF SCHOLARSHIP TO AVOIDANCE
The Endless Investigation

Should scholarly investigation suspend judgment in an inquiry into a clear scriptural text that conveys an unconditional requirement?

It is never dangerous that one finds out the true state of affairs . . . It can, however, be dangerous for Christianity if the truth is set aside, if not unjustly then at least by way of equivocation. For example, if someone got the notion that the version was problematic or the words "No one can serve two masters" were difficult to understand, so that in the first case there must be profound investigation and in the second case prolonged research, and of course (since investigation and research are not everyone's business) there must also be a few professors, whose livelihood would then be to investigate and do research, and for that reason they certainly (for the sake of scholarship or at least for the sake of their livelihood) would see to it that the investigation or research would last as long as they lived.

—*Judge for Yourself!*
For Self Examination; Judge for Yourself!
158–59 (KW 21)

THE DANGER IN READING SCRIPTURE

Salvation by Commentaries

What makes it possible for one to feel safe reading Holy Scripture?

When a profoundly stirred contemporary steps forth, someone who sets the price of being a Christian at a mere fifth the price the Gospel puts on it, people shout, "Watch out for that person! Do not read what he writes, least of all in solitude. Do not talk with him, above all not alone—he is a dangerous person." But Holy Scripture! Why, almost everyone owns it; one does not hesitate to present this book to each confirmand (consequently at the most dangerous age). . . .

To be alone with Holy Scripture! I dare not! If I open it—any passage—it traps me at once; it asks me (indeed, it is as if it were God himself who asked me): Have you done what you read there? And then, then—yes, then I am trapped. Then either straightway into action—or immediately a humbling admission.

Oh, to be alone with Holy Scripture—and if you are not, then you are not reading Holy Scripture.

That being alone with God's Word is a dangerous matter is implicitly admitted also by more competent people. Possibly there was someone (a competent and earnest person, even if we cannot laud his conclusion) who said to himself, "I am no good at doing anything halfway—and this book, God's Word, is an extremely dangerous book for me. And it is an imperious book—if one gives it a finger, it takes the whole hand; if one gives it the whole hand, it takes the

144

whole man and may suddenly and radically change my whole life on a prodigious scale. No, without allowing myself one single derogatory or disparaging word (something I abhor) about this book, I put it in some out-of-the-way place, I refuse to be alone with it." We do not approve of this, but nevertheless there is always something in this that we do approve of—a certain honesty.

But, asserting defiantly that one certainly does dare to be alone with it, which nevertheless is not true, one can also defend oneself against God's Word in quite a different way. Take Holy Scripture, lock your door—but then take ten dictionaries, twenty-five commentaries, then you can read it, just as calmly and coolly as you read newspaper advertising. If, as you sit there reading a passage, you happen, curiously enough, to get the idea: Have I done this? Do I act according to this (of course, you can hit upon such ideas only in distraction, in an absentminded moment when you are not concentrating with your usual seriousness), then the danger is still not very great. Look, perhaps there are several variations, and perhaps a new manuscript has just been found—good Lord!—and the prospect of new variations, and perhaps there are five interpreters with one opinion and seven with another and two with a strange opinion and three who are wavering and have no opinion, and "I myself am not absolutely sure about the meaning of this passage, or, to speak my mind, I agree with the three wavering interpreters who have no opinion" etc.

—For Self-Examination
For Self-Examination; Judge for Yourself!
31–32 (KW 21)

GENIUS

WHETHER THE APOSTLE PAUL HAD A GENIUS FOR UPHOLSTERY

How great a literary genius was the Apostle Paul?

As a genius Paul can sustain no comparison with Plato or with Shakespeare, as an author of beautiful similes he ranks rather low, as stylist his is an obscure name, and as an upholsterer—well, I may admit that in this respect I don't know

145

where to place him. One always does well to transform stupid serious-ness into a jest—and then comes the really serious thing, the serious fact that Paul was an apostle, and as an apostle has no affinity either with Plato or Shakespeare or a stylist or an upholsterer, who are all of them (Plato as the upholsterer Hansen) beneath any comparison with him.

*On Authority and Revelation: The Book
on Adler, or a Cycle of Ethico-Religious
Essays 105*

SCRIPTURE CRITICISM   THE AUTHORITY OF THE
                        ASSISTANT PROFESSOR

**How does the authority of the apostle compare to that of the
assistant professor in a course on scripture?**

Nowadays it is perhaps all too easy to understand that Peter was an apostle, but in those days people found it far easier to understand that he was a fisherman. . . . Divine au-thority is the category. Here there is little or nothing at all for a *privat-docent* or a licentiate or a paragraph-swallower to do—as little as a young girl needs the barber to remove her beard, and as little as a bald man needs the *friseur* to "accommodate" his hair, just so little is the assistance of these gentlemen needed. The question is quite sim-ple: Will you obey? or will you not obey? . . .

Now, as a matter of course, from generation to generation, in every university, in every semester, there is a course about *how*, etc. etc. Yea, that is an excellent means of diversion. In that way we are diverted farther and farther from the task of obeying. . . . In this way one can easily be done with Paul without even beginning with him, or beginning with the fact that he possessed divine authority. People treat the Scriptures so scientifically that they might quite as well be anonymous writings.

*On Authority and Revelation: The Book
on Adler, or a Cycle of Ethico-Religious
Essays 25–27*

The Clergy

VERACITY

What is the difference between the theater and the church?

The difference between the theater and the church is essentially this: the theater honorably and honestly acknowledges being what it is. The church, however, is a theater that in every way dishonestly seeks to conceal what it is.

An example. On the theater poster it always states plainly: money will not be returned. The church, this solemn holiness, would shrink from the offensiveness, the scandalousness, of placing this directly over the church door, or having it printed under the list of preachers on Sundays. . . .

The actor is an honest man who says outright: I am an actor.

Never for any price, never for any price would one get a pastor to say that.

No, "the pastor" is just the opposite of an actor; indeed, altogether disinterestedly (since he knows that it does not pertain to him) he raises and answers the question whether an actor may be buried in Christian ground. It never crosses his mind at all (a masterpiece of theatrical art, if it is not obtusity) that he does indeed have a co-interest in the settlement of this question—yes, that even if it is decided in favor of the actor, it still could remain doubtful whether it is defensible that the pastor be buried in—Christian ground.

—*The Moment,* no. 6
The Moment *and Late Writings* [221],
349 (KW 23)

147

RELIGION BUSINESS   The Stock Company Dedicated to "Fishing for Men"

How has evangelization been drastically refashioned within modern "Christendom"?

Just as one company is formed to speculate in the herring-fishery, another in cod-fishing, another in whaling, etc., so man-fishing was carried on by a stock company which guaranteed its members a dividend of such and such a per cent. . . .

It proved indeed that even the most successful herring company did not make nearly so big a profit as did man-fishery. And one thing further, an extra profit, or at least a piquant seasoning on top of the profit, namely, that no herring company is able to quote words of Scripture when they send boats out for the catch.

Kierkegaard's "Attack upon
'Christendom'" [203]–4

THE CHOSEN PEOPLE   The Trick of Living off of Nothing

How do the clergy manage to survive on nothing?

In the splendid cathedral the Honor-able Right Reverend *Geheime-General-Ober-Hof-Prædikant* [Private Chief Royal Chaplain] comes forward, the chosen favorite of the elite world; he comes forward before a chosen circle of the chosen ones and, deeply *moved*, preaches on the text he has himself chosen, "God has chosen the lowly and the despised in the world"—and there is no one who laughs. . . .

A Swedish pastor, shaken by the sight of the effect his discourse had on the listeners, who were swimming in tears, is reported to have said reassuringly: Do not weep, children, it may all be a lie. . . .

One cannot live on nothing. One hears this so often, especially from pastors.

And the pastors are the very ones who perform this feat: Christianity does not exist at all—yet they live on it.

—*The Moment*, no. 6
The Moment *and Late Writings* [203]–5
(KW 23)

ORDINATION FRAUD   THE MOLE IN CLERICAL GARB

Is Christianity endangered by those who misrepresent their way through ordination?

Let us suppose that a theological candidate in our time had adopted the notion that the oath of office is unjustifiable. Well then, he can say this freely and openly, if he thinks it expedient. "But by this he will close the road to advancement, and perhaps not accomplish anything, not even arouse a sensation, for a candidate is far too small an entity, and moreover he has no monopoly on the State-Church, since he has no official position." So (now I will think of a selfish man who not only does not love the Establishment but at bottom is an enemy of it) what can he do? He keeps silent for the time being. Then he seeks a position as teacher in the State-Church; he gets it; he takes the oath. So now he is an office-bearer in the State-Church. Thereupon he publishes a book wherein he sets forth a revolutionary view. The whole situation is now changed. It would have been easy for the State-Church to bounce a theological candidate, easy to say to him, Very well then, having these views, you cannot become an office-bearer—and the State-Church would not have had to take any action at all with regard to this case, at the very most it would have to take a preventive measure against him quite particularly by not promoting him. But the theological candidate was shrewd and shrewdly understood how to make himself far more important. The responsibility which he as a candidate would have to assume for his peculiar view and would have bought dearly by sacrificing his future in the service of a higher call, while seeking to make the affair as easy as possible for the Establishment—this responsibility is now devolved upon the State-Church, which is required to take positive action to *deprive* of his

149

office a man who by having become an office-bearer has at the same time made an attempt to interest the whole body of office-bearers in his fate. . . .

Therefore, even though the State or the State-Church is sound enough in health to separate from it the revolutionary member, it is nevertheless deleterious that this gives rise to reflection. To everything hidden and concealed applies the saying of the ballad: "Merely one word thou hast uttered." It is easy enough to utter such a fateful word, but it is incalculable what harm may be occasioned by it, and a giant will be needed to stop the injurious effect of one word such as Peer Ruus let out in his sleep. And if the State or the State-Church must often suspend many such individuals, then at last an appearance is conjured up as though the State itself is *in suspenso*.

> On Authority and Revelation: The Book
> on Adler, or a Cycle of Ethico-Religious
> Essays 28–30

"HALLOWING" THE MUNDANE
THE PRIESTLY BLESSING OF
EXCURSIONS TO DEER PARK

How do the charlatans of "Christendom" turn ordinary experiences into profit?

Let us assume that God's will was that we men must not go out to the Deer Park.

This of course "man" could not put up with. What then would be the upshot? The upshot would be that the "priest" would make out that if, for example, one blessed the four-seated Holstein carriage and made the sign of the cross over the horses, then taking a drive to the Deer Park would be well pleasing to God.

The consequence therefore would be that people would go out to the Deer Park just as much as they do now, without any change, except that it had become dearer, cost perhaps five dollars for persons of rank, five dollars for the priests, and four cents for poor people. But then the excursion to the Deer Park would also have the enchantment of being at the same time . . . . . divine worship.

150

Perhaps the priests would have hit upon the thought of taking in hand themselves the business of hiring out horses and carriages, so that if it were to be thoroughly pleasing to God that one went out to the Deer Park, the carriage must be hired from the priests.

Kierkegaard's "Attack upon 'Christendom'" 288

CONSIDERING THE VOCATION OF PASTOR
The Fantasy of
Shepherding Others

How does one, considering ordination, keep all options open while imagining a life of service?
Now all your passionate energy is aroused; reflection with its hundred arms seizes the idea of becoming a pastor. You find no rest; day and night you think about it; you read all the books you can find, go to church three times every Sunday, make the acquaintance of pastors, write sermons yourself, deliver them to yourself, and for half a year you are dead to the whole world. Now you are ready; you can speak with more insight and seemingly with more experience about being a pastor than many a one who has been a pastor for twenty years. When you meet them, it arouses your exasperation that they do not know how to pour out their hearts with a completely different eloquence. You say: "Is this enthusiasm? Compared with them, I, who am not a pastor, who have not dedicated myself to being a pastor, I speak with the voice of angels." That may very well be true, but you nevertheless did not become a pastor.

—*Or*
Either/Or 2:165 (KW 4)
[Voice: Judge William]*

THE PRIESTHOOD OF ALL BELIEVERS

The Missing Middle Term
between "We Pastors" and
"Everyone Else"

Must one who preaches the way also follow it?

It is quite true that a person who cannot shave himself can set up shop as a barber and serve others according to their needs, but in the world of spirit this is meaningless.

It is, however, regarded as part and parcel of earnestness to want to be readily available to exert an influence upon others, yet without necessarily wanting to be an apostle (how humble!)—and yet without being able to determine one's similarity to and one's dissimilarity from such a person (how meaningless!). Everyone wants to work for others. This is a rule in the civic address, although it is more understandable there, but it is also a rule in the rhetorical form of the religious address. I do not doubt that it is found in printed sermon outlines, and one hears it ever so often, unless one is listening to an individual who has been personally tested and knows how to speak and knows whereof he speaks.

If the sermon is about preparing the way of the Lord, then the first point is that everyone does his part in spreading Christianity, not just we pastors but also everyone else as well etc. This is indeed fascinating! Not just we pastors. Here at the outset the dialectical middle terms, whether a pastor is an apostle, are lacking, and if not, then how is he different from one and how is he like one? The ecclesiastical points of difference with regard to ordination increase the difficulties, and the principal middle term is pushed back by decisions in the realm of the undecided. So, then, not just we pastors. This passage looks very hopeful at the beginning. But that to which "not just" refers is not given at all, and now follows the apodisis with the earnestness of exhortation: Heed my words, dear listeners, it is not just I and we pastors who should work in this manner, but you also should work in this way! How? Well, that is the only thing that does not become clear in this earnest discourse, the earnestness of which does not lie exactly in the subject matter. Now the first point has been made. The pastor wipes away the sweat, and the listeners do likewise just at the thought that in this way they have become missionaries.

The speaker begins again. One hopes to receive a little more detailed enlightenment, but look! The next point is that each person prepares the way of the Lord within himself.

Stages on Life's Way 341–42 (KW 11)
[Voice: Quidam]

Repentance

EXCOMMUNICATION   The Prescribed Punishment

What chastisement is devised by Danish establishment clergy for those who refuse repentance?

Indeed the punishment is cruelly devised; it is so cruel that I counsel the women to have their smelling salts at hand in order not to faint when they hear it. If I do not reform, the church door should be closed to me. Horrible! So then, if I do not reform, I should be shut out, excluded from hearing on Sundays during the quiet hours the eloquence of the witnesses to the truth, which if it is not literally *unbezahlbare* [incalculable], is yet priceless. And I, silly sheep, who can neither read nor write, and therefore, being thus excluded, must spiritually pine away, die of hunger, by being excluded from what can be truly called nourishing, seeing that it nourishes the priest and his family! . . .

So if this punishment [excommunication] should be inflicted upon me, I shall live on without noticing it any more than I notice here in Copenhagen that in the distant town of Aarhus a man is giving me a thrashing. Only I have one wish. If that is fulfilled, the infliction of this punishment will not cause even the very least change in my customary mode of life upon which I set such great store. The wish is that I may be permitted to continue without any change to pay the tithes (which we call priest's money), lest the altered form of the tax bill might cause me to notice the change.

Kierkegaard's "Attack upon
'Christendom'" 45–46*

Can one who intensely fears disapproval admonish another or call for contrition?

It is like the case of a teacher who is too much concerned about [some] judgment his pupils may pass upon his instruction, his knowledge, &c. Such a teacher when he tries to teach is unable to move hand or foot. Suppose, for example, he thought it best for his pupils' sake to say of something he understood quite well that he did not understand it. Good gracious! This he could not venture to do, for fear the pupils might really believe that he did not understand it. That is to say, he is not fit to be a teacher—though he calls himself a teacher, he is so far from being such a thing that he actually aspires to be cited for commendation . . . . . by his pupils. Or as in the case of a preacher of repentance who, when he wants to chastise the vices of the age, is too much concerned about what the age thinks of him. He is so far from being a preacher of repentance that he resembles rather a New Year's visitor who comes with congratulations. He merely makes himself a bit interesting in a costume which is rather queer for a New Year's visitor.

—*The Point of View for My Work as an Author*
The Point of View for My Work as an Author: A Report to History, and Related Writings 33–34*

PERFECTION   A HARD JOURNEY MADE EASY

By what conveyance does modern "Christendom" travel toward perfection?

In the old days, the road to perfection was narrow and solitary. The journey along it was always disturbed by aberrations, exposed to predatory attacks by sin, and pursued by the arrow of the past, which is as dangerous as that of the

Scythian hordes. Now one travels to perfection by railway in good company, and before he knows it, he has arrived.

The Concept of Anxiety 117 (KW 8)
[Voice: Vigilius Haufniensis]

PENITENCE   Ash Wednesday in Berlin

With what special enthusiasm do the Germans love to repent?

I became completely out of tune, or, if you please, precisely in tune with the day, for fate had strangely contrived it so that I arrived in Berlin on the *allgemeine Buszund Bettag* [Universal Day of Penance and Prayer]. Berlin was prostrate. To be sure, they did not throw ashes into one another's eyes with the words: *Memento o homo! quod cinis es et in cinerem revertaris* [Remember, O man! that you are dust and to dust you will return]. But all the same, the whole city lay in one cloud of dust. At first I thought it was a government measure, but later I was convinced that the wind was responsible for this nuisance and without respect of persons followed its whim or its bad habit, for in Berlin at least every other day is Ash Wednesday.

—*Repetition*
Fear and Trembling; Repetition 152–53
(KW 6) [Voice: Constantin
Constantius]

HABIT   The Hundred-Cannon Reminder

What is to prevent repentance and love from becoming habituated as a routine?

Let the thunder of a hundred cannons remind you three times a day to resist the force of habit. Like that mighty Eastern emperor, keep a slave who reminds you daily, keep hundreds. Have a friend who reminds you every time he sees you. Have a wife who, in love, reminds you early and late—but take care that this does not also become a habit! You can become so habituated to hearing the thunder of a hundred cannons that you can sit at the table and hear the slightest triviality much more clearly than the thunder of the hundred cannons—which you have become habituated to hearing. You can become so habituated to having hundreds of slaves remind you every day that you no longer hear them, because through habit you have acquired ears that hear and yet do not hear. No, only eternity's *you shall*—and the listening ear that wants to hear this *shall*—can save you from habit.

Works of Love 37 (KW 16)

Denmark

MISFORTUNE   THE ORDEAL OF BEING AN AUTHOR
IN DENMARK

Are there advantages to being an author in an inconsequential, hideaway country?

When a land is little, the proportions are in every respect small in the little land. So in respect to literature: the honorarium and all that goes with it will be insignificant. If one is not a poet, and more particularly a dramatist, and does not write textbooks or is not supported in some other way by one's profession, then the business of being an author is about the most wretchedly rewarded, the least secure, and so to that extent the most thankless occupation. If there lives a man possessed of the talents requisite for authorship, who in addition to that is so fortunate as to have some property, he can then become an author more or less at his own expense.

—"My Activity as a Writer"
*The Point of View for My Work as an
Author: A Report to History, and Related
Writings* 141*

LITERARY PAROCHIALISM WALKING AROUND ONE ANOTHER

What do authors do for exercise in a small country?

When there are many springs it is not so dangerous that one of them is muddled, but in a little land, where in every direction there is hardly more than one spring, anyone who muddles it assumes a high degree of responsibility. . . . How strange the whole thing looks. About an author who till now has not had many readers I write a book which presumably will not be read. As it is related of two princely personages who were very fat that they took their exercise by walking around one another, so in a little land the exercise of the authors consists in walking around one another.

> *On Authority and Revelation: The Book*
> *on Adler, or a Cycle of Ethico-Religious*
> *Essays 17–18*

THE PUBLIC EXPOSURE OF AN AUTHOR IN DENMARK
Hiding Oneself on a Plate

When a writer is cursed by being born in a small country with an odd language, why might he prefer to address a single reader rather than a thousand?

To be an author in Denmark is nearly as bothersome as to have to live exposed to view [*paa en Præsenteer-Bakke*]. It is especially nerve-racking for a lyric author who, even though as a person he is the opposite, yet qua author is always a bit shy of people, flees from everything clamorous, regardless of whether it is praise or blame, and abandons himself in solitude to the refreshing, cozy, sweet romance that here and there there sits in secret a reader who makes the reception warm, who, purely esthetically speaking, closes his door and talks with the author in secret. If anyone finds my first statement exaggerated, then perhaps he will still have patience to wait for my next, that to be an author in Denmark is to a large extent identical with being an author in Copenhagen, which is nearly as bothersome as having to hide oneself on a plate [*paa en Tallerken*].

> *Prefaces: Light Reading for Certain Classes*
> *as the Occasion May Require 33* [Voice:
> Nicolaus Notabene]

THE "CHRISTIAN" DESIGNATION

Why does "Christendom" have such trouble with one who will not play along with its major premise?

Just because I do not call myself a Christian, it is impossible to get rid of me, having as I do the confounded capacity of being able, also by means of not calling myself a Christian, to make it manifest that the others are even less so.

O Socrates! If with kettledrums and trumpets you had proclaimed yourself to be the one who knew the most, the Sophists would soon have been finished with you. No, you were the ignorant one; but you also had the confounded capacity of being able (also by means of being yourself the ignorant one) to make it manifest that the others knew even less than you—they did not even know that they were ignorant. . . .

My task is to audit the definition: Christian.

—Appendix: *The Moment*, no. 10
The Moment *and Late Writings* 342–43
(KW 23)

SCALE

Does abstract thinking provide a useful map for human existence?

Having to exist with the help of the guidance of pure thinking is like having to travel in Denmark with a small map of Europe on which Denmark is no larger than a steel penpoint.

Concluding Unscientific Postscript to
Philosophical Fragments 1:310–11
(KW 12) [Voice: Johannes Climacus]

160

RELATIONSHIPS

The Hazards of Love

LOVE AS A DEVALUATED CURRENCY

THE INFLATIONARY TREND IN

ARDENT LANGUAGE

What recourse is left to language when love has come to mean almost anything, hence nothing?

It is comic that a mentally disordered man picks up any piece of granite and carries it around because he believes it is money, and in the same way it is comic that Don Juan has 1,003 mistresses, for the number simply indicates that they have no value. Therefore one should stay within one's means in the use of the word "love." . . . In Prussia an order was established for those who participated in the War of Independence and an order also for those who stayed home.

Stages on Life's Way 293 (KW 11)

[Voice: Quidam]

THE DANGER OF LOVE   ON KEEPING THE OTHER FOOT OUT

OF THE FOX TRAP

Should a warning sign be posted wherever love surfaces?

When a wall is being torn down, a sign is posted, and I make a detour. When a fence is being painted, a warning is put up. When a coachman is about to drive over someone, he shouts: Look out! When there is cholera, a soldier is stationed outside the house, etc. What I mean is that when there is danger the danger can be indicated, and one succeeds in avoiding it by paying attention to the signs. Now since I am afraid of becoming ludicrous

163

through love, I certainly do regard it as a danger—what, then, must I do to avoid it, or what must I do to avoid the danger of having a woman fall in love with me? . . . I am in the same situation as the man Jean Paul tells about—standing on one foot, he reads the following notice: Fox traps are set here, and he does not dare to walk or put his foot on the ground.

> *Stages on Life's Way* 37–38 (KW 11)
> [Voice: The Young Man, quoted by
> William Afham]*

THE AUTHOR'S IMPEDIMENT
THE MANUSCRIPT SET AFLAME

What is the special difficulty of arguing with one's wife?

Although happily married as only few are and also thankful for my happiness as perhaps only few are, I have nevertheless run up against difficulties in my marriage, the discovery of which is due to my wife, because I suspected nothing. Several months had passed by since the wedding. I had gradually become somewhat practiced in the pattern of marital life. Then little by little there awakened again in me a desire that I had always nourished and in which I in all innocence thought I might indulge myself: engagement in some literary task. The subject was chosen, books along this line that I myself owned were set out, particular works were borrowed from the Royal Library, my notes were arranged synoptically and my pen was, so to speak, dipped. Meanwhile, my wife had scarcely conceived a suspicion that some such thing was in the wind before she began watching my movements very carefully. Occasionally she dropped an enigmatic word, vaguely suggested that all my busyness in the study, my longer sojourns there, and my literary ruminations were not altogether to her liking. I did, however, keep all my wits about me and pretended not to understand her, which I actually did not at first. Then one day she catches me off guard and extracts from me the formal confession that I was on the way to wanting to be an author. If until now her conduct had been more a reconnoitering, she

164

now zeroed in more and more definitely, until she finally declared open war, *et quidem* [and this] so openly that she intended to confiscate everything I wrote, in order to use it in a better way as backing for her embroidery, for curlers, etc. . . . Even if I can debate with the devil himself, I cannot debate with my wife. She has, namely, only one syllogism, or rather none at all. What learned people call sophistry, she, who wants nothing to do with being learned, calls teasing. . . . The consequence of this is that all my skill in debating becomes a luxury item for which there is no demand at all in my domestic life. If I, the experienced dialectician, fairly well exemplify the course of justice, which according to the poet's dictum is so very long, my wife is like the royal Danish chancery, *kurz und bündig* [short and to the point], except that she is very different from that august body in being very lovable. It is precisely this lovableness that gives her an authority that she knows how to maintain in a charming way at every moment. . . .

She came over to the table where I was sitting, put her arm intimately around my neck, and asked me to read a passage again. I begin to read, holding the manuscript high enough so that she can see to follow me. Superb! I am beside myself but am not quite through that passage when the manuscript suddenly bursts into flames. Without my noticing it, she had pushed the single candle under the manuscript. The fire won out; there was nothing to save; my introductory paragraph went up in flames—amid general rejoicing, since my wife rejoiced for both of us. Like an elated child she clapped her hands and then threw herself about my neck with a passion as if I had been separated from her, yes, lost to her. I could not get in a word. . . .

If in a doctoral dissertation defense I was in the position that an opponent offered similar arguments, I would probably turn my back on him and say about him what the *Magister* [Master of Arts] says in Holberg: An ignoramus who does not know how to distinguish between *ubi praedicamentale* [the where predicative] and *ubi transcendentale* [the where transcendental]. With my wife it is something else. Her argumentation comes straight from the shoulder—and to the heart, from which it actually comes. In this regard she has taught me to understand how a Roman Catholic can be built up by a service in

Latin, because her argumentation, viewed as such, is what Latin is for the one who does not understand it, and yet she always builds me up, moves and affects me. . . .

The whole thing is declared to be teasing, and "moreover, she has not forgotten what is said about marriage in the catechism, that it is the husband's duty in particular." I futilely seek to explain to her that she is in linguistic error, that she is construing these words illogically, ungrammatically, against all principles of exegesis, because this passage is only about the husband's particular duties with regard to marriage, just as the very next paragraph is about the wife's particular duties. It is futile. . . .

And what, then, was the end of this conflict? Who was victorious, my *hostis domesticus* [domestic enemy] or the author? It certainly is not difficult to guess, even though it is momentarily difficult for the reader when he reads this and thus sees that I became an author. The end was that I promised not to insist on being an author. But just as at academic disputations, when the author has disarmed all of one's objections, one comes forward with some linguistic triviality in order nevertheless to turn out to be right about something, and the author politely agrees that one is right in order nevertheless to admit that one is right about something, I thus reserved for myself permission to venture to write "Prefaces." In this connection I appealed to analogies, that husbands who had promised their wives never to use snuff any more had as recompense obtained permission to have as many snuffboxes as they wished. She accepted the proposal, perhaps with the idea that one could not write a preface without writing a book, which I indeed do not dare to do, unless one is a famous author who writes such a thing on request, which, to be sure, could not possibly be the case with me.

—Preface to *Prefaces*
Prefaces; Writing Sampler 6–10, 12
(KW 9) [Voice: Nicolaus Notabene]*

Love and Duty

REGIMEN Accomplishing Marital Chores on Cue

Does duty have a stifling effect upon erotic love?

How disgusting it is to see the dullness with which all such things are done in marital life, how superficially, how apathetically they take place, almost on the stroke of a clock, much as in the tribe the Jesuits discovered in Paraguay, a tribe so apathetic that the Jesuits found it necessary to have a bell rung at midnight as a pleasant reminder to all married men to attend to their marital duties. In this way, because of discipline, everything takes place at the right time.

—*Or*
Either/Or 2:140 (KW 4) [Voice: "A,"
quoted by Judge William]

BREAKING UP Into the Loony Bin

How is the duty of fidelity in love viewed from outside the circle of that love by aesthetic observers?

If I were to say, "I took that crucial step [breaking up the relationship] because I felt bound, because I had to have my freedom, inasmuch as the lustfulness of my desire embraces a world and cannot be satisfied with one girl," then the chorus would reply, "That makes sense! Good luck, you enlightened man!" But if I were to say, "She was the only one I have loved; if I had not been sure of that when I left her, I would never have dared to leave her," then the answer would be, "Away to the loony bin with him!" If I were to say, "I was tired of her," then the chorus would answer, "Now you're talking! That is understandable!" But if I were to say, "Then I cannot understand it, for one certainly does not dare to break a relationship of duty because one is tired of it," then they would say "He is crazy."

Stages on Life's Way 339 (KW 11)
[Voice: Quidam]*

MARITAL DUTY

OUT OF THE LOVER LOOMS
MASTER ERIK

Is there a demon that hides beneath eros in marriage?

Within itself, marital love is hiding something completely different; it seems so gentle and beautiful and tender, but as soon as the door is shut on the married couple and before one can say Jack Robinson, out comes Master Erik; then the tune is changed to duty. And now you can decorate this scepter for me as much as you please, turn it into a Shrovetide birch switch; it is still a Master Erik.

—*Or*

Either/Or 2:145 (KW 4) [Voice: "A,"
quoted by Judge William]

DEBT

THE LOVER'S DESIRE TO REMAIN
IN ARREARS

Does the lover seek to end indebtedness to the beloved, or rather seek to be in debt?

To remain in a debt! But should that be difficult? After all, nothing is easier than to remain in a debt! On the other hand, should remaining in a debt be the task! After all, we think just the opposite, that the task is to get out of a debt. Whatever the debt happens to be—a money debt, a debt of honor, a prom-

168

ise debt—in short, whatever the debt, the task is always the opposite, to get out of the debt, the sooner the better. But here [in the case of love] it is supposed to be the task, an honor, to remain in it! . . . Let us begin with a little thought-experiment. If a lover had done something for the beloved that, humanly speaking, was so extraordinary, so magnanimous, so self-sacrificing, that we human beings were obliged to say, "This is absolutely the highest that one human being can do for another"—this certainly would be beautiful and good. But suppose he added, "See, now I have paid my debt"—would this not be speaking unlovingly, coldly and harshly? Would it not be, if I may say so, an impropriety that ought never to be heard and ought never to be heard in the good company of true love either! If, however, the lover had done this magnanimous and self-sacrificing thing and then added, "But I have one request—please let me remain in debt," would not this be speaking lovingly! . . .

The one who actually loves continually has a head start, and an infinite head start, because every time the other has come up with, figured out, invented a new expression of devotion, the one who loves has already carried it out, because the one who loves needs no calculation and therefore does not waste a moment in calculating.

Works of Love 177–78, 181 (KW 16)*

Marriage and the Single State

THE SINGLE STATE WHAT THE BACHELOR
CANNOT CELEBRATE

What makes a golden wedding golden?

I do not know what age the world happens to be in at present, but you know as well as I do that we customarily say that first came the Golden Age, then the Silver Age, then the Copper Age, then the Iron Age. In marriage it is the reverse—first the silver wedding, and then the golden wedding. Or is recollection not the real point in such a wedding—and yet the terminology of marriage declares them to be even more beautiful than the first wedding. But this must not be misinterpreted, as would be the case if you were inclined to say, "Then it would be best to be married in the cradle in order to begin at once with one's silver wedding and have a chance to be the first to coin a brand new term in the dictionary of marital life." You yourself probably perceive what constitutes the falsity in your jest, and I will not linger further on it. . . . Incidentally, I have frequently wondered why it is that, according to the common way of speaking and thinking, the single state has no such prospects at all, that on the contrary a bachelor who celebrates an anniversary is held up to ridicule instead.

—Or
Either/Or 2:142–43 (KW 4) [Voice:
Judge William]

170

THE INGREDIENTS OF MARRIAGE
A LITTLE OF EVERYTHING

What is the unifying idea of marriage?

Just as turtle meat has a taste of all kinds of meat, so marriage has a taste of everything, and just as the turtle is a slow creature, so also is marriage. Falling in love is indeed something simple, but a marriage! Is it something pagan or something Christian, or something sacred or something secular, or something civil or a little of everything? Is it the expression of that inexplicable eroticism, that *Wahlverwandtschaft* [elective affinity] between kindred souls, or is it a duty, or is it a partnership or an expediency in life or the custom in certain countries, or is it a little of everything? Is the town musician or the organist to furnish the music—or should one have a little of both; should the pastor or the police sergeant give the talk and inscribe their names in life's register—or in the municipal register; is it in comb-and-paper music that marriage can be heard or does it listen to that whisper that sounds like "the fairies' from the grottos on a summer night"? [from A. G. Oehlen Schläger, *Aladdin*]. Every benedict believes that when he entered upon marriage he performed a very composite number, a very complex passage, more complicated than anything else, and expects to go on performing it as a married man.

My dear drinking companions! For want of another wedding gift and congratulations, should we not give each of the married folks *one* NB [*nota bene*, note well] and marriage *two* NBs for repeated inattention! . . . I wait in vain for the unifying idea that holds these most heterogeneous *disjecta membra* [separated members] of life-views together.

Stages on Life's Way 63–64 (KW 11)
[Voice: Victor Eremita]*

CLIMBING THE LADDER OF SUCCESS
First Find a Wife, Then Preach

How can a young, single pastor acquire a growing audience?

In former days people required that the proclaimer's life should express the doctrine. This was called earnestness; it was, as we say nowadays, the guarantee the proclaimer had to make. In these days (when a totally secular sensibleness has thrust itself between the prototypes and ourselves, that is, has removed them or put them at an almost ridiculous distance from us, so that we *in contemporaneity* with such a life, a striving such as that, would regard it as the most ridiculous exaggeration of all that is ridiculous)—in these days, that kind of proclamation of Christianity certainly could become too earnest a matter for the Christian public. Therefore the requirement now is different. If you wish to be a success in the world with your proclamation of Christianity, it is now required that your life express the very opposite of the proclamation, or it is required that your life, by expressing the opposite of the proclamation, provide the guarantee that the proclamation is an artistic enjoyment, a dramatic production with tears, gestures, and the like. . . .

First of all obtain a high rank for yourself, then acquire a few, or rather not a few, the more the better, medals and ribbons—and then preach with all your might that the Christian disdains rank and titles, medals and ribbons. You will have the applause of the Christian public. . . .

Is this what you want to tell them, that Christianity prefers the single state, and you yourself are unmarried? My dear fellow, this is not something for you to speak about; the Christian public might be capable of believing that it should be taken seriously, and then God help you. No, take your time, first of all find yourself a wife—and then preach that Christianity has a preference for the single state. Weep a little about it; the Christian public will be moved to weep along with you in the quiet hour, because your life guarantees that the proclamation is an artistic work.—Is this the message you want to give, that Christianity holds that one ought to marry only once—

and you yourself are married for the first time? My dear fellow, this is still not something for you. It may be a long time before you can preach about such things; perhaps you never will be able to. In any case, wait; if and when your first wife has died and you have married a second time—then is the time—now preach that Christianity is of the opinion that one is to marry only once! You will have the Christian public's applause, because your life guarantees that your proclamation is objective.

—*Judge for Yourself!*
For Self-Examination; Judge for Yourself!
138–39 (KW 21)

THE PLEASURE OF SOLITUDE
WHY MYSON LAUGHED

Why did Myson laugh, and did his laughter make him wise?

There was in Greece a wise man. He enjoys the singular honor of being counted among the seven wise men if it is assumed that the number of these was fourteen. If I am not mistaken his name is Myson. An ancient author states that he was a misanthrope. He is very brief: "It is said of Myson that he was a misanthrope and that he laughed when he was alone. When someone asked him why he did so, he answered: Simply because I am alone." You see, you have a predecessor; you will aspire in vain to be included among the number of the seven wise men, even if the number were set at twenty-one, for Myson stands in your way.

—*Or*
Either/Or 2:320–21 (KW 4) [Voice:
Judge William]

The Vulnerability of the Male

EROTIC INSURANCE   THE UNINSURABILITY OF
                     SEXUAL COMPLEMENTARITY

Is a man fulfilled by an emancipated woman?

It is the man's function to be absolute, to act absolutely, to express the absolute; the woman consists in the relational. Between two such different entities no real interaction can take place. This misrelation is precisely the joke, and the joke entered the world with woman. It goes without saying that the man must know how to maintain himself under the absolute, for otherwise nothing manifests itself; that is, something very ordinary manifests itself—namely, that the man and the woman are suited to each other, he as a half man, and she as a half man. . . . If a man in all earnestness surrenders in erotic love, he can say that he is well insured—that is, if he can be insured at all, because the insurance company must inevitably be dubious about something as inflammable as a woman. What, then, has he done? He has identified himself with her; if she goes off with a bang on New Year's Eve, he goes along, too. . . . Here in life one must take her for what she is. What that is will soon be manifest, for she, too, is not satisfied with the esthetic. She goes further; she wants to be emancipated—she is man enough to say that. If that happens, the joke will exceed all bounds.

Stages on Life's Way 48–49, 55–56
(KW 11) [Voice: Constantin
Constantius, quoted by
William Afham]*

PROMISES

Can marriage be temporary?

If, instead of saying "throughout eternity," the couple would say "until Easter, until next May Day," then what they say would make some sense, for then they would be saying something and also something they perhaps could carry out. . . .

Since marriage is like that, it is not strange that attempts are made in many ways to shore it up with moral props. If a man wants to be separated from his wife, the cry goes up: He is a mean fellow, a scoundrel, etc. How ridiculous, and what an indirect assault upon marriage! Either marriage has intrinsic reality [*Realitet*], and then he is adequately punished by losing it, or it has no reality, and then it is unreasonable to vilify him because he is wiser than others. If someone became weary of his money and threw it out the window, no one would say he is a mean fellow, for either money has reality, and then he is adequately punished by not having it anymore, or it has no reality, and then, of course, he is indeed wise.

—*Either:* "The Rotation of Crops"
Either/Or 1:296–97 (KW 3)
[Voice: "A"]

OBSTACLES TO SECRET LOVE

The Rooster Who Would Dearly Love to Have Laid an Egg

At what point does love become a public matter?

In our time, when the social situation makes a secret love affair almost impossible, when the city or commune most often has already had the banns of the happy couple read several times from the pulpit before the parson has done it once; in our time, when society would consider itself robbed of one of its dearest prerogatives did it not have the power to fasten the knot of love, and, at its own invitation (not the parson's) to have much to say about it, so that a love affair only acquires its validity by being publicly discussed, while an understanding entered into without the knowledge of the community is almost regarded as invalid, or at least as a shameful invasion of its prerogatives—just as a sexton regards suicide as a disgraceful stratagem designed to sneak oneself out of the world—in our time, I say, it may occasionally seem necessary for a person to play false if he does not wish the city to take upon itself the honorable task of proposing for him, so that he need only present himself with the customary facial expression of one about to propose, in the manner of Peder Erik Madsen, with white gloves and a written sketch of his future prospects in his hand, together with the other magical charms (not to mention a trustworthy *aide-memoire*) to be used in the final assault. . . . Similar mystifications are sometimes also necessary in literature when one is everywhere surrounded by a multitude of vigilant literati who discover authors about the same way that Poly Panderer arranges matches. . . . And should it progress so far that it is possible to induce some crowing rooster, who would so dearly love to lay an egg, to allow the paternity to be imputed to him, half averting and half reinforcing people in their delusion, then the ironist has won the day.

The Concept of Irony, with Constant Reference to Socrates 268–69

THE CUCKOLD

Xanthippe Surprised *in Flagranti* by Socrates

Supposing Socrates caught Xanthippe in the act—what would be a distinctively Socratic response?

Imagine Socrates surprising Xanthippe *in flagranti* [in the act] (for it would already be un-Socratic to imagine Socrates essentially concerned about or even spying on Xanthippe's faithfulness)—I think that that subtle smile which turned the ugliest man in Athens into the most beautiful would for the very first time change into a roar of laughter. On the other hand, since Aristophanes at times wanted to portray Socrates as ludicrous, it is

176

inconceivable that it never occurred to him to have Socrates come running on stage shouting: Where is she, where is she, so that I can murder her, that is, the unfaithful Xanthippe. Whether Socrates was made a cuckold or not really makes no difference; anything Xanthippe does in this respect is a waste of effort, like snapping one's fingers in one's pocket. Socrates, even with horns on his forehead, remains the same intellectual hero; but that he could become jealous, that he could want to murder Xanthippe—ah, then Xanthippe would have had a power over him that the whole Greek state and the death penalty did not have: to make him ridiculous. A cuckold is therefore comic in his relation to his wife, but in his relation to other men he can be regarded as tragic.

> Stages on Life's Way 50–51 (KW 11)
> [Voice: Constantin Constantius, quoted
> by William Afham]

TRAITORS TO MARRIAGE A Wedding Congratulation

**What does a man look like who has inwardly rebelled against
marriage so as to feel like a slave?**

Every order [*Stand*] of life has its traitors. The order of marriage [*Ægtestand*] also has its traitors. Of course, I do not mean seducers, for they, after all, have not entered into the holy estate of marriage (I hope that this inquiry will find you in a mood in which you will not smile at this expression); I do not mean those who have withdrawn from it by a divorce, for they nevertheless have had the courage to be flagrant rebels. No, I mean those who are rebels merely in thought, who do not even dare let it manifest itself in deed; those wretched husbands who sit and lament that love vanished from their marriage long ago; those husbands who, as you once said of them, sit like lunatics, each in his marital cubicle, slave away in chains, and fantasize about the sweetness of engagement and the bitterness of marriage; those husbands who, according to your own correct observation, are among those who with a certain malicious glee congratulate anyone who becomes engaged.

—Or

Either/Or 2:32–33 (KW 4) [Voice: Judge William]

The Strength of Woman

A Woman's Pleas

Is it fair that a woman's pleas convey such special moral authority?

A woman's pleas! Who inexcusably put this weapon into her hands, who gives the madman a sword, and how powerless he is compared with the pleading of the powerless!

Stages on Life's Way 213 (KW 11)
[Voice: Quidam]

FASHION   The Ladies' Tailor Speaks

Of what about the feminine is male consciousness most densely ignorant?

Just as the robber has his hideout beside the noisy highway and the anteater its funnel in the loose sand and the pirate ship its hiding place by the roaring sea, so I have my fashion boutique right in the middle of the human swarm, as seductive and irresistible to a woman as Venusberg to the man. Here in a fashion boutique one learns to know her practically and from the ground up without all that theoretical fuss. Indeed, if fashion meant nothing more than that a woman in the concupiscence of desire put everything aside, that would still be something. But that is not the way it is; fashion is not open sensuality, is not tolerated dissipation, but is a sneaky trafficking in impropriety that is authorized as propriety. And just as in pagan Prussia the marriageable girl carried a bell whose ringing was a signal to the men, so a woman's existence in fashion is a perpetual carillon. . . . If one wishes to learn to know

179

women, one hour in my boutique is worth more than years and days on the outside. . . .

You may think that it is only in odd moments that she wishes to be in fashion. Far from it, she wants to be that at all times, and it is her one and only thought. Woman does have spirit, but it is invested just about as well as the prodigal son's resources; and woman is reflective to an incomprehensibly high degree, for there is nothing so sacred that she does not immediately find it suitable for adornment, and the most exclusive manifestation of adornment is fashion. No wonder she finds it suitable, for fashion, after all, is the sacred. And there is nothing so insignificant that she does not in turn know how to relate it to adornment, and the manifestation of adornment most devoid of ideas is fashion. And there is nothing, not one thing in her whole attire, not the smallest ribbon, without her having a notion of its relevance to fashion, and without her detecting at once whether the lady passing by has noticed it—because for whom does she adorn herself if it is not for other ladies! Even in my boutique, where she comes, of course, to be fitted out in fashion, even there she is in fashion. Just as there are a special bathing costume and a riding costume, so there is also a special attire that is in vogue to wear for going to the boutique. . . . Whether Diogenes disturbed the woman praying in a somewhat immodest position by asking her whether she did not believe that the gods could see her from behind, I do not know, but this I do know—if I were to say to her kneeling ladyship: The folds of your gown do not fall in a fashionable way, she would dread this more than offending the gods. Woe to the outcast, the Cinderella who does not understand this. . . .

What blissful hours the lover spends with the beloved before the wedding. I do not know, but the blissful hours she spends in my boutique pass him by. Without my special license and my sanction, a wedding is still an invalid act or else a very plebian affair. Suppose the time has already come when they are to meet at the altar, suppose she comes forward with the clearest conscience in the world since everything has been bought in my boutique and in every way put to the test before me—if I were to rush up and say: But good heavens, my lady, the myrtle wreath is fastened entirely wrong—the ceremony would very likely be postponed. But men are ignorant of all

180

such things; to know that, one must be a fashion designer. It takes such prodigious reflection to supervise a woman's reflection that only a man who devotes himself to it is able to do it, and then only if he is originally so endowed. Lucky, then, is the man who does not become involved with any woman; even if she belongs to no other man, she does not belong to him, for she belongs to that phantom produced by feminine reflection's unnatural intercourse with feminine reflection: fashion. . . . From my boutique has gone out to the elite world the glad gospel for all ladies of distinction that fashion decrees that a certain kind of headgear be worn when one goes to church, and that in turn this headgear must be different for the morning service and for vespers. So when the bells ring, the carriage stops at my door. Her ladyship steps out (for it has also been proclaimed that no one but me, the fashion designer, can adjust the headgear properly); I rush to greet her with a deep bow, lead her into my dressing room; while she softly vegetates, I put everything in order. She is ready, has looked at herself in the mirror. Swiftly as an emissary of the gods, I hurry ahead, open the door of the dressing room and bow, hurry to the boutique door, place my arm across my chest like an oriental slave, but then, encouraged by a gracious nod, even dare to throw her an adoring and admiring kiss. She sits down in the carriage—but look! she has forgotten her hymnbook; I hurry out and hand it to her through the window, allowing myself once again to remind her to hold her head just a trifle to the right and to adjust her headgear herself if in stepping out she should disarrange it a bit. She drives off and is edified. . . . No one, not even a god, could dismay her, for she is indeed in fashion.

Stages on Life's Way 66–71 (KW 11)
[Voice: The Fashion Designer]

WOMEN'S EMANCIPATION

Why Woman Is Stronger
than Man

In what way is a woman likely to be closer to perfection than a man?

She [woman] is more perfect than man, for surely the one who explains something is more perfect than the one who is hunting for an explanation. Woman explains the finite; man pursues the infinite. . . .

That is why I hate all that detestable rhetoric about the emancipation of women. God forbid that it may ever happen. I cannot tell you with what pain the thought can pierce my soul, nor what passionate indignation, what hate, I harbor toward anyone who dares to express such ideas. It is my consolation that those who propound such wisdom are not wise as serpents but ordinarily are like oafs whose blabbing can do no harm. Indeed, if the serpent could manage to delude her about this, could tempt her with this seemingly delightful fruit, if this infection were to spread, if it pushed its way through even to her whom I love, my wife, my joy, my refuge, the root of my life, yes, then my courage would be crushed, then freedom's passion in my soul would be exhausted. Then I know very well what I would do—I would sit in the market place and weep, weep like that artist whose work had been destroyed and even he could not remember what it represented. . . . No black-hearted seducer could think up a more dangerous theory for the woman than this, for once he has deluded her into thinking this, she is completely in his power, abandoned to his conditions; she can be nothing for the man except a prey to his whims, whereas as woman she can be everything to him. But the poor [male] wretches do not know what they are doing. They themselves are not much good at being men, and instead of learning how to be men they want to corrupt the woman and be united on the condition that they themselves remain what they are, half-men, and the woman advances to the same wretchedness. . . .

This is why, as I already pointed out previously, Scripture does not say that a woman should leave father and mother and cling to her husband, which one would expect, for, after all, woman is the weaker one who seeks protection from the man—no, it says that the man should leave father and mother and cling to his wife, because to the extent she bestows the finite on him, she is stronger than he.

—Or
Either/Or 2:311–13 (KW 4) [Voice: Judge William]*

MARRIAGE AND OTHER RELATIONSHIPS
A Management Exercise

Can one learn from marriage how to weather other relationships?

That Socrates was not quite the model husband is surely felt by all. The conception of his relationship to [Xanthippe was, as] attributed to Socrates by Xenophon—that he had the same benefit from this shrewish wife as trainers of wild horses, namely, learning how to manage them, that she was for him an exercise in mastering people, inasmuch as when he had done with her he could easily put up with other people.

The Concept of Irony, with Constant Reference to Socrates 217n*

WOMAN AS FANTASY   When the Executioner Goes a-Wooing

How drastic is the reversal that occurs in romantic idealism at the point of marriage?

If a feminine existence is summed up to show the decisive elements in its totality, then every feminine existence makes a thoroughly fantastic impression. The critical turning points in her life are quite different from man's, for her critical turning points turn everything upside down. In Tieck's romantic plays we sometimes find a character who, formerly king of Mesopotamia, is now a grocer in Copenhagen. Every feminine existence is precisely as fantastic as this. If the girl's name is Juliane, then her life is as follows: "Formerly empress in the vast outskirts [*Overdrev*] of erotic love and titular queen of all exaggerations [*Overdrivelser*] of giddiness, now Mrs. Petersen on the corner of Badstustraede [Bathhouse Street]."

As a child, a girl is regarded as inferior to a boy. When she is a little older, one does not quite know what to do with her; finally comes that decisive period that makes her the sovereign. Adoring, man approaches her; he is the suitor. Adoring, for every suitor is that; it is not an invention of a cunning deceiver. Even the public executioner, when he lays down his *fasces* to go a-wooing, even he bends the knee, even though he intends as soon as possible to devote himself to domestic executions, which he takes so much for granted that he is far from trying to make the excuse that public executions are becoming so rare. The cultured gentleman conducts himself in the same way. He kneels, he adores, he conceives of the beloved in the most fantastic categories and thereupon very quickly forgets his kneeling position and would know full well while he was kneeling that it was fantasy. If I were a woman, I would prefer being sold by my father to the highest bidder, as in the Orient, for a business transaction nevertheless does have meaning.

Stages on Life's Way 57–58 (KW 11)
[Voice: Victor Eremita]

HOW MEN ARE TRANSFORMED BY WOMEN
The Girl He Got and the Girl He Lost

Is one more likely to become a poet (or genius or hero or saint) by getting the girl or by not getting her?

Many a man became a genius because of a girl, many a man became a hero because of a girl, many a man became a poet because of a girl, many a man became a saint because of a girl—but he did not become a genius because of the girl he got, for with her he became only a cabinet official; he did not become a hero because of the girl he got, for because of her he became only a general; he did not become a poet because of the girl he got, for because of her he became only a father; he did not become a saint because of the girl he got, for he got none at all and wanted only to have the one and only whom he did not get, just as each of the others became a genius, a hero, a poet with the aid of the girl he did not get.

Stages on Life's Way 59 (KW 11) [Voice: Victor Eremita]

EVE'S PROFICIENCIES   Defense of Woman's
Native Abilities

Through what lens do men view the particular excellence of women?

History throughout the ages shows that woman's great abilities have at least in part been recognized. Hardly was man created before we find Eve already as audience at the snake's philosophical lectures, and we see that she mastered them with such ease that at once she could utilize the results of the same in her domestic practice. . . .

As a speaker, woman has so great a talent that she made history with her own special line: the so-called bed-hangings sermons, curtain lectures, etc., and Xanthippe is still remembered as a pattern of feminine eloquence and as founder of a school that has lasted to this very day, whereas Socrates' school has long since disappeared. . . . And when the rabbis forbade [women] to put in their word, it was solely because they were afraid that the women would outshine them or expose their folly.

—"Articles from Student Days,
1834–1836"
Early Polemical Writings [3] (KW 1)*

185

Children and Youth

FATHERLY AMBIVALENCE THE BLESSING OF CHILDREN — AT
A DISTANCE

Why are children sent to boarding school?

Our age has had a hard time effect-
ing the resignation it takes to enter into a marriage; if one has denied
oneself to that extent, one thinks that this is enough and cannot
really put up with such tedious difficulties as a flock of children. It is
alleged frequently enough in novels, albeit casually but nevertheless
as a reason for a particular individual not to marry, that he cannot
endure children; in life in the most civilized countries this is expressed by the removal of the children from the parental house as
soon as possible and their placement in a boarding school etc. How
often have you not been amused by these tragi-comic family men
with four darling children whom they secretly wished were far, far
away? How often have you not gloated over the outraged sensibilities
of such family men at all the petty details that life entails, when the
children have to be spanked, when they spill on themselves, when
they scream, when the great man—father—feels frustrated in his
venturesomeness by the thought that his children tie him to the
earth? How often have you not with well-deserved cruelty brought
such noble fathers to the peak of suppressed rage when you, occupied
exclusively with his children, dropped a few words about what a
blessing it really is to have children?

—Or
Either/Or 2:69 (KW 4) [Voice: Judge
William]

186

Why is roguish piety so disarming?

In Christianity we see at times a vague and yet—precisely because of this vagueness and ambiguity—appealing blend of the erotic and the religious that has just as much brave and bold roguishness as it has childlike piety. This is found most often, of course, in Catholicism, and with us in its purest form among the common folk. Imagine (and I know you enjoy doing this, for it is indeed a situation) a young peasant girl with a pair of eyes audacious and yet modestly hiding behind her eyelashes, healthy, and freshly glowing, and yet there is something about her complexion that is not sickness but a higher healthiness. Imagine her on a Christmas eve: she is alone in her room; midnight is already past, and nevertheless sleep, which ordinarily visits her so faithfully, is elusive; she feels a sweet, pleasant restlessness; she opens the window halfway and alone with the stars gazes out into the infinite space. A little sigh lightens her heart; she closes the window. With an earnestness that is continually on the verge of roguishness she prays:

You wise men three,
Tonight let me see
Whose bread I shall bake
Whose bed I shall make
Whose name I shall carry
Whose bride I shall be,

and then, hale and hearty, she jumps into bed. To be honest, it would be a disgrace for the three kings if they did not take care of her.

—*Or*
Either/Or 2:44–45 (KW 4) [Voice: Judge William]

Is time experienced in the same way by both the unhappy and the happy?

What is the happiest life? It is that of a young girl sixteen years old, when she, pure and innocent, possesses nothing, neither a chest of drawers nor a tall cupboard, but makes use of the lowest drawer of her mother's bureau to hide all her treasures: a confirmation dress and a hymnbook. Fortunate is he who possesses no more than he could manage with the next drawer. What is the happiest life? It is that of a young girl sixteen years old, when she, pure and innocent, indeed can dance but goes to a ball only twice a year. What is the happiest life? It is that of a young girl sixteen summers old, when she, pure and innocent, sits busy at her work and still has time to steal a glance at him, at him, who owns nothing, neither a chest of drawers nor a tall cupboard, but is only a copartner in the shared wardrobe, and nevertheless has a completely different explanation, since in her he possesses the whole world, although she possesses nothing at all. And who, then, is the unhappy one? It is that rich young man, twenty-five winters old, who lives across the street. If someone is sixteen summers old and another sixteen winters, are they not the same age? Alas, no! Why not? Is the time not the same when it is the same? Alas, no! The time is not the same.

Stages on Life's Way 262–63 (KW 11)
[Voice: Quidam]

LOVE COVERS SIN   The Child in the Den of Thieves

What will a child see in a den of thieves?

Even a youth upon first stepping out into life is very eager to divulge how he knows and has discovered evil (because he is reluctant to have the world call him a simpleton). . . . If someone has discovered how fundamentally good-natured almost every human being is, he would hardly dare to acknowledge his discovery, and he would fear becoming ludicrous, perhaps even fear that humanity would feel insulted by it. If, however, someone pretends that he had discovered how fundamentally shabby every human being is, how envious, how selfish, how faithless, and what abomination can lie hidden in the purest, that is, in the one regarded by simpletons and silly geese and small-town beauties as the purest—that person conceitedly knows that he is welcome, that it is the yield of his observing, his knowledge, his story that the world longs to hear. Thus sin and evil have one power more over people than we ordinarily think of: that it is so stupid to be good, so shallow to believe in the good, so small-townish to betray ignorance . . .

Put a child in a den of thieves (but the child must not remain there so long that it is corrupted itself); that is, let it remain there only for a very brief time. Then let it come home and tell everything it has experienced. You will note that the child, who is a good observer and has an excellent memory (as does every child), will tell everything in the greatest detail, yet in such a way that in a certain sense the most important is omitted. Therefore someone who does not know that the child has been among thieves would least suspect it on the basis of the child's story. What is it, then, that the child leaves out, what is it that the child has not discovered? It is the evil. Yet the child's story about what it has seen and heard is entirely accurate. What, then, does the child lack? What is it that so often makes a child's story the most profound mockery of the adults? It is knowledge of evil, that the child lacks knowledge of evil, that the child does not even feel inclined to want to be knowledgeable about evil. In this the one who loves is like the child.

Works of Love 283–87 (KW 16)

EDITOR AS TEMPTER   THE SEDUCTION OF A
                          YOUNG AUTHOR

What changes a talker into an author, and a young author into one not so young?

If a person belongs to "the readers' sect," if he in one way or another distinguishes himself as an alert and diligent reader, others begin to nurture the notion that a minor author might emerge, for as Hamann says: ". . . [out of children come adults, out of virgins come brides, out of readers come writers]."

Now a rose-tinted life begins, much like a girl's early youth. Editors and publishers begin to pay court. It is a dangerous period, for the conversation of editors is very seductive, and soon one is in their power; but they deceive only us poor children, and then—well, then it is too late. Watch out, young man, and do not go too often to the cafés and restaurants, for that is where editors spin their webs. And when they see an innocent young man who talks straight from the shoulder, fast and loose, with no idea whether what he says is worth anything or not, but merely rejoices in letting his words freely flow forth, in hearing his heart pound as he speaks, pounding in what is said—then a dark figure approaches him, and this figure is an editor. He has a subtle ear; he can hear immediately whether what is being said will look good in print or not. Then he tempts the young fellow; he shows him how indefensible it is to cast his pearls away in this manner; he promises him money, power, influence, even with the fair sex. The heart is weak, the editor's words beautiful, and soon he is trapped. Now he no longer seeks solitary places in order to yearn and sigh; he does not hurry eagerly to the happy haunts of youth to become intoxicated with talk; he is silent, for one who writes does not talk. He sits pallid and cold in his workroom; he does not change color at the kiss of the idea; he does not blush like a young rose when the dew sinks into his cup. He has no smiles, no tears; calmly he watches the pen glide across the paper, for he is an author and not young anymore.

—*Either:* "The First Love"
Either/Or 1:245–46 (KW 3) [Voice: "A"]

TRUTH AND COMMUNICATION

Literary and Artistic Criticism

THE UNWRITTEN BUT
WELL-REVIEWED BOOK

**Might a book achieve the distinction of being well reviewed, even
if never written?**

"Have you read the excellent re-
view?" "No." "Then you must read it. You must definitely read it. It is
absolutely as I would have written it myself."—"Strangely enough,
what the interesting reviewer says was the same as I said when I had
merely leafed through the book in Reitzel's."—"I haven't read it yet,
but I've heard from a friend in the country, who is damned bright and
a connoisseur, that the book is a failure, although there are really
beautiful passages in it."—It hangs together in this way. That friend
in the country has not read the book but got a letter from a man in
the capital who has not read the book either, but read the review,
which in turn was written by a man who had not read the book, but
heard what that reliable man said who had leafed through it a bit in
Reitzel's. *Summa summarum* [all in all] it is not unthinkable that a
book could be published, cause a sensation, occasion a review that
was read, while the book could just as well be unwritten . . .

A cellarman wanted to rent a cellar from me. In spite of his known
integrity, etc., he was not found, on a landlord's gold-scales, to be a
24-karat tenant. There was, then, a question of guarantee. In all politeness I let myself betray my misgivings—but he looked at me with
a smile and said, "Don't worry, I'm good enough, damn it all, for I am
myself guarantor for a cellarman in Strandstræde [Beach Street]." I
had to steady myself with a chair, for at the very moment I tried to

think through what he said, everything went black. In this way the common reviewers guarantee the reading public's judgment.

Prefaces: Light Reading for Certain Classes as the Occasion May Require 35–36
[Voice: Nicolaus Notabene]

CRITICISM   THE ACTING WATER INSPECTOR

What function do reviewers perform for the literary world?

The reviewer is the acting water inspector who sees to it that the drain water runs free and unhindered. With this everything is consummated in itself: the water comes from the public and runs back to the public. . . .

I could at most suggest that a committee be appointed to inquire into how one could interrupt the critical proceedings.

Prefaces: Light Reading for Certain Classes as the Occasion May Require 38–40
[Voice: Nicolaus Notabene]

THE AIM OF A PREFACE   ON TIPPING ONE'S HAT WHEN NO
                         ONE IS THERE

What is a preface supposed to accomplish?

The preface as such, the emancipated preface, must then have no subject to discuss but must deal with nothing, and as far as it is thought to deal with something, this must be an appearance and a feigned movement. . . .

Writing a preface is like sharpening a scythe; like tuning a guitar; like chatting with a child; like spitting out of the window. . . . Writing a preface is like ringing at a man's door to bamboozle him; like walking past a young girl's window and looking at the cobblestones; it is like lashing with one's stick in the air at the wind; like tipping one's hat though one greets no one. Writing a preface is like having done something that entitles one to a certain amount of attention; like having something on one's conscience that tempts one to confide; like bowing in invitation to dance, then not moving; like pressing the left leg in, tightening the reins to the right, and hearing the steed say, "Prrf." . . . Thus, oh thus, it is to write prefaces. And what is the one who writes them like? . . . He does not go to the Stock Exchange to scrape money together but only strolls through it. He does not talk about annual general meetings, because the air is too stuffy; he does not propose toasts in any Society because one has to give notice several days in advance; he does not run errands for the System; he pays no installments on the national debt, indeed he does not even take it seriously.

> *Prefaces: Light Reading for Certain Classes*
> *as the Occasion May Require* 19–21
> [Voice: Nicolaus Notabene]

ADULATION   IMMORTAL MOZART!

Who among artists ranks first?

I am infatuated, like a young girl, with Mozart, and I must have him rank in first place, whatever it costs. And I will go to the deacon and the pastor and the dean and the bishop and the whole church council, and I will beseech and implore them to grant my request, and I will challenge the whole congregation on the same matter, and if my appeal is not heard, my childish wish not fulfilled, then I will secede from the association, then I will divorce myself from its way of thinking, then I will form a sect that not only places Mozart first but has no one but Mozart. And I will beseech Mozart to forgive me that his music did not inspire me to great deeds but made me a fool who, because of him, lost the little sense I had and now in quiet sadness usually passes the time humming something I do not understand, and like a ghost prowls night and day around something I cannot enter. Immortal Mozart! You to whom I owe everything—to whom I owe that I lost my mind, that

my soul was astounded, that I was terrified at the core of my being—
you to whom I owe that I did not go through life without encounter-
ing something that could shake me, you whom I thank because I did
not die without having loved, even though my love was unhappy.

—*Either:* "The Immediate Erotic Stages"
Either/Or 1:48–49 (KW 3) [Voice: "A"]

COMPLIANCE   WHEN I SPEAK GERMAN

**What personal transformation occurs when one converses in
German?**

When I speak German, I am the
most accommodating man in the world.

—*Repetition*
Fear and Trembling; Repetition 152 (KW
6) [Voice: Constantin Constantius]

Comedy and Contradiction

INDULGING ONESELF IN A GESTURE

The Dancer Whom Nothing
Would Satisfy but Leaping

How does humor enter just at that point where all else fails?

There probably is no person who has not gone through a period when no richness of language, no passion of interjection was adequate, since no expression, no gesture sufficed, since nothing satisfied him other than breaking into the strangest leaps and somersaults. Perhaps the same individual learned to dance. Perhaps he went frequently to the ballet and admired the art of the dancer. Perhaps there came a time when ballet no longer stirred him, and yet he had moments when he could return to his room and, indulging himself, find indescribably humorous relief in standing on one leg in a picturesque pose or, giving not a damn for the world, settle everything with an *entrechat*.

—*Repetition*
Fear and Trembling; Repetition 158 (KW
6) [Voice: Constantin Constantius]

THE COMIC

Plunging into the Abyss
of Laughter

How is comic genius in farce to be evaluated?

For a cultured person, seeing a farce is similar to playing the lottery, except that one does not have the annoyance of winning money. . . . For the same farce can produce very different impressions, and, strangely enough, it may so happen that the one time it made the least impression it was performed best. Thus a person cannot rely on his neighbor and the man across the street and statements in the newspaper to determine whether he has enjoyed himself or not. . . . A completely successful performance of a farce requires a cast of special composition. It must include two, at most three, very talented actors or, more correctly, generative geniuses. They must be children of caprice, intoxicated with laughter, dancers of whimsy who, even though they are at other times like other people—yes, the very moment before—the instant they hear the stage manager's bell they are transformed and, like a thorough-bred Arabian horse, they begin to snort and puff, while their distended nostrils betoken the chafing of spirit because they want to be off, want to cavort wildly. They are not so much reflective artists who have studied laughter as they are lyricists who themselves plunged into the abyss of laughter and now let its volcanic power hurl them out on the stage. Thus they have not deliberated very much on what they will do but leave everything to the moment and the natural power of laughter. They have the courage to venture what the individual makes bold to do only when alone, what the mentally deranged do in the presence of everybody, what the genius knows how to do with the authority of genius, certain of laughter. They know that their hilarity has no limits, that their comic resources are inexhaustible, and they themselves are amazed at it practically every moment. They know that they are able to sustain laughter the whole evening without its costing them any more effort than it takes me to scribble this down on paper. . . . Beckmann is unquestionably a comic genius who purely lyrically frolics freely in the comic, one who does not distinguish himself by character portrayal but by ebullience of mood.

—*Repetition*
Fear and Trembling; Repetition
159–61, 163 (KW 6) [Voice:
Constantin Constantius]

COMIC AUTHORITY   THE COMIC SCYTHE IN THE WORLD
                         OF SPIRIT

In what does the power of the comic consist?

The power in the comic is the po-
liceman's badge, the emblem of jurisdiction that every agent who in
our day actually is an agent must carry. But this comic power is not
impetuous or reckless, its laughter not shrill; on the contrary, it is
careful with the immediacy that it lays aside. Similarly, the reaper's
scythe is equipped with wooden slats that run parallel to the sharp
blade, and while the scythe cuts the grain, the grain sinks down almost voluptuously upon the supporting cradle, thereupon to be laid
neatly and beautifully in a swath. So it is with the legitimized comic
power in relation to matured immediacy. The task of cutting down is
a solemn act. The one who cuts down is not a dreary reaper, but
nevertheless it is the sharpness and the biting blade of the comic
before which the immediacy sinks, not unbeautifully, supported by
the cutting down even in the falling. This comic power is essentially
humor. If the comic power is cold and bleak, it is a sign that there is
no new immediacy sprouting. Then there is no harvest, only the
empty passion of a sterile wind storming over bare fields.

> *Concluding Unscientific Postscript to*
> Philosophical Fragments 1:281–82 (KW
> 12) [Voice: Johannes Climacus]

SUFFERING AND THE AUTHORITY OF THE COMIC
                    THE SECOND RAP OF
                    THE NIGHTSTICK

How does one gain competence in comic awareness?

The more one suffers, the more
sense, I believe, one gains for the comic. Only by the most profound
suffering does one gain real competence in the comic, which with a
word magically transforms the rational creature called man into a

Fratze [caricature]. This competence is like a policeman's self-assurance when he abruptly grips his club and does not tolerate any talk or blocking of traffic. The victim protests, he objects, he insists on being respected as a citizen, he demands a hearing—immediately there is a second rap from the club, and that means: Please move on! Don't stand there!

> *Stages on Life's Way* 245–46 (KW 11)
> [Voice: Quidam]

MORPHOLOGY OF THE UNEXPECTED
WUNDERLICH!

How is the comic intensified by the unexpected?

When a peasant knocks on the door of a man who is German and talks with him to find out whether there is a man living in the house whose name the peasant has forgotten but who has ordered a load of peat, and the German, impatient at being unable to understand what the peasant is saying, bursts out, "*Das ist doch wunderlich* [That is strange]," to the immense joy of the peasant, who says, "That's right! The man's name is Wunderlich"—then the [double] contradiction is that the German and the peasant are unable to speak together because the language is a hindrance, and that the peasant nevertheless obtains the information by means of the language.

> *Concluding Unscientific Postscript to*
> Philosophical Fragments 1:516n
> (KW 12) [Voice: Johannes Climacus]

LANGUAGE AND COMEDY
WHEN THE WORD BECAME PORK

Does miscommunication elicit comedy?

When a German-Danish pastor declares in the pulpit, "The Word became pork (*Fleisch*)," this is comic.

The comic is not just the ordinary contradiction that arises when someone speaks a foreign language he does not know and evokes by the words an effect totally different from the one he wants. But because he is a pastor and he is preaching the contradiction is sharpened, since in a pastor's discourse speaking is used only in a more special sense, and the least that is assumed as a given is that he can speak the language. Moreover, the contradiction also strays into ethical territory: a person may innocently make himself guilty of blasphemy.

Concluding Unscientific Postscript to
Philosophical Fragments 1:518n
(KW 12) [Voice: Johannes Climacus]

PRATTFALLS   Vanishing into the Basement
                        while Gazing at the Stars

Why is falling down more amusing precisely when the performer gazing upward?

When a soldier stands in the street staring at the glorious window display in a fancy gift shop and comes closer in order to see better, when with his face really aglow and his eyes fixed on the finery in the window he does not notice that the basement entrance extends out inordinately far so that he vanishes into the basement just when he is about to have a proper look—then the contradiction is in the movement, the upward direction of the head and gaze and the underground direction down into the basement. If he had not been gazing upward, it would not have been so ludicrous. Thus it is more comic if a man who is walking and gazing at the stars falls into a hole than if it happens to someone who is not as elevated above the earthly.

Concluding Unscientific Postscript to
Philosophical Fragments 1:516n
(KW 12) [Voice: Johannes Climacus]

COMIC REPETITION   <small>THE QUEEN AND THE
                        DEAF MINISTER</small>

At what point does repetition turn comic?

When the queen had finished telling a story at a court function and all the court officials, including a deaf minister, laughed at it, the latter stood up, asked to be granted the favor of also being allowed to tell a story, and then told the same story.

—*Repetition*
Fear and Trembling; Repetition 150 (KW 6) [Voice: Constantin Constantius]

Laughter as the Test of Truth

LAUGHTER'S AUTHORITY The Revivalists' Fight over
"Greatest-Sinner" Status

Can comedy be objectively researched?

If three revivalists have a dispute of
honor with one another about which one of them is the greatest
sinner, a bare-knuckle fight over this rank—then, of course, this
godly expression has become for them a worldly title.

In the previous century, a thesis propounded by Lord Shaftesbury
that makes laughter the test of truth engendered several little research projects to find out whether it is so. In our day, Hegelian
philosophy has wanted to give predominance to the comic, which
might seem especially odd on the part of Hegelian philosophy, which
of all philosophies was least able to stand a blow from that corner.

> *Concluding Unscientific Postscript to*
> Philosophical Fragments 1:512 (KW 12)
> [Voice: Johannes Climacus]*

LEGITIMATING COMEDY IN RELIGIOUS SPEECH
Buying Permission on Sunday to
Laugh All Week Long

Is comedy a legitimate expression of religious consciousness?

The religious [awareness] does not
dare ignore what occupies people's lives so very much—what continually comes up again every day in conversations, in social intercourse, in books, in the modification of the entire life-view—*unless*

203

the Sunday performances in church are supposed to be a kind of indulgence in which with morose devoutness for one hour a person buys permission to laugh freely all week long. The question of the legitimacy of the comic, of its relation to the religious, whether it itself has legitimate significance in the religious address, this question is of essential importance for a religious existence in our time, in which the comic runs off with the victory everywhere. To cry "alas and woe" over this manifestation merely shows how little the defenders respect the religious [life] that they are defending, since it shows far greater respect for the religious to demand that it be installed in its rights in everyday life rather than affectedly to hold it off at a Sunday distance. The matter is very simple. The comic is present in every stage of life *(except that the position is different)*, because whereever there is life there is contradiction, and wherever there is contradiction, the comic is present.

Concluding Unscientific Postscript to
Philosophical Fragments 1:513–14
(KW 12) [Voice: Johannes Climacus]*

THE HUMAN COMEDY

The Speaker Who Still in His Speaking Gown Disavows His Speech

How may the truth become untruth instantly after having been spoken?

A man, stirred to tears so that not only sweat but also tears pour down his face, can sit and read or hear an exposition on self-denial, on the nobility of sacrificing his life for the truth. Then in the next moment, *ein, zwei, drei, vupti,* almost with tears still in his eyes, he can be in full swing helping untruth to be victorious—in the sweat of his brow and to the best of his modest ability. It is exceedingly comic that a speaker with sincere voice and gestures, deeply stirred and deeply stirring, can movingly depict the truth, can face all the powers of evil and of hell boldly, with cool self-assurance in his bearing, a dauntlessness in his air, and an appropriateness of movement worthy of admiration—it is exceedingly comic that almost simultaneously, practically still "in his dressing gown," he can timidly and cravenly cut and run away from the slightest inconvenience. It is exceedingly comic that someone is able to understand the whole truth about how mean and sordid the world is etc.—that he can understand this and then the next moment not recognize what he has understood, for almost at once he himself goes out and participates in the very same meanness and sordidness, is honored for it, and accepts the honor, that is, acknowledges it.

The Sickness unto Death 90–91 (KW 19)
[Voice: Anti-Climacus]*

INTERRUPTION   ANSWERING A QUESTION THAT HAS
                      ONLY A RHETORICAL PURPOSE

What comic transition occurs when a rhetorical question is seriously answered?

It is comic when in everyday conversation a man uses the sermonic rhetorical question form (which does not require an answer but merely forms the transition for answering it oneself). It is comic when the person with whom he is speaking misunderstands it and chimes in with the answer.

Concluding Unscientific Postscript to Philosophical Fragments 1:517n
(KW 12) [Voice: Johannes Climacus]

SEEMING TO BE ENSNARED BY THE
OTHER'S COMPULSION   THE IRONIST'S INTENSE SATISFACTION
                            IN DISCOVERING WEAKNESSES

How does the ironist trap the pretentious?

One sometimes sees it employed against a man who is on his way toward suffering from some fixed idea, against a man who deludes himself into thinking he is handsome or has especially handsome side-whiskers, or imagines he is witty or that he once said something so funny that it cannot be repeated often enough, or against a man whose whole life is contained in a single event, as it were, which he constantly reverts to and which anyone can induce him to relate at any moment if one but knows the right spring to press, etc. In all these instances it is the ironist's pleasure to seem ensnared by the same prejudice imprisoning the other person. It is one of the ironist's chief satisfactions to discover such weaknesses everywhere, and the more distinguished the person in whom they are found, so much the more does it please the ironist to make a fool of him unawares. . . . In relation to a superabundance of wisdom, [the ironist appears] to be ignorant, so stupid, to be as much of a bumpkin as possible, yet always so amiable and eager to learn that the landlords of wisdom take pleasure in letting him poach on their well-stocked preserves.

The Concept of Irony, with Constant Reference to Socrates 267*

CONTEXT · BUSTLING ACTIVITY ON THE SINKING SHIP

What is funny about extreme busyness amid extreme danger?

Insofar as money is a something, the relativity between richer and poorer is not comic, but if it is token money, it is comic that it is a relativity. If the reason for people's hustle-bustle is a possibility of avoiding danger, the busyness is not comic; but if, for example, it is on a ship that is sinking, there is something comic in all this running around, because the contradiction is that despite all this movement they are not moving away from the site of their downfall.

Concluding Unscientific Postscript to Philosophical Fragments 1:555 (KW 12) [Voice: Johannes Climacus]

THE PRIMITIVITY OF WIT THE RING OF REAL COINS AFTER
THE WHISPER OF PAPER MONEY

**Can one understand the comic without the exquisite timing
wrought out of the depths of inward suffering and passion?**

To aspire to wittiness without pos-
sessing the wealth of inwardness is like wanting to be prodigal on
luxuries and to dispense with the necessities of life; as the proverb
puts it, it is selling one's trousers and buying a wig. But an age without passion possesses no assets. Everything becomes, as it were, trans-
actions in *paper money*. Certain phrases and observations circulate
among the people, partly true and sensible, yet devoid of vitality, but
there is no hero, no lover, no thinker, no knight of faith, no great
humanitarian, no person in despair to vouch for their validity by
having primitively experienced them. Just as in our business transac-
tions we long to hear the ring of real coins after the whisper of paper
money, so we today long for a little primitivity. But what is more
primitive than wit, more primitive, at least more amazing, than even
the first spring bud and the first delicate blade of grass? Yes, even if
spring were to come according to a prior arrangement, it would still
be spring, but a witticism by prior arrangement would be an abomination. Suppose, then, that as a relief from the feverishness of flaring
enthusiasm a point were reached where wit, that divine happening,
that bonus given by divine cue from the enigmatic origins of the
inexplicable . . . suppose that wit were changed to its most trite and
hackneyed opposite, a trifling necessity of life, so that it would become a profitable industry to fabricate and make up and renovate and
buy up in bulk old and new witticisms: what a frightful epigram on
the witty age!

*Two Ages: The Age of Revolution and the
Present Age, a Literary Review* 74–75
(KW 14)

The Vocation of Authorship

MAKING DIFFICULTIES EVERYWHERE

How did Johannes Climacus [SK's humorist pseudonym] become an author?

It is now about four years since the idea came to me of wanting to try my hand as an author. I remember it very clearly. It was on a Sunday; yes, correct, it was a Sunday afternoon. As usual, I was sitting outside the café in Frederiksberg Gardens, that wonderful garden which for the child was the enchanted land where the king lived with the queen, that lovely garden which for the youth was a pleasant diversion in the happy gaiety of the populace, that friendly garden which for the adult is so cozy in its wistful elevation above the world and what belongs to the world, that garden where even the envied glory of royalty is what it indeed is out there—a queen's recollection of her late lord. There as usual I sat and smoked my cigar. Regrettably, the only similarity I have been able to detect between the beginning of my fragment of philosophic endeavor and the miraculous beginning of that poetic hero is that it was in a public place. Otherwise there is no similarity at all, and although I am the author of *Fragments*, I am so insignificant that I am an outsider in literature. I have not even added to subscription literature, nor can it truthfully be said that I have a significant place in it.

I had been a student for a half score of years. Although I was never lazy, all my activity was nevertheless only like a splendid inactivity, a kind of occupation I still much prefer and for which I perhaps have a little genius. I read a great deal, spend the rest of the day loafing and thinking, or thinking and loafing, but nothing came of it. The productive sprout in me went for everyday use and was consumed in its first greening. An inexplicable power of persuasion, both strong and cunning, continually constrained me, captivated by its persuasion. This power was my indolence. It is not like the vehement craving of erotic love or like the intense incitement of enthusiasm; it is instead like a woman in the house who constrains one and with whom one gets on very well—so well that one never dreams of wanting to marry. This much is certain: although I am generally not unacquainted with the comforts of life, of all comforts indolence is the most comfortable.

So there I sat and smoked my cigar until I drifted into thought. Among other thoughts, I recall these. You are getting on in years, I said to myself, and are becoming an old man without being anything and without actually undertaking anything. On the other hand, wherever you look in literature or in life, you see the names and figures of celebrities, the prized and highly acclaimed people, prominent or much discussed, the many benefactors of the age who know how to benefit humankind by making life easier and easier, some by railroads, others by omnibuses and steamships, others by telegraph, others by easily understood surveys and brief publications about everything worth knowing, and finally the true benefactors of the age who by virtue of thought systematically make spiritual existence easier and easier and yet more and more meaningful—and what are you doing?

At this point my introspection was interrupted because my cigar was finished and a new one had to be lit. So I smoked again, and then suddenly this thought crossed my mind. You must do something, but since with your limited capabilities it will be impossible to make anything easier than it has become, you must, with the same humanitarian enthusiasm as the others have, take it upon yourself to make something more difficult. This idea pleased me enormously; it also flattered me that for this effort I would be loved and respected, as much as anyone else, by the entire community. In other words, when all join together to make everything easier in every way, there remains only one possible danger, namely, the danger that the easiness would become so great that it would become all too easy. So only one lack remains, even though not yet felt, the lack of difficulty. Out of love of humankind, out of despair over my awkward predicament of having achieved nothing and of being unable to make anything easier than it had already been made, out of genuine interest in those who make everything easy, I comprehended that it was my task: to make difficulties everywhere. . . .

When at a banquet where the guests have already gorged themselves, someone is intent on having more courses served and someone else on having an emetic ready, it is certainly true that only the former has understood what the guests demand, but I wonder if the latter might not also claim to have considered what they might require.

From that moment I have found my entertainment [*Underholdning*] in this work.

> Concluding Unscientific Postscript to
> Philosophical Fragments 1:185–87
> (KW 12) [Voice: Johannes Climacus]

COMPULSIVE SELF-DISCLOSURE

THE WOULD-BE AUTHOR WHO LEPT OUT OF BED TO DIVULGE HIS SYMPTOMS

What becomes of the writer who has nothing to communicate, least of all himself?

A young man shows up in a family, passes himself off as a cousin who has been away for many years. He himself does not know what the cousin is called until a bill received for the cousin is presented to him and helps him out of the predicament. He takes the bill and in a not unwitty aside says: It can always be good to find out what my name is. Similarly, the premise-author also produces a comic effect when he passes himself off as something other than he is by passing himself off as an author, and he finally must wait for something from the outside that will inform him about who he really is, that is, spiritually understood, what he really wants. . . .

The premise-author has no need to *communicate himself* because essentially he has nothing to communicate; indeed, he lacks precisely the essential, the conclusion, the meaning in relation to the presup-

210

positions. He has no *need to communicate* himself; he is *one who is in need*. And just as other needy persons fall as a burden on the state and the welfare department, so all premise-authors are basically needy persons who fall as a burden on the generation, since they want to be supported by it rather than that they themselves work and support themselves with the understanding that they themselves earn. . . .

It is one thing when a physician, who is informed about treatment and healing, which he discusses in his medical practice, relates a case history. A physician at a sickbed is one thing, and a sick person, one who has leaped out of bed and by becoming an author, immediately describing his symptoms, obviously confuses being sick with being a physician, is something else. . . .

See, in those distant times when a man was vouchsafed lofty revelations, he used a long time to understand himself in this marvel before he began to want to guide others. . . . Now, however, immediately the next morning one puts in the newspaper that one had a revelation last night.

The Book on Adler 13–14, 17, 23
(KW 24)

THE HAZARDS OF AUTHORSHIP
What Could Possibly Go Wrong
on the Way to the Printer?

Even after the author has done the hard work of coming to know himself and writing accurately of his self-knowledge, can he know beforehand what uncertainties still may lie ahead?

Whether one who wants to write a book is capable of it, time will teach him; whether he will finish with it, whether in just that same moment he will not, as ill luck would have it, upset the inkhorn over it, or mislay the manuscript, or the printer throw it away, or the delivery boy lose it, or the compositor's burn down, or the edition be spoiled, or it become apparent that not

211

one person likes what he writes—no person can get to know all this beforehand.

> *Prefaces: Light Reading for Certain Classes as the Occasion May Require* 73 [Voice: Nicolaus Notabene]

DISCONNECTED SENTENCES

The Book Whose Typesetting Occurred through a Misunderstanding

Can one cohesively review disconnected scraps of paper?

It is well known that as a task for composition in the mother tongue one sometimes uses single disconnected words from which the pupils must form a connected sentence. So it is that [Magister Adolf Peter] Adler throws out quite abruptly brief clauses, sometimes meaningless, perhaps to give the reader an opportunity of practicing the composition of connected sentences. In other places he seemed to behave quite as if the reader did not exist, that is to say, as though what he wrote were not meant to be printed, but as though from time to time it had been written in a notebook and got printed through a misunderstanding. . . .

One cannot help thinking of him as walking to and fro on the floor, constantly repeating the same particular phrase, supporting the particular phrase by altering his voice and gesticulating, till he has bewitched himself into a sort of intoxication so that he is aware of a wondrous and solemn buzzing in his ears—but this is not thinking. In case a person wanted to put himself into a solemn mood and therefore were to walk back and forth on the floor and say incessantly: 7–14–21; 7–14–21; 7–14–21—then would this monotonous repetition have the effect of a magical formula or of a strong drink upon a neurasthenic, it would seem to him that he had got into touch with something extraordinary. In case another to whom he imparted his wisdom were to say, "But what then is there in this 7–14–21?" he likely would reply, "It depends upon what voice you say it with, and that you continue to say it for a whole hour, and moreover that you

212

gesticulate—then you will surely discover that there is something in it." In case one were to write on small scraps of paper such short phrases as, "He went out of the castle," "He drew the knife," "I must have dislocated my hip"—in case one were to hide all these scraps in a drawer, take out a single slip of paper and repeat uninterruptedly what was written on it, he would in the end find himself in a fantastic state of mind and it would seem to him that there was something extraordinarily deep in it. . . . When one in rummaging among old papers finds such short phrases the whole connection of which has long been forgotten, there is some amusement in giving oneself over to the play of imagination. When one has done that he burns the papers. Not so Adler—he publishes them. . . . In case a man could make a multitude believe that he possesses a hidden wisdom, and thereupon he were to write abrupt phrases on small scraps of paper, in case he borrowed, moreover, the entire scenarium used in drawing the lottery, the big tent, the wheel of fortune, a company of soldiers, a minister of chancery before whom the soldiers would present arms, while one stepped out on the balcony, then to the accompaniment of soft festal music mingled with a swirl of notes in a higher pitch, let the wheel turn round and the boy in festal costume draw a ticket the content of which was read out—on that occasion several women at least would lose their senses. What is said here about Adler's passion for raising himself into a state of exaltation contains absolutely no exaggeration.

> *On Authority and Revelation: The Book*
> *on Adler, or a Cycle of Ethico-Religious*
> *Essays* 135–38*

AUTHORSHIP MADE SIMPLE
ON HANGING OUT A SHINGLE AS AN AUTHOR

Is there any completely painless way to become a writer?

It is the easiest thing of all in our time to write a book if, according to custom, one takes ten older ones that treat of the same topic and from those compiles an eleventh on the same topic. In this way one obtains the honor of being an author just as easily as, according to Holberg's advice, one obtains the dignity of being a practicing doctor and in possession of fellow townsmen's money, confidence, and respect by providing oneself with a new black suit and writing on one's door: "*N.N. praktisirender Arzt*" [N.N. Practicing Physician]. . . .

The eleventh book, which is the mediation, produces no new thought, but is different from the earlier ones only in that the word *mediation* is found several times on every page and that the author in the introduction to every section reels off with unction the creed that one must not stop with the ten but must mediate. Now, as this is not deemed more difficult to learn to say than that even an industrious parrot could learn it, so with this word the gospel is preached for all commonplace topics on a scale unprecedented in the world, and this word proclaims an indulgence as no pope ever proclaimed it, since, at the same time as it proclaims indulgence from work and the agony of punishment, it proclaims the big prize more surely than any lottery.

*Prefaces: Light Reading for Certain Classes
as the Occasion May Require 63–65*
[Voice: Nicolaus Notabene]*

WRITING ABOUT ORDINARY HUMAN EXISTENCE
The Challenge of Describing Everyday Life

Is description of ordinary mundane life more difficult to write than logical argumentation?

Since I am now forced into the sorry admission that I am unable to speak about China, Persia, the system, astrology, or veterinary science, I have (in order to come up with at least something in my predicament) trained my pen, in proportion to the capabilities granted me, to be able to copy and describe as concretely as possible everyday life, which quite often is different from Sunday life. If anyone finds this kind of presentation or my presentation boring, then let him. I am not writing for any prize medal. I shall gladly admit, if this is required of me, that it is much more difficult and involves much more commotion and an entirely different kind of responsibility than to kill a rich uncle in a novel in order to get money into the story (or to skip ten years, let time go by in which the most important thing happened, and then begin with its having happened). It takes a totally different pithy brevity to describe the victory of faith in a half hour—than to describe that with which an ordinary person fills up a day in the living room . . . It is in the living room that the battle must be fought, lest the skirmishes of religious-ness become a changing-of-the-guard parade one day a week. It is in the living room that the battle must be fought, not imaginatively in church, with the pastor shadowboxing and the listeners looking on. . . . The main point still is that the single individual will go home from church willing wholeheartedly and eagerly to battle in the living room. If the pastor's activity in the church is merely a once-a-week attempt to tow the congregation's cargo ship a little closer to eternity, the whole thing comes to nothing. A human life, unlike a cargo ship, cannot lie in the same place until the next Sunday.

Concluding Unscientific Postscript to
Philosophical Fragments 1:464–65
(KW 12) [Voice: Johannes Climacus]*

THE CULTURE OF MODERNITY

The Present Age

GETTING READY TO SAVE THE WORLD

SERIOUS BANQUETING

What form does self-denial take in a culture absorbed with its own self-esteem?

A penetrating religious renunciation of the world and what is of the world, adhered to in daily self-denial, would be inconceivable to the youth of our day. Every second theological graduate, however, has enough virtuosity to do something far more marvelous. He is able to found a social institution with no less a goal than to save all who are lost. . . .

Just like a young man who, having resolved to study earnestly for his exams after September 1, fortifies himself for it by taking a vacation in the month of August, so the present generation—and this is much more difficult to understand—seems to have determined in earnest that the next generation must attend to the work in earnest, and in order not to frustrate or deter them in any way, the present generation attends banquets. But there is a difference: the young man understands that his enterprises are rash and reckless. The present age is sober and serious—even at banquets.

Two Ages: The Age of Revolution and the Present Age, a Literary Review 71
(KW 14)

DYING MODERNITY   CAN A DEAD BODY STILL
LOOK ALIVE?

Is modernity dying or flourishing?

Our age reminds one very much of
the disintegration of the Greek state. Everything continues, and yet
there is no one who believes in it. The invisible spiritual bond that
gives it validity has vanished, and thus the whole age is simultaneously comic and tragic: tragic because it is perishing, comic because it continues. For it is still always the incorruptible that bears
the corruptible, the intellectual-spiritual that bears the physical. And
it if were possible to imagine that an inanimate body could still perform the usual functions for a little while, it would be comic and
tragic in the same way.

—Or
Either/Or 2:19 (KW 4) [Voice: Judge
William]

MODERN CHAUVINISM   CHASTISING THE DEAD

**On what grounds are recent times assumed to be morally superior
to all previous times?**

Three hundred years ago they said,
"So it was fifteen hundred years ago, and a thousand years ago, and
three hundred years ago; but it is not so now—well, well, at all
events, not in the most recent times." There must be something lurking at the bottom of this expression, "the most recent times." Yes,
undoubtedly. One comes as close as possible without actually speaking to the living—and in fact the living generation represents "the
most recent times." If the address was made to a gathering of young
people, one would doubtless say, "the very most recent times," for
then the old folks and elders would not be present, so one might well
chastise them—but always preferably the dead, one chastises them at

a convenient distance, unmindful of the fine rule of speaking only good of the dead.

—*Christian Discourses*
Christian Discourses; and the Lilies of the Field and the Birds of the Air, and Three Discourses at the Communion on Fridays 237*

ILLUSION   INVENTING EXCUSES FOR STAYING IN BED

Is the modern age understood better as concerned with actuality or illusion? With energy or indolence?

Just as scurvy is cured by green vegetables, so a person worn out in reflection perhaps does not need strength as much as a little illusion. . . .

Exhausted by its chimerical exertions, the present age then relaxes temporarily in complete indolence. Its condition is like that of the stay-abed in the morning who has big dreams, then torpor, followed by a witty or ingenious inspiration to excuse staying in bed. . . .

The age of great and good actions is past. The present age is the age of anticipation. No one is willing to be satisfied with doing something specific. Everyone wants to luxuriate in the daydream that he at least may discover a new part of the world.

Two Ages: The Age of Revolution and the Present Age, a Literary Review 67, 69, 71 (KW 14)

Objective Knowledge and Science

ARCHIMEDES' DISCOVERY

BIRD-DROPPINGS ON MERCHANT
BEAREND'S TABLE

**When Archimedes ran naked through the streets did that prove
that he had made a fabulous discovery?**

Running naked through the streets of
Syracuse has thus nothing whatever to do with [Archimedes'] discovery, which therefore remains absolutely just as good as before. Hence
it is quite right that the discovery serves as an excuse for the offense,
that because of that one quite forgets that Archimedes was naked, as
he himself did. Only prudery could dwell long on the offensiveness of
the act, and only a crazy Philistinism triumphant in a small town
could turn everything round about and reach the conclusion: It is
certain that Archimedes ran naked through the streets—*ergo* he has
made no great discovery. . . . Philistinism in interpreting the distinguished man would say as did the merchant Bearend, according to a
well-known story, when a bird dropped something on the table: "If I
had done that," said he, "you would have heard a great row."

*On Authority and Revelation: The Book
on Adler, or a Cycle of Ethico-Religious
Essays 162–63**

FORGETTING THAT THE INVESTIGATOR EXISTS
Knowing Too Much
for Inwardness

What happens when one remembers everything except that one actually exists?

The misfortune with our age was just that it had come to know too much and had forgotten what it means to exist and what inwardness is. . . . The person who is so fortunate as to be dealing with multiplicity can easily be entertaining. When he is finished with China, he can take up Persia. When he has studied French, he can begin Italian, and then take up astronomy, veterinary science, etc., and always be sure of being regarded as a great fellow. But inwardness does not have the kind of range that arouses the amazement of the sensate. For example, inwardness in erotic love does not mean to get married seven times to Danish girls, and then to go for the French, the Italian, etc., but to love one and the same and yet be continually renewed in the same erotic love, so that it continually flowers anew in mood and exuberance—which, when applied to communication, is the inexhaustible renewal and fertility of expression.

Concluding Unscientific Postscript to
Philosophical Fragments 1:259–60
(KW 12) [Voice: Johannes Climacus]

INFORMATION OVERLOAD
The Stuffed Mouth That
Hinders Eating

Under what circumstances does feeding elicit starvation?

When a man has filled his mouth so full of food that for this reason he cannot eat and it must end with his dying of hunger, does giving food to him consist in stuffing his mouth even more or, instead, in taking a little away so that he can eat? Similarly, when a man is very knowledgeable but his knowledge is meaningless or virtually meaningless to him, does sensible communication consist in giving him more to know, even if he loudly proclaims that this is what he needs, or does it consist, instead, in taking something away from him?

Concluding Unscientific Postscript to
Philosophical Fragments 1:275n
(KW 12) [Voice: Johannes Climacus]

PRECISION REGARDING THE FANTASTIC
THE GREAT HOLOPHERNES

Is there a precise measurement for a fantasy?

Holophernes is said to be fourteen and one-fourth feet tall. The contradiction is essentially in the latter part. The fourteen feet is fantastic, but the fantastic does not as a rule speak of fourths. The fraction "one-fourth" calls actuality to mind. The person who laughs at the fourteen feet does not laugh appropriately, but the person who laughs at fourteen and one-fourth feet knows what he is laughing at.

Concluding Unscientific Postscript to
Philosophical Fragments 1:514–15n
(KW 12) [Voice: Johannes Climacus]

SOCRATIC MIDWIFERY   TOO MUCH KNOWLEDGE

Which does modern culture need most, an honest man, or a new plan for social transformation?

Socrates, Socrates, Socrates! Yes, we may well call your name three times; it would not be too much to call it ten times, if it would be of any help. Popular opinion maintains that the world needs a republic, needs a new social order and a new religion—but no one considers that what the world, confused simply by too much knowledge, needs is a Socrates. Of course, if anyone thought of it, not to mention if many thought of it, he would be less needed. Invariably, what error needs most is always the last thing it thinks of—quite naturally, for otherwise it would not, after all, be error.

The Sickness unto Death 92 (KW 19)
[Voice: Anti-Climacus]

THE TRIVIAL ACCUMULATION OF DATA

A Precise Chronological Table
for Dating Any Historical Event

Does raw data contribute to the inward story of the soul?

Mr. Bonfils, M.A., has published a table by which the year can be determined with given dates. I, too, benefit from his services; I have calculated and calculated and finally worked out that the year that fits the given dates is the year 1751, or that remarkable year when Gregor Roghfischer joined the Lutheran Church, a year which for anyone who with one deeply profound eye cyclopeanly contemplates the marvels in the course of history is also noteworthy in that precisely five years later the Seven Years War broke out.

Stages on Life's Way 190 (KW 11)
[Voice: Frater Taciturnus]

Medicine

HEARTACHE   IT HURTS EVERYWHERE

Where in the body precisely does one suffer in suffering heartache?

"Where exactly do you suffer?" the physician asks the patient. "Alas, dear doctor, everywhere," he answers. "But how are you suffering?" continues the physician, "so that I can diagnose the illness." No one asks me this, nor do I need it. I know very well how I suffer—I suffer sympathetically. This is exactly the suffering that is really able to shake me deeply. Even though I am depressingly and sincerely convinced that I am good for nothing, as soon as there is danger I really have the strength of a lion. When I suffer autopathetically [inwardly toward myself], I am able to stake all my will. Depressed as I am and depressingly brought up, the appalling finds me all the more prepared for what is even more appalling. But when I suffer sympathetically, I have to use all my power, all my ingenuity, in the service of the appalling to reproduce the other's pain. That exhausts me.

Stages on Life's Way 265 (KW 11)
[Voice: Quidam]*

DIAGNOSIS   THE ANSWER TO ALL RIDDLES

Is there a hypothesis that covers every possible symptom?

With existence, things go just as they did with me and my physician. I complained about not feeling well. He answered: No doubt you are drinking too much coffee and don't walk enough.

Three weeks later I speak with him again and say: I really do not feel well, but now it cannot be from drinking coffee, because I do not touch coffee, nor can it be from lack of exercise, because I walk all day long. He answers: Well, then the reason must be that you do not drink coffee and that you walk too much. So it was: my not feeling well was and remained the same, but when I drink coffee, it comes from my drinking coffee, and when I do not drink coffee, it comes from my not drinking coffee.

And so it is with us human beings. Our entire earthly existence is a kind of ill health. If someone asks the reason, he is first asked how he has organized his life. As soon as he has answered that, he is told: There it is—that is the reason. If someone else asks the reason, one goes about it in the same way, and if he answers the opposite, he is told: There it is—that is the reason. Then the adviser leaves with the superior air of one who has explained everything—until he has turned the corner, and then he sticks his tail between his legs and sneaks away. Even if someone gave me ten rix-dollars, I would not take it upon myself to explain the riddle of existence. Indeed, why should I? If life is a riddle, in the end presumably the one who has proposed the riddle will himself explain it.

> *Concluding Unscientific Postscript to*
> Philosophical Fragments 1:450–51
> (KW 12) [Voice: Johannes Climacus]

SCIENTIFIC INVENTIONS BARBER LÜTZOV'S STETHOSCOPE

How does one "keep up with the times"?

Barber Lützov's already commendably famous and much frequented barbershop now has, on the basis of a new improvement, a new claim on the discerning acknowledgment by the most esteemed public. Herr Lützov is a well-read man who keeps up with the times and the discoveries of the times. Assured that a new era is beginning with the stethoscope, not only in the history of medicine but in the history of human life, he has decided to stethoscope everyone who comes into his barbershop, completely *gratis* and without costing anything.

—*Writing Sampler*, no. 5
Prefaces; Writing Sampler 82 (KW 9)
[Voice: Godthaab]

INCOMMENSURABILITY OF LIFE'S VALUE
Disproportional Assessment of the Gold in the Book Binding

Can the value of life be quantified?

If someone were to say, "I venture to stake my life on there being at least four and a half shillings' worth of gold in the binding of this book," that would be comic. The contradiction is between the highest pathos (to stake his life) and the object; it is teasingly intensified by the phrase "at least," which holds out the prospect of four and a half shillings' worth, as if that were less contradictory.

Concluding Unscientific Postscript to
Philosophical Fragments 1:514n
(KW 12) [Voice: Johannes Climacus]

Authority and Establishment

THE TALENT OF THE EXECUTIONER
The Distinct Gifts of a
Master Hangman

For an audience that values taste, where is it to be found?

The execution of the two notorious murderers, Ole Hansen and Hans Olsen, brought a sizable and most esteemed cultured crowd out to Amager. Even though the weather was not at all favorable, the happiest and most loyal mood generally reigned. That worthy artist, Copenhagen's executioner, Herr Madsen, performed his difficult task with a rare virtuosity and bravado and mastery. Favorably thought of earlier, he has now truly made himself deserving of the name by which he is called: the master hangman. It was therefore well-earned acknowledgment when his appearance and also his exit were greeted with loud applause. The executioner from Roskilde, who was also present to flog a third criminal, possesses an unmistakable talent and gave a praiseworthy performance. In this his first attempt, he satisfactorily distinguished himself with taste and correctness in every respect.

—*Writing Sampler*, no. 4
Prefaces; Writing Sampler 81 (KW 9)*

TAKING OFFICE   Beware the Title

What is the down side of accepting a title?

A title can never be disposed of; it would take a criminal act for that, which would incur a public whip-

229

ping. Even then one cannot be sure of not being pardoned by royal decree and acquiring the title again.

—*Either:* "The Rotation of Crops"
Either/Or 1:298 (KW 3) [Voice: "A"]

CORRECTING MISTAKES The Major Who Took the Wrong Way on the Parade Grounds

How are leadership errors typically corrected?

In my younger days, I liked to watch the National Guard drill at the parade grounds. During a royal review, it so happened that a major stood facing his battalion when he should have been facing the other way. An experienced army officer present, no doubt fearful that this mistake would not escape the late king's sharp scrutiny, rode over to him and whispered softly. "Major, you are facing the wrong way. You must turn around." The major was no pighead. He willingly took the advice and in a loud voice shouted, "Battalion, all together, about face!"

—*Public Confession*
The Corsair *Affair and Articles Related to the Writings* 8–9 (KW 13)

THE DISAVOWAL OF AUTHORITY
Offering Counsel with
the Authority of an
Alehouse Keeper

How can one avoid being taken seriously as an authority?

Concerning my own humble person, I frankly confess—no matter how my confession is understood—that I am fully aware that as an author I am a king without a country. I have endeavored to cut my coat from my own cloth and to be an author without any claims. If in the best sense of the word it seems

230

too much to zealous envy that I bear a Latin name, it may serve as pleasant news that if anyone desires and I can be of service, I shall gladly assume the name Christen Madsen. Most of all I wish to be regarded as an alehouse keeper, innkeeper, or as a plain layman who walks the floor and speculates without wishing that his speculative result should be regarded as speculation. I would not for anything in the world want to be an authority, not even for the most insignificant man, because I regard being an authority as the most boring of all things. But in relation to everyone else, I apply myself to be as devout in my belief in authority as the Roman was tolerant in his worship of God. When it comes to human authority, I profess to fetishism and worship anyone whomsoever with equal piety, provided it is made sufficiently clear by a proper beating of drums that he has become the authority and the *imprimatur* for the current year, whether this is decided by lottery or whether the honor is passed around, just as one of the 36 representatives takes his turn on the board of arbitration.

The Concept of Anxiety 179–80 (KW 8)
[Voice: Vigilius Haufniensis]

LEGITIMACY

Turning Down the
Innkeeper's Application

Can one add by subtracting?

When a man applies for a permit to go into business as an innkeeper and the application is turned down, this is not comic. But if it is turned down because there are so few innkeepers, it is comic, because the reason for the application is used as the reason against it. For example, there is a story about a baker who said to a poor woman, "No, mother, she does not get anything; there was another one recently who didn't get anything, either. We can't give to everybody." The comic aspect lies in his appearing to arrive at the sum total "everybody" by subtracting.

Concluding Unscientific Postscript to
Philosophical Fragments 1:515n
(KW 12) [Voice: Johannes Climacus]*

EUROCENTRISM   So Few Chinese — So Many Germans

Why in Hegel's philosophy of world history do there appear so many Germans and so few Chinese?

It has not yet become world-historically clear where China is to be placed in the [Hegelian] world-historical process, in which every assistant professor since the day before yesterday clearly and definitely finds plenty of room. In other words, all assistant professors are included, and as soon as the method reaches our day, it will go like a prairie fire, and we shall all find a place. The method admits only one Chinese, but not a single German assistant professor is excluded, especially no Prussian, because whoever has the cross blesses himself first. But then the system is not entirely finished yet; perhaps it expects to be able systematically, one, two, three, to make capital of the arduous work of a genuine scholar by having a few extra Chinese placed at its disposal. Then it will be all right. Now it certainly looks a little embarrassing to have only one Chinese when there are so many Germans.

Concluding Unscientific Postscript to
Philosophical Fragments 1:150n
(KW 12) [Voice: Johannes Climacus]*

THE COMPLETELY RATIONAL SYSTEM

The Proper Beginning Point for
Explaining World History

Is there any end to a system which never begins?

A pamphlet writer such as I am has no seriousness, as you presumably will hear about me—why, then, should I now in conclusion pretend seriousness in order to please people by making a rather big promise? In other words, to write a pamphlet is frivolity—but to promise the system, that is seriousness and has made many a man a supremely serious man both in his own eyes and in the eyes of others. . . . As is well known, Christianity is the only historical phenomenon that despite the historical—indeed, precisely by means of the historical—has wanted to be the single individual's point of departure for his eternal consciousness, has wanted to interest him otherwise than merely historically, has wanted to base his happiness on his relation to something historical. No philosophy (for it is only for thought), no mythology (for it is only for the imagination), no historical knowledge (which is for memory) has ever had this idea—of which in this connection one can say with all multiple meanings that it did not arise in any human heart . . . The monks never finished narrating the history of the world because they always began with the creation of the world. If in discussing the relation between Christianity and philosophy we begin by narrating what was said earlier, how shall we ever, not finish, but ever manage to begin, for history just keeps on growing. If we begin with "that great thinker and sage Pontius Pilate, *executor Novi Testamenti*," . . . and if, before beginning with him, we have to wait for one or two decisive books (perhaps the system) that have already been announced *ex cathedra* [with authority] several times, how shall we ever manage to begin?

—*Philosophical Fragments*
Philosophical Fragments; Johannes
Climacus 109–10 (KW 7) [Voice:
Johannes Climacus]

How profoundly do historians understand history?

Then come the [quasi-Hegelian] parrots, who despite their survey of world history unfortunately lack all contemplation, and who know as much about the concepts as that noble youth knew about raisins, who, when asked in the test for a grocer's licence where raisins come from, answered: We get ours from the professor on Cross Street.

The Concept of Anxiety 134–35 (KW 8)
[Voice: Vigilius Haufniensis]*

SOCIOLOGICAL AND CULTURAL ANALYSIS

Cheap Talk on a Grand Scale

EXTERNAL SOCIAL CHANGE

An Announcement of a Reward

Are external changes in society or politics being here advocated?
In Ursin's *Arithmetic*, which was used in my school days, a reward was offered to anyone who could find a miscalculation in the book. I also promise a reward to anyone who can point out in these numerous books [Kierkegaard's pseudonymous writings] a single proposal for external change, or the slightest suggestion of such a proposal, or even anything that in the remotest way, even for the most nearsighted person at the greatest distance, could resemble an intimation of such a proposal or of a belief that the problem is lodged in externalities, that external change is what is needed, that external change is what will help us.

—"An Open Letter"
The Corsair *Affair, and Articles Related to the Writings* 53 (KW 13)*

POLITICAL REFORM   Freedom of Conscience by a
                          Simple Majority

Can one achieve political reform by knowledge of "numerical ratios"?
It is apparent from his latest work that Dr. R. [Rudelbach] believes that Christianity and the Church are to be saved by "the free institutions." If this faith in the saving power of politically achieved free institutions belongs to true Christianity, then I am no Christian, or, even worse, I am a regular child

of Satan, because, frankly, I am indeed suspicious of these politically achieved free institutions, especially of their saving, renewing power. Such is my "Christendom" [*Christendom*] or so "Christian-dumb" [*Christendum*] am I, who, incidentally, have had nothing to do with "Church" and "state"—this is much too immense for me. Altogether different prophets are needed for this, or quite simply, this task ought to be entrusted to those who are regularly appointed and trained for such things. I have not fought for the emancipation of "the Church" any more than I have fought for the emancipation of Greenland commerce, of women, of the Jews, or of anyone else. With my sights upon "the single individual," aiming at inward deepening in Christianity in "the single individual," with the weapons of the spirit, simply and solely with the weapons of the spirit, I have, as an individual, consistently fought to make the single individual aware of the "illusion" and to alert him against letting himself be deceived by it. . . .

Christianity will not be helped from the outside by institutions and constitutions, and least of all if these are not won through suffering by martyrs in the old-fashioned Christian way but are won in a social and amicable political way, by elections or by a lottery of numbers. . . .

[Luther] did not go around with hearty nonsense to every Tom, Dick and Harry, friends and acquaintances, casting a world-historical glance at the Church's past and ditto at its future. Nor did he [say]: ". . . If we get together with them in the voting, according to my exact knowledge of numerical ratios (knowledge of numerical ratios—fix this in your memory, preserve it for the historian, for this phrase is the secret of my life—knowledge of numerical ratios is really what makes 'the reformer'), it is not impossible, it is not impossible that we can squeeze a few points from the opposition and squeeze our way through—to freedom of conscience!—by a very scant simple majority."

—"An Open Letter"
The Corsair Affair, and Articles Related to the Writings 54–55, 58n (KW 13)*

CHEAP TALK LOVES A GRAND SCALE
The Movement Dilettante

What has gone awry when naughty children imagine themselves to be reformers, and when the grandiose political scale is easier to manage than one's own personal life?

It is perhaps not beside the point to remind people of this, for our age, the age of movement, tends to bring fundamental assumptions under discussion, so that the consequence is that a marvelous number of men in the mass get on their feet and open their mouths all at once in the game of discussion, along with the public which understands absolutely nothing about it, whereas the prodigious size of the problem advantageously hides the ignorance of the discussers and the speakers respectively. In case a teacher wants to favor a know-nothing of a pupil, he can do it in various ways, but among others he can do it by assigning to him such a prodigious problem that the examiners can infer nothing whatever from the triviality of his reply, because the immense magnitude of the subject deprives them of any standard of judgment. Perhaps I can illuminate this by an example from the world of learning. A learned twaddler who at bottom knows nothing can seldom be got to deal with anything concrete; he does not talk of a particular dialogue of Plato, that is too little for him—also it might become apparent that he had not read it. No, he talks about Plato as a whole, or even perhaps of Greek philosophy as a whole, but especially about the wisdom of the Indians and the Chinese. This Greek philosophy as a whole, the profundity of Oriental philosophy as a whole, is the prodigiously great, the boundless, which advantageously hides his ignorance. So also it is much easier to talk about an alteration in the form of government than to discuss a very little concrete problem like sewing a pair of shoes. . . .

So it is much easier for a dunce to criticize our Lord than to judge the handiwork of an apprentice in a shop, yea, than to judge a sulphur match. . . . When the father becomes weak, when the family life is stirred by a rebellious reflection, then the naughty children easily confuse themselves with a sort of reformer. When the schoolmaster loses the reins, then it is very easy for a pert pupil to regard himself as a kind of reformer. In our age therefore it has indeed gone so far that it really requires no courage to defy the King, to vex and disturb the government of the State; but indeed it requires no little courage to say a word to the opposition.

On Authority and Revelation: The Book on Adler, or a Cycle of Ethico-Religious Essays 31–34

Journalism and the Press

ESTABLISHING HISTORICAL TRUTH
Who Bumped the Gravy Boat?

What news of importance occurred yesterday?

Merchant Marcussen in Badstuestræde had a large dinner party yesterday. At the table there occurred, however, the misfortune that the merchant knocked a gravy boat over himself and the lady next to him. This is how it happened. Just at the very moment when the servant offered the gravy boat, the merchant stood up to make a toast. With a movement of his arm, he bumped the servant and the gravy boat. This is the historical truth. We are well aware that a rumor is circulating that tells the story otherwise, namely, that with a movement of her head the lady bumped the servant. But this is only a rumor without any official standing. We have received no information as to the lady's name. Some mention Miss Lindvad; others say it was Gusta Jobbe. As soon as we learn it, we will immediately report it. The name is of enormous importance, because for the first week there will, of course, be talk of nothing else in all Copenhagen and in all Denmark.

—*Writing Sampler,* no. 5
Prefaces; Writing Sampler 81–82 (KW 9)
[Voice: Godthaab]

SCANDALMONGERING   WHY THE PRESS REGARDS SETTING
FIRE TO THE CITY AS A VIRTUE

How has broadcasting another's faults become in our time a highly profitable business in which consumers pay money to become infected?

It is only too clear that every man, unfortunately, has a great inclination to see his neighbor's faults and perhaps an even greater inclination to want to tell about them. If it is nothing else, it is, alas, to use the mildest expression, a kind of nervousness which makes men so weak in this temptation, in this dizziness of being able to tell something evil about their neighbors, of being able for a moment to create for themselves an attentive audience with the aid of such entertaining reports. But what is already corrupting enough as a nervous urge which cannot keep quiet is sometimes a raging, demonic passion in a man, developed on the most terrifying scale. I wonder whether any robber, any thief, any man of violence, in short, any criminal is in the deepest sense as depraved as such a man who has taken upon himself as his contemptible means of livelihood the task of proclaiming on the greatest possible scale, loudly as no word of truth is heard, widely over the whole land in a way seldom achieved by something worthy, penetrating into every nook where God's word hardly penetrates, his neighbor's faults, his neighbor's weaknesses, his neighbor's sins and to press upon everyone, even upon unformed youth, this polluting knowledge . . . But the most terrible of all must be to have guilt, heinous guilt, and to add guilt and more guilt and new guilt day in and day out—and not to become conscious of it, because one's whole environment, because existence itself had become transformed into an illusion which strengthened one in his view that it was nothing, not only that there was no guilt but that it was something almost meritorious. O, there are criminals whom the world does not call criminals, whom it rewards and almost honors—and yet, yet I would rather, God forbid, but I nevertheless would rather enter eternity with three repented murders on my conscience than as a retired scandalmonger with this horrible, incalculable load of criminality which was heaped up year after year, which was able to spread on an almost inconceivable scale, to put men in their graves, embitter the most intimate relationships, injure the most innocent sympathizers, besmirch the young, mislead and corrupt both young and old, in short, to spread itself on a scale which even the most vivid power of phantasy cannot imagine—this horrible load of criminality which I nevertheless never got time to begin repenting of, because the time had to be used for new offences, and because these innumerable offences had secured money for me, influence, prestige almost, and above all a pleasurable life! In connection with arson a distinction is made between setting fire to a house in the full knowledge of its being inhabited by many or being uninhabited. But scandalmongering is like setting fire to a whole community and it is not even regarded as a crime! We quarantine for diseases—but this disease which is worse than the bubonic plague, scandalmongering, which corrupts the mind and soul, we invite into all the houses; we pay money to become infected; we greet as a welcome guest one who brings the infection!

Works of Love: Some Christian Reflections in the Form of Discourses 269–71

BANALITY AS A COMIC PREMISE
The Exile and Recall of an Ostracized Nobody

Why do journalists tend to glorify the banal?

It would be ironically in the spirit of Aristophanes to have an utterly insignificant man be exiled by ostracism. This irony would be even higher comedy than, for example, ironically elevating a nobody like that to the position of ruler, simply because exile by ostracism is already the negative manifestation [obverse expression] of excellence. Therefore, it would in turn be even higher ironical comedy to have it end with the people recalling the banished one because they could not get along without him, which of course would be a total enigma to the people with whom he lived in exile, since they naturally had been unable to find any excellence in him at all. In *The Knights*, Aristophanes portrays the ultimate state of

243

decay: just as the Dalai Lama's excrement is reverenced, the rabble ends by adoring the dregs of society, the first to come along, the best, or adoringly seeing itself in them, a situation that in its degeneracy corresponds to a democracy's decision to put imperial dignity up for auction.

> Two Ages: The Age of Revolution and the
> Present Age, a Literary Review 82–83
> (KW 14)*

APPLYING TO BE ABUSED THE INSULT OF BEING PRAISED BY A SCURRILOUS JOURNALIST

What ironic remedy is fitting if one is praised by a journal that persistently does not tell the truth?

With a paper like *The Corsair*, which hitherto has been read by many and all kinds of people and *essentially* has enjoyed the recognition of being ignored, despised, and never answered, the only thing to be done in writing in order to express the literary, moral order of things—reflected in the inversion that this paper with meager competence and extreme effort has sought to bring about—was for someone praised and immortalized in this paper to make application to be abused by the same paper. . . . So *The Corsair* can be hired to abuse just as a hand organ can be hired to make music. . . . I cannot do any more for others than to request to be abused myself. . . .

Anyone who is insulted by being praised by this paper—if he happens to find out about it—will protest if he so pleases and thereby confirm the judgment of decent literature upon *The Corsair*: it is to be permitted to continue its trade of attacking and vilifying at will, but if it has the nerve to praise, it must on this occasion encounter the brief protest: May I ask to be abused—the personal injury of being immortalized by *The Corsair* is just too much. The inconvenience will not be great, as if one now had to read *The Corsair* in order to see if one has been praised. . . . I do not doubt that the police superintendent, Councilor Reiersen, who as a matter of fact is obliged to take the trouble of reading the paper through, will, if asked, do the favor of briefly informing a person that he has been praised.

—"The Dialectical Result of a Literary Police Action"
The Corsair *Affair and Articles Related to the Writings* 47, 50 (KW 13) [Voice: Frater Taciturnus]

SENSATIONALISM   THE POWER OF POPULAR OUTRAGE TO SUMMON DESTINY'S FORCES

Does writing in a loud voice something that everyone will read thereby make it true?

In spite of the fact that the man [Magister Adler] writes, he is not essentially an author. He will be capable of writing the first part, but he cannot write the second part, or (to avoid any misunderstanding) he can write the first and also the second part, but he cannot write the third part—the last part he cannot write. If he goes ahead naively (led astray by the reflection that every book must have a last part) and so writes the last part, he will make it thoroughly clear by writing the last part that he makes a written renunciation to all claim to be an author. . . .

All [speculative, tendentious] premise-authors, whatever their relative differences may be, have one thing in common: they all have a *purpose*, they all wish to produce an effect, they all wish that their works may have an extraordinary diffusion and may be read if possible by all mankind. . . . The premise-writer has neither time nor patience to think it out more precisely. His notion is: "If only an outcry is raised in a loud voice that can be heard all over the land, and it is read by everybody and is talked about in every company, then surely it will turn out all right." The premise-author thinks that the outcry is like a wishing rod. . . . One smiles at reading all the romantic tales of a bygone age about how knights fared forth into the forest and killed dragons and liberated princes from enchantment, etc.—the romantic notion that in the forests such monsters dwelt, along with

245

enchanted princes. And yet it is quite as romantic that in a whole generation everyone believes in the power of outcry to summon such monstrous forces.

On Authority and Revelation: The Book
on Adler, or a Cycle of Ethico-Religious
Essays 3–4, 6–7*

TALKATIVENESS   THE WIDE-OPEN MOUTH OF THE
                       PRESENT AGE

In the absence of the quiet cultivation of inwardness, what does the modern age demand?

Our age demands something more. It demands, if not lofty then at least loud-voiced pathos, if not speculation then surely results, if not truth then conviction, if not honesty then certainly affidavits to that effect, if not emotion then incessant talk about it. It therefore mints quite a different species of privileged faces. It will not tolerate the mouth to be closed defiantly nor the upper lip to quiver prankishly. No, it demands that the mouth drop open, for how else is one to visualize a true and genuine patriot except he be making speeches, how else should one visualize the dogmatic face of a profound thinker except with a mouth able to swallow the whole world, how else could one imagine a virtuoso on the cornucopia of the living word except with a mouth wide open? It will not tolerate a man to stand still and become immersed in himself; to walk slowly is already suspect.

The Concept of Irony, with Constant
Reference to Socrates 263

STATISTICS ON PRUDENCE
Suicide by Discussion

What happens to the culture when there is too much prudence and deliberation, when people are strangled by calculation?

If we had statistics on the use of prudence from generation to generation as we have them on the consumption of liquor, we would be amazed to see the enormous quantity used these days. What a quantity of weighing and deliberating and considering even a small non-official family uses although it has ample income. What a quantity even children and young people use. For just as the children's crusade symbolizes the Middle Ages, so the shrewdness of children symbolizes ours. I wonder if there is a person anymore who ever makes just one big stupid blunder. Not even a suicide these days does away with himself in desperation but deliberates on this step so long and so sensibly that he is strangled by calculation, making it a moot point whether or not he can really be called a suicide, inasmuch as it was in fact the deliberating that took his life.

*Two Ages: The Age of Revolution and the
Present Age, a Literary Review* 68
(KW 14)*

Public Opinion and the Crowd

THE PUBLIC

How has the idea of "public opinion" become an agent of anonymity and leveling?

The public is a corps, outnumbering all the people together. But this corps can never be called up for inspection. Indeed, it cannot even have so much as a single representative, because it is itself an abstraction. Nevertheless, if the age is reflective, devoid of passion, obliterating everything that is concrete, the public becomes the entity that is supposed to include everything. . . . The public may take a year and a day to assemble, and when it is assembled it still does not exist. . . .

A people, an assembly, a person can change in such a way that one may say: they are no longer the same; but the public can become the very opposite and is still the same—the public. But if the individual is not destroyed in the process, he will be educated by this very abstraction . . . The bleakness of antiquity was that the man of distinction was what *others could not be*. The inspiring aspect [of the modern era] will be that the person who has gained himself religiously is only what *all can be*. . . . For a few hours of the day he perhaps is part of the public, that is, during the hours when he is a nobody, because during the hours in which he is the specific person he is, he does not belong to the public. Composed of someones such as these, of individuals in the moments when they are nobodies, the public is a kind of colossal something, an abstract void and vacuum that is all and nothing. . . . The drunken sailor has absolutely the same right to a public as the most distinguished of men, the absolute right to place all these many, many zeros *in front of* his figure [the number] one. . . .

In this state of indolent laxity, more and more individuals will aspire to be nobodies in order to become the public, that abstract aggregate ridiculously formed by the participant's becoming a third party. That sluggish crowd which understands nothing itself and is unwilling to do anything, that gallery-public, now seeks to be entertained and indulges in the notion that everything anyone does is done so that it may have something to gossip about.

> *Two Ages: The Age of Revolution and the Present Age, a Literary Review* 91–94 (KW 14)*

EVADING RESPONSIBILITY
THE MIRAGE OF "THE OTHERS"

When everyone blames everyone else, where will blame settle?

When out of seven people who are all charged with having committed a crime others could not have committed, the seventh says, "It was not I, it was the others," "the others" are understood to be the six others, and so on down the line. But what if all seven, each one separately, said, "It was the others"?—what then? Does that not conjure up a mirage that has multiplied the actual seven in an attempt to fool us into thinking that there were many more, although there were only seven? So, too, when the whole human race, each one separately, hits upon saying "the others," an apparition is conjured up, as if the race existed one more time in addition to the time of its actual existence, except that it is very difficult here to point out the falsity, the bedazzlement with the appearance of profundity, because the race is innumerable . . . Who would stop such a mutiny, if there is one?

Should we perhaps repeat the fallacy of the mutiny, but in a new pattern, and each one separately say: I cannot stop it; "the others must"?

> *Works of Love* 116–17 (KW 16)

THE MAN OF MOVEMENT Racing to Get ahead of the New Direction

How does one lead a relativistic movement?

He who would move anything must himself stand firm, but the man of movement has nothing firm about him, he is firm only when he is taken into custody [*blevet fast*]—i.e., afterwards. He might therefore wish that the established order were weak and decrepit, in order that he might the more easily conquer. If such is not the case, then he must resort to every expedient to conquer, to cunning and wiliness, to handshaking, to conciliation, exclaiming as his trump card "the devil take me," or a concessive "beg your pardon." The reformer's behavior must be like his who seeks a position and runs errands all over the town, or like a huckster selling his vegetables on a busy Thursday. . . . Such a man of movement is unable—unable even to venture—to stand alone as an individual and thereby find room to venture life and all. On the contrary he has need of the majority to be certified if it is true, if what he wants is any good. He wishes to move others, and at bottom he wants the others to hold on to him in order that he may stand firm. . . . As when children are at play and one of them suddenly shouts, "Why not play this game?" so the man of movement shouts, "Why not do this now?" Thereupon when they have become many, when the majority is on their side and the cause is forced through—then the man of movement is for the first time really recognizable. He goes about with New Year's congratulations and says, "It was really I who stood at the head of the Movement and the New Direction." Sometimes it comes to pass that men behold with wonder several men going about with congratulations, each one of them saying, "It was really I who stood at the head of the Movement, etc." So it appears that there was not merely one but several men at the head. This comical confusion contains a deep truth, namely, that no one at all stood at the head.

On Authority and Revelation: The Book on Adler, or a Cycle of Ethico-Religious Essays 41–44*

Advertising and Impression Management

THE CONCEPT OF QUANTITY IN MASS ADVERTISING
The Bargain Price of Ale

How has the inflation of the value of huge quantities risen to an art form within modernity?

In our day some have become perfectly adept at thoughtlessly wasting lives, at participating noisily and thoughtlessly whenever there is talk about one or another imposing, prodigious idea, in the fulfillment of which they unite in an unshakable faith that in union there is strength. This is a faith as marvelous as that of the alehouse keeper who sold his beer for a penny less than he paid for it and still counted on a profit, "for it is the *quantity* that does it."

The Concept of Anxiety 67–68 (KW 8)
[Voice: Vigilius Haufniensis]*

REGRESSION AS PERFECTIBILITY
Walking Again on All Fours

Is "Christendom" within modernity a further step toward human perfectibility, or a retrogression which has learned to manipulate the impression of progress?

Just as a dog which is compelled to walk on two feet has every instant a tendency to go again on all four, and does so as soon as it sees its chance, waiting only to see its chance, so is Christendom an effort of the human race to go back to walking on all fours, to get rid of Christianity, to do it knavishly under the pretext that this is Christianity, claiming that it is Christianity perfected. . . .

By the help of dogmas, the preachers of diluted "Christendom" have secured themselves against everything which with any semblance of truth could be called a Christian pattern, and then they went with full sail in the direction of . . . . . perfectibility.

Kierkegaard's "Attack upon
'Christendom'" 160–61*

REVOLUTIONARY IMPRESSION MANAGEMENT
The Impression That Something Decisive Is Happening

What central impression does the modern age seek to give of itself?

Just as weapons were freely distributed in the age of revolution and the insignia of the enterprise was conferred publicly during the crusades, so today we are everywhere lavishly regaled with pragmatic rules, calculus of considerations, etc. Suppose a whole generation could be presumed to have the diplomatic task of procrastinating and of continually frustrating any action and yet make it seem as if something were happening. We cannot deny that our age is performing just as amazingly as such an imagined age of revolution. If someone were to make an experiment and forget all he knows about the age and the plain fact of its habitual and excessive relativity, if he were to come as if from another world and were to read some books, an article in the paper, or merely talk with a passer-by, he would get the impression: By Jove, something is going to happen this very night—or something must have happened the night before last!

Two Ages: The Age of Revolution and the
Present Age, a Literary Review 69–70
(KW 14)*

THE HEGELIAN TECHNIQUE OF MEDIATION
A MODEST OFFER IN THE
ADVERTISER TO BECOME THE
FULFILLMENT OF WORLD HISTORY

What does it take to identify the conclusion to which the whole of past world history is tending?

It is strange, therefore, that no one offers in *Adresseavisen* [the *Advertiser*] to everyone who has merely a moderate previous knowledge, in less than three hours to perfect him in the idea of mediation—by which everyone becomes the conclusion to which the whole of past world history is tending. If one has thus secured for oneself the several millennia of the past, then it merely remains to perfect oneself in the idea of society, by which one conquers the whole of future time. . . . Therefore, as I gazed into the future, which still hides itself in the veil of mist of what is to come and hides the achievement of the generation, there appeared then before my eye a huge temple or festal building from which there issued a confused noise, that was, however, sometimes interrupted only to rise higher again, mixed with a flourish of kettledrums and trumpets, and over the entrance to this building my eye discovered with amazement the following inscription: Here's cheers.

Prefaces: Light Reading for Certain Classes as the Occasion May Require 66 [Voice: Nicolaus Notabene]

253

Politics, Revolution, and Reform

SHREWDNESS   THERE ARE NO BACKSTAIRS

How desperately does God need political expertise?

God is not like a king in a predica-
ment, who says to the highly trusted Minister of the Interior, "You
must do everything; you must create the atmosphere for our proposal
and win public opinion to our side. You can do it. Use your sagacity.
If I cannot depend upon you, I have no one." But in relation to God,
there are no secret instructions for a human being any more than
there are any backstairs. Even the most eminent genius who comes to
give a report had best come in fear and trembling, for God is not
hard-pressed for geniuses. He can, after all, create a few legions of
them; and wanting to make oneself indispensable in the service of
God means *eo ipso* dismissal.

> *Concluding Unscientific Postscript to*
> Philosophical Fragments 1:260–61n
> (KW 12) [Voice: Johannes Climacus]

REFORMING THE AGE   THE FANTASY THAT THE WHOLE
                              WORLD DEPENDS UPON ME

**Must I take upon myself responsibility for radically recasting my
era of history?**

Each generation has its own task and
need not trouble itself unduly by being everything to previous and
succeeding generations. Just as each day's trouble is sufficient for the
day, so each individual in a generation has enough to do in taking
care of himself and does not need to embrace the whole contempo-

rary age with his paternal solicitude or assume that era and epoch begin with his book, and still less with the New Year's torch of his promise or with the intimations of his farseeing promises or with the referral of his reassurance to a currency of doubtful value. Not everyone who is stoop-shouldered is an Atlas, nor did he become such by supporting a world. Not everyone who says Lord, Lord, shall enter the kingdom of heaven. Not everyone who offers himself as surety for the whole contemporary age proves by such action that he is reliable and can vouch for himself. Not everyone who shouts Bravo, schwere Noth, Gottsblitz, bravissimo has therefore understood himself and his admiration.

The Concept of Anxiety [7] (KW 8)
[Voice: Vigilius Haufniensis]

REVOLUTIONARY HEEDLESSNESS

THE TOLL CLERK WHOSE WRITING
COULD NOT BE DECIPHERED

What typifies revolutionary idealists who pay no heed to secondary consequences?

He was like that toll-clerk who wrote so that nobody could read, and considered it his business to write and the business of the tariff commission to read—so he thought it was his business to cast a firebrand into the established order, and its business to take care of the consequences.

On Authority and Revelation: The Book on Adler, or a Cycle of Ethico-Religious Essays 55–56

THE SWARM OF HELPFUL PEOPLE
PITCHERS AND SQUIRTS

How much do good intentions help in a crisis?

Hardly is the cry of "Fire!" heard before a crowd of people rush to the spot, nice, cordial, sympathetic, helpful people, one has a pitcher, another a basin, the third a squirt, etc., all of them nice, cordial, sympathetic, helpful people, so eager to help put out the fire.

But what says the Fire Chief? The Fire Chief, he says—yes, generally the Fire Chief is a very pleasant and polite man; but at a fire he is what one calls coarse-mouthed—he says, or rather he bawls, "Oh, go to hell with all your pitchers and squirts. . . . Rid me of these damn people with their pitchers and squirts; and if they won't yield to fair words, smear them a few over the back [tan their hides], so that we may be free of them and get down to work" . . .

Their presence and effect is the most dangerous assistance the fire could have.

Kierkegaard's "Attack upon
'Christendom'" 193–94*

COURAGE
THE POLITICIAN WHOM ANY BREEZE COULD WAFT

What is the price of success for the hollow genius of trendy political adaptation?

If a man is to succeed, he must be like a reed before the wind, for even the least bush can put up at least a little bit of resistance; he must be without any deeper conviction, hollow within, so that, if one would liken time to the wind, he easily can be wafted by every breath of air, and, if one would liken time to a stream, he can as easily float upon the surface; he must be silent when he should speak, speak when he should be silent, say yes when he should say no, and no when he should say yes, answer evasively when he should answer decisively, answer decisively even though it

256

were unto blood, sleep when he should be vigilant, yea, do his part to make others sleep, flee every danger in which forsaken truth can find a stay, and take part in every popular folly; he must entirely forget God and the seriousness of eternity and everything that is high and holy: thus perhaps he may succeed—woe unto him!

> —*Christian Discourses*
> *Christian Discourses; and the Lilies of the*
> *Field and the Birds of the Air, and Three*
> *Discourses at the Communion on Fridays*
> 236

MOVEMENT CONSCIOUSNESS
The Vacillating Age
of Movement

Does the movement-oriented activist live as a premise with no conclusion?
Since, as says the barber (and one who has no opportunity of keeping abreast of the age by the aid of newspapers may well rest satisfied with the barber, who in olden times when there were as yet no newspapers was what the newspapers are now: universal intelligence), "our age is the age of movement," it is not improbable that the lives of many men go on in such a way that they have indeed premises for living but reach no conclusions— quite like this stirring age which has set in movement many premises but also has reached no conclusion.

> *On Authority and Revelation: The Book*
> *on Adler, or a Cycle of Ethico-Religious*
> *Essays 3**

SOBRIETY   THE UNAMBIGUOUS PROOF
ON THE TEMPERANCE
SOCIETY'S SIGNIFICANCE

By what logic does revolutionary rhetoric proceed?

Only the sound of the crowd acts on
the speaker like martial music, like the whine of the bowstring on the
one fighting. Yet the great aim of the Society, a member of which I
have the honor to be, demands that I seek also in print to dissemi-
nate the address on distilled spirits, for which assuredly I demand no
other reward than the applause that fell to my lot that evening, that
unforgettable evening that will ever remain unforgettable to me. Yet
the interest of the Society, to which my life belongs with its sole
desire to be its active member, this Society's interest demands that by
the publication of this address I strive to draw attention to our undertaking, to invite those who stand more distant to come closer. For
indeed, the one who just once attends our meeting will be faithful to
us forever. The Temperance Society seeks its equal in vain and knows
with proud self-confidence that this search is in vain. . . . One forms
a Society and one wants to be active, but the Society's activity is
perceived not to have any significance for the individual members.
Even though the Scandinavian Society wrought the astounding,
there nevertheless had to be a microscopic observation to discover
how much advantage accrues to the individual member. . . . Praised
be our Society; glorious is its reward. That is to say, when the individual does what is usually even a matter of indifference to the individual, then he thereby becomes, if he joins our Society, important
for the whole Society. Is this not a marvel, is this not a proof of the
Society's enormous significance! That a person out of regard for his
spiritual or physical health totally abstains from strong drink, that he
knows this in himself, what sort of a reward is this—or has it ever
occurred to any such person to pride himself on it? But if he joins
our Society then by so doing he acquires infinite significance for
the whole Society, which of course everyone who is a member
knows. . . .

What wonder is it, really, that the significance is significant? But to

258

do what is insignificant in itself more significantly than the most significant—this is still certainly a task. And this task has never before been fulfilled in the world, unless by those morally perfect people, monks and nuns, and will never be fulfilled on such a scale as when the Temperance Society consistently expands more and more. For that a man is faithful to his wife, that he knows this himself and is happy to know it along with her, what reward is this? But if the Temperance Society also accommodates this side of life: if he then joins our Society, then he will become infinitely important, indeed, is it not marvelous, infinitely important by doing what every husband ought to do and what most people do without knowing how infinitely important it is? But so it is, everywhere outside the Temperance Society the old saying still applies that a person, if he does his duty, is an unworthy servant. In the Temperance Society this saying has been abolished. And how is a person's moral power to be strengthened and encouraged if he always has to be reminded that he cannot do more than his duty? But how will the moral power not be raised far above and beyond the universal ethic [det Almene], even to taking the great by force, when one becomes infinitely important merely by doing the trivial!

Yet, however big the reward is, neither shall I hide what it cannot be the Society's purpose to hide, that the danger too can be manifold—precisely because the trivial, which has been transformed into the infinitely important by the Society's almighty words, has a constant inclination to rebel. Besides, the Society and each of its members are struggling, struggling against the whole of the remaining, imperfect, indeed addicted, humanity. . . .

The thought about our Society and its endeavors carries me away at once, more than Bacchus carried away the poet, for every member ought to be just as intoxicated as a drunk man, but, mark well, intoxicated with enthusiasm, which is the more marvelous the less there is of what causes the intoxication.

Prefaces: Light Reading for Certain Classes as the Occasion May Require 51–55
[Voice: Nicolaus Notabene]

THE MONARCHY

Should the monarchy be abolished?

I once visited a family with a grand-father clock that for some reason or other was out of order. But the trouble did not show up in a sudden slackness of the spring or the breaking of a chain or a failure to strike; on the contrary, it went on striking, but in a curious, abstractly normal, but nevertheless confusing way. It did not strike twelve strokes at twelve o'clock and then once at one o'clock, but only once at regular intervals. It went on striking this way all day and never once gave the hour. So it is in an enervating tension: the relations remain, but in a state of abstract non-cessation . . . The established order continues to stand, but since it is equivocal and ambiguous, passionless reflection is reassured. We do not want to abolish the monarchy, by no means, but if little by little we could get it transformed into make-believe, we would gladly shout "Hurrah for the King!"

Two Ages: The Age of Revolution and the Present Age, a Literary Review 80–81 (KW 14)

Equality

FACTIONS   A CLUB FOR EVERY
CONCEIVABLE PARTISAN

How many factions are allowed in a sane society?

We have Liberals, Ultra-Liberals,
Conservatives, Ultra-Conservatives, *juste-milieu*. In politics we have
every conceivable and inconceivable worthiness. We have Kantians,
Schleiermacherians, and Hegelians. These in turn are divided into
two large parties: the one party comprises those who have not
worked their way into Hegel but nevertheless are Hegelians. The
other comprises those who have gone beyond Hegel but nevertheless
are Hegelians. The third party, the genuine Hegelians, is very small.
We have five anti-infant Baptists, seven Baptists, nine Anabaptists.
Among the Baptists there are three who think the adults should be
baptized in salt water, two who think they ought to be baptized in
fresh water, and one who mediates between the two factions and
insists on brackish water. We have two Straussians. We have a tailor
on Utterslev Heath who has formed a new sect consisting of himself
and two tailor apprentices. For some time there was a lot of talk that
he had gained a third disciple from another trade, but just as he was
about to capture him there was a quarrel that caused the neophyte to
forsake him and take one of the apprentices along, and the person
from the other trade also came up with a new belief. Right now in
Pistol Street someone is supposed to have retired into solitude to
think up a new religion, and his conclusions are expectantly awaited
in the neighboring streets, Christian Bernikov Street and Peder Madsen's Alley. Party spirit is stirring everywhere. Soon there will be
insufficient manpower to have one person for each party. . . . Soon
one may well have to represent several parties, just like that remark-

261

able man who was mustered by Lippe-Detmold and Schaumburg-Lippe in the field as a company, who on one side represented Lippe-Detmold and on the other Schaumburg-Lippe, on the one side was an infantryman and on the other was a cavalryman.

—"Public Confession"
The Corsair *Affair and Articles Related to
the Writings* 6–7 (KW 13)

COMMUNIST "EQUALITY" AS SURROGATE
RELIGIOUSNESS   Into the Common Tub

Suppose a communistic political regime took on the task of enforcing the equalitarian ideal quantitatively, what is likely to result?

How self-contradictory all this is, that men in general assembly or by casting their votes, or by hand-shaking, shall be, if you please, a surrogate for religiousness. . . .

With amendments to the Constitution, with the fourth estate, with all men wishing to solve the problem of likeness and equality between man and man in the medium of worldliness, i.e., in the medium the nature of which is difference and inequality. Though all travel in Europe must stop because one must wade in blood, and though all ministers were to remain sleepless for ruminating, and though every day ten ministers were to lose their reason, and every next day ten new ministers were to begin where the others left off, only to lose their reason in turn—with all this not one step forward is made. . . . For give us eternity, a prospect of eternity every instant, its seriousness and its blessedness, its relief; give eternity again to every individual—then no more blood-shedding will be needed, and the ministers may be allowed to retain their respective reasons. . . .

But the understanding in the service of worldly passion will constantly imagine that it can reckon this out and get likeness and equality in worldliness. Every new construction becomes then—yes, in the now antiquated style it becomes a paragraph with the appropriate sign—it now has become, *stili novi*, a new [government] ministry. And then when the new ministry goes out, or is convulsively

262

thrust out, has one then reached the conclusion that the misfortune did not lie in the accidental mistakes or defects of the combination but in the fact that what was needed was something entirely different, namely, religiousness? No, this conclusion one will not draw. There will immediately be a new combination and a new ministry in the offing, which having shaken the relativities kaleidoscopically in a somewhat different way imagines that it has found what it sought. And one will say almost quite systematically, "Well, no, in the way the former ministry wanted to do it it cannot be done, but if only one reckons rightly it must come out all right"—and there comes the new ministry which does less for the beer-sellers, more for the candle-makers, and then you take more from landowners and bring the proletariat more to the fore, equalize priests and deacons, and above all make a humpback watchman and a bowlegged blacksmith's apprentice into straight and equal men. . . .

The reaction (conversely to that of the Reformation) will transfigure what seemed to be, and imagined itself to be, politics into a religious movement. . . .

To be selected to be the ruler in a worldly sense is regarded as good fortune, but to be selected to serve as a ruler in a religious sense is, humanly speaking, rather like a punishment, in any case, humanly speaking, it is suffering; humanly speaking, it is the opposite of an advantage.

Discontented, unsatisfied, with the State, with the Church and with everything related to them (art, learning, etc., etc.) the human race, if allowed to follow its own devices, would resolve itself into a world of atoms—whereby nevertheless this progress will be made that now God will himself come directly into relation with the single individuals, not through abstractions, neither through representative persons, but God will himself, so to speak, undertake to educate the countless individuals of the generations, to become himself the schoolmaster who looks after all, everyone in particular. Here thought comes to a stop. The form of the world would be like—well, I know not with what I should liken it. It would resemble an enormous version of the town of Christenfeld [an example of Christian Communism], and so there would be present the two greatest possible contrasts, striving with one another about the interpretation of

263

this phenomenon. On the one hand *communism*, which would say, This is the correct worldly way, there must not be the slightest difference between man and man; riches, art, learning, rule, etc., etc., are of the evil one, all men ought to be equal like laborers in a factory, like cattle in a barnyard, partake of the same food, be washed in one common tub at the same stroke of the clock, be of the same dimensions, etc., etc. On the other hand *pietism*, which would say, This is the right Christian way, that one make no difference between man and man, we ought to be brothers and sisters, have all in common; riches, art, learning, etc., etc., are of the evil one; all men should be equal as it was once in little Christenfeld, all dressed alike, all pray at fixed times, marry by casting lots, go to bed at the stroke of the clock, partake of the same food, out of one dish, at the same time, etc., etc.

On Authority and Revelation: The Book on Adler, or a Cycle of Ethico-Religious Essays xx–xxiii, xxv–xxvi*

THE MAN OF DISTINCTION
A View from the Upper Class

What modes of consciousness are required for one to become "well-bred"?

This distinguished corruption teaches the man of distinction that he exists only for distinguished men, that he shall live only in their social circle, that he must not exist for other men, just as they must not exist for him. But he must be circumspect, as it is called, in order with smoothness and dexterity to avoid getting people excited; that is to say, the secret and the art of the secret consist in keeping this secret to oneself. This avoidance of disturbance must not be an expression for the relationship, and it must not be done in a striking manner that might awaken attention. No, the evasiveness must be for the purpose of shielding oneself and therefore must be practiced so carefully that no one becomes aware of it, to say nothing of being offended by it. Consequently he will go about as if with closed eyes (alas, but not in the Christian sense) when he travels amid the human throng. Proudly, and yet quietly, he will flit, as it were, from one distinguished circle to another. He must not look at those other men—lest he be seen; yet behind this screen his eyes will be all attention, just in case he should happen to meet a fellow-being or an even more distinguished person. His glance will float vaguely about, sweeping over all these men so that no one may catch his eye and remind him of their kinship. He must never be seen among less important people, at least never in their company, and if this cannot be avoided, it must appear as a stately condescension—although in the subtlest guise in order not to offend and hurt. He must be prepared to employ extreme courtesy towards common people, but he must never associate with them as equals, for thereby expression would be given to his being—a human being—whereas he is a distinguished personage. And if he can do this easily, smoothly, tastefully, elusively and yet always keeping his secret (that those other men do not really exist for him and he does not exist for them), then this refined corruption will confirm him as being—a well-bred man.

> *Works of Love: Some Christian Reflections*
> *in the Form of Discourses* 85

THE IDEAL OF ABSOLUTE EQUALITY
In Love with Impracticality

Can complete equality be attained?

An impatient politician who hurriedly peeps into these pages will find little to edify him; so be it. Yet I am convinced that even he, if only he would be so kind as to bestow upon himself a little patience, will become aware, by merely the brief suggestions communicated in these pages, that the religious is the transfigured rendering of that which the politician has thought of in his happiest moment, if so be that he truly loves what it is to be a man, and loves people really, although he is inclined to regard religion as too lofty an ideal to be practical. . . .

Even a pagan, and precisely that "practical philosopher" of antiquity [Socrates] was one who declared himself head over heels in love with *this* unpracticality.

But "unpractical" as he is, the religious man is nevertheless the transfigured rendering of the politician's fairest dream. No politics ever has, no politics ever can, no worldliness ever has, no worldliness ever can, think through or realize to its last consequences the thought of human equality [*Menneske-Lighed*]. To realize complete equality in the medium of worldliness [*Verds-Lighed*], i.e. to realize it in the medium the very nature of which implies differences, and to realize it in a worldly [*verds-ligt*] way, i.e., by positing differences— such a thing is forever impossible, as is apparent from the categories. For if complete equality were to be attained, worldliness would be at an end. But is it not a sort of obsession on the part of worldliness that it has got into its head the notion of wanting to enforce complete equality, and to enforce it by worldly means . . . . . in a worldly medium? It is only religion that can, with the help of eternity, carry human equality to the utmost limit—the godly, the essential, the non-worldly, the true, the only possible human equality.

—"'The Individual': Two 'Notes'
Concerning My Work as an Author"
*The Point of View for My Work as an
Author: A Report to History, and Related
Writings* 107–8*

Economics

THE AUTHORIZATION TO SELL CHRISTIANITY
The Marketing of Town Hall

Who is the one duly authorized to "sell Christianity"?

After all, Stundenstrup is clearly in the right about the Town Hall, that it is a very handsome building, and that for the song at which these "honest men" are willing to dispose of it, it is the most brilliant transaction that can well be imagined. This must be conceded by his paternal uncle at the town of Thy, by all the kindred in Alling, and by all shrewd men wherever they are.

What Stundenstrup neglected to consider was whether these honest men stood in such a relation to the Town Hall that they were able to dispose of it. If not, then, the price, if it were only four shillings and sixpence, would be very dear . . . . . for the Town Hall. So then, cheapness is not to be extolled unconditionally . . .

So it is with Christianity. That an eternal blessedness is an inestimable good, far more considerable than the Town Hall, and if it can be bought for the song at which the priests dispose of it, it may be considered a far, far, far more brilliant transaction than that of Stundenstrup's in buying the Town Hall—that I am willing to concede.

The only difficulty I feel is whether the priests stand in such a relation to the blessedness of eternity that they are able to dispose of it. For if not, then, though it were only four shillings sixpence, it is an enormous price.

Kierkegaard's "Attack upon
'Christendom'" 50–51

WITNESSING TO THE TRUTH

The Stubborn Shopkeeper with Spoiled Goods

Should entrepreneurial religious leaders be viewed as a part of the mercantile class?

If it was possible to attack a merchant in such a way that one showed that his goods were bad but this still did not have the slightest influence on his customary sales of goods, he would presumably say, "Such an attack is of no importance to me at all, because whether the goods are good or bad does not in itself concern me. After all, I am a merchant, and what concerns me is the sales. Indeed, I am to such a degree a merchant that if it could be shown not only that the coffee I sell is damaged, spoiled, but that what I am selling under the name of coffee is not coffee at all—if only I am assured that this attack has no influence whatever on the sales, such an attack is of no importance to me at all. Why should I care about what people guzzle under the name of coffee; I care only about the sales." . . .

Have I protested against the clergy's being regarded as a merchant class? No, I have protested against their wanting to be regarded as truth-witnesses. . . .

It would cause great confusion and disorder, indeed, in many a case probably harm, if a number of people hit upon the idea of placing over their door "Practicing Physician" and hanging out a red light. The social order would have to demand that all those signs be removed. It is the same with hanging up the sign "Practicing Truth-Witnesses."

—"Newspaper Articles 1854–1855"
The Moment *and Late Writings* 61–62
(KW 23)

THE WAY AS THE TRUTH How Long Did It Take Not to Invent Gunpowder?

What is the relation between what one does and the way one does it?

Someone invents something—gunpowder, for example. He, the inventor, has perhaps spent many, many years of his life in pondering and devising; many before him have perhaps spent a long time in like manner, but in vain. Now he has succeeded, now gunpowder is invented. At the very same moment the way almost entirely drops out; to such an extent it is shortened. That for which he has used twenty years, someone else can now learn in half an hour with the help of his instructions about how one proceeds with it. The twenty years stand in an altogether accidental relation to the invention. It cannot really be said that he has used the twenty years to invent gunpowder. No, he really invented the gunpowder in half an hour. One must rather say that during those twenty years he did not invent gunpowder; in a certain sense they are worthless since they were not spent in inventing but in a vain attempt to invent gunpowder; consequently they were spent in not inventing gunpowder. . . . Since the truth is not different from the way but is precisely the way, no essential shortening can possibly take place in relation between the predecessor and the successor.

Practice in Christianity 207–8 (KW 20)
[Voice: Anti-Climacus]

THE LURE OF DISCOVERING EVIL
The One Who Imagined He Invented Gunpowder

What is the fate of one who thinks he invented gunpowder long after its actual invention?

If one wants to single out someone as especially shallow and obtuse, one says, "He for sure didn't invent gunpowder," which of course hardly needs to be done in our day, since it has already been invented; so it would be even more dubious if someone in our time were to think that he was the one who had invented gunpowder. Oh, but to discover something is so admired in the world that it is impossible to forget the enviable fate of having invented gunpowder!

So, then, it is certainly easy to see that the one who loves, who discovers nothing, makes a very poor showing in the eyes of the world. To make discoveries even with regard to evil, with regard to sin and the multitude of sins, to be the shrewd, sly, foxy, perhaps more or less corrupt observer who can really make discoveries—this is highly regarded in the world . . . Finally there is no limit to his discovery. Now he discovers sin even where he himself knows it does not exist.

Works of Love 283–87 (KW 16)

PSYCHOLOGICAL ANALYSIS

Behavior Change

ADDICTIVE BEHAVIORS   The Grandiose Resolution of
the Gambler

**By what behavior change strategy is obsessive craving overcome,
so as to "fool the craving"?**

                          Earnestness is precisely this kind of
honest distrust of oneself, to treat oneself as a suspicious character, as
a financier treats an unreliable client, saying, "Well, these big promises are not much help; I would rather have a small part of the total
right away." . . .

    Imagine a person who has been and is addicted to a passion. . . .
Imagine that one morning he said to himself (let us suppose him to
be a gambler), "I solemnly vow that I will never more have anything
to do with gambling, never—tonight will be the last time"—ah, my
friend, he is lost! I would rather bet on the opposite, however strange
that may seem. If there was a gambler who in such a moment said to
himself, "Well, now, you may gamble every blessed day all the rest of
your life—but tonight you are going to leave it alone," and he did—
ah, my friend, he is saved for sure! The first gambler's resolution is a
trick by the craving, and the second gambler's is to fool the craving.
The one is fooled by the craving, and the other fools the craving.
The craving is strong only momentarily; if it has its way only momentarily, then from its side there is nothing against making a lifetime promise. But to reverse the situation and say, "No—only not
today, but tomorrow, and the day after tomorrow, etc."—that fools
the craving, since if there is waiting to do, then the craving loses the
craving. If the craving is not granted entrance the moment it announces itself, ahead of every other, if it is told that it cannot be
admitted until tomorrow, then the craving understands (even more
swiftly than the most ingratiating and ingenious courtier or the wili-

est woman understands what it means when this happens to them in the reception room), then the craving understands that it no longer is the one and only.

—*For Self-Examination*
For Self-Examination; Judge for Yourself!
44–45 (KW 21)

LUST   SUBDUING THE IMMEDIACY OF DESIRE THROUGH DELAY

How is lust mastered?

The art of mastering desire is not so much in exterminating it or utterly renouncing it as in determining the moment. Take whatever desire you please—the secret in it, the power in it, is in its being absolutely in the instant. It is often said that the only way is to refrain altogether. This is a very wrong method, which also succeeds only for a time. Imagine a person who has become addicted to gambling. Desire awakens in all its passion; it is as if his life would be at stake if his desire is not satisfied. If he is able to say to himself: At this moment I will not do it; I will not do it for an hour—then he is cured.

—*Or*
Either/Or 2:230 (KW 4) [Voice: Judge William]

THE PSYCHOLOGIST   THE POLICE AGENT WITH EVIDENCE AT HAND

What special competencies distinguish the astute psychologist?

One who has properly occupied himself with psychology and psychological observation acquires a general human flexibility that enables him at once to construct his example which even though it lacks factual authority nevertheless has an authority of a different kind. The psychological observer ought to be

274

more nimble than a tight-rope dancer in order to incline and bend himself to other people and imitate their attitudes, and his silence in the moment of confidence should be seductive and voluptuous, so that what is hidden may find satisfaction in slipping out to chat with itself in the artificially constructed nonobservance and silence. Hence he ought also to have a poetic originality in his soul so as to be able at once to create both the totality and the invariable from what in the individual is always partially and variably present. Then, when he has perfected himself, he will have no need to take his examples from literary repertoires and serve up half-dead reminiscences, but will bring his observations entirely fresh from the water, wriggling and sparkling in the play of their colors. Nor will he have to run himself to death to become aware of something. On the contrary, he should sit entirely composed in his room, like a police agent who nevertheless knows everything that takes place. What he needs he can fashion at once; what he needs he has at hand at once by virtue of his general practice, just as in a well-equipped house one need not carry water from the street but has it on his level by high pressure.

The Concept of Anxiety 54–55 (KW 8)
[Voice: Vigilius Haufniensis]

EMPIRICAL PSYCHOLOGY On Wasting Time Explaining Sin
                                   under Deterministic Models

Viewed empirically, what is the precise cause of sin?

I do not intend to repeat all the ingenious and stupid hypotheses with which thinkers and speculators have encumbered the beginning of history, men who only out of curiosity were interested in the great human concern called sin, partly because I do not wish to waste the time of others in telling what I myself wasted time in learning, and partly because the whole thing lies outside of history, in the twilight where witches and speculators race on broomsticks and sausage-pegs. The science that deals with the explanation is psychology, but it can explain only up to the ex-

275

planation and above all must guard against leaving the impression of explaining that which no science can explain and that which ethics explains further only by presupposing it by way of dogmatics.

The Concept of Anxiety 38–39 (KW 8)
[Voice: Vigilius Haufniensis]

Anxiety, Guilt, and Boredom

FATE   THE URGENT BATTLE DIRECTIVE
                             THAT WAITED UNTIL JUNE 14

What special form of anxiety seizes the genius of fate?

A second lieutenant, if he is a genius [of fate], is able to become an emperor and change the world, so that there becomes one empire and one emperor. But therefore, too, the army may be drawn up for battle, the conditions for the battle be absolutely favorable, and yet in the next moment wasted; a kingdom of heroes may plead that the order for battle be given—but he cannot: he must wait for the fourteenth of June. And why? Because that was the date of the battle of Marengo. So all things may be in readiness, he himself stands before the legions, waiting only for the sun to rise in order to announce the time for the oration that will electrify the soldiers, and the sun may rise more glorious than ever, an inspiring and inflaming sight for all, only not for him, because the sun did not rise as glorious as this at Austerlitz, and only the sun of Austerlitz gives victory and inspiration. Thus the inexplicable passion with which such a one may often rage against an entirely insignificant man, when otherwise he may show humanity and kindness even toward his enemies. Yes, woe unto the man, woe unto the woman, woe unto the innocent child, woe unto the beast of the field, woe unto the bird whose flight, woe unto the tree whose branch comes in his way at the moment he is to interpret his omen.

The Concept of Anxiety 99–100 (KW 8)
[Voice: Vigilius Haufniensis]*

Is any player in the game of conscience fast enough to run away from guilt?

The person sitting in a showcase is not as embarrassed as every human being is in his transparency before God. This is the relationship of conscience. The arrangement is such that through the conscience the report promptly follows each guilt, and the guilty one himself must write it. But it is written with invisible ink and therefore first becomes clearly legible only when it is held up to the light in eternity while eternity is auditing the consciences. Essentially, everyone arrives in eternity bringing along with him and delivering his own absolutely accurate record of every least trifle he has committed or omitted. Thus a child could hold court in eternity; there is really nothing for a third party to do, everything down to the most insignificant word spoken is in order. The situation of the guilty person traveling through life to eternity is like that of the murderer who fled the scene of his act—and his crime—on the express train: alas, just beneath the coach in which he sat ran the telegraph wires carrying his description and orders for his arrest at the first station. When he arrived at the station and left the coach, he was arrested— in a way, he had personally brought his own denunciation along with him.

The Sickness unto Death 124 (KW 19)
[Voice: Anti-Climacus]

SPIRITLESSNESS THE MANUSCRIPT WITHOUT PUNCTUATION MARKS

What turns rational creatures into perpetual mutterers?

The life of Christian paganism . . . really knows no distinction between the present, the past, the future, and the eternal. Its life and its history go on crabbedly like the writing in ancient manuscripts, without any punctuation marks, one word, one sentence after the other. From an esthetic point of view, this is very comical, for while it is beautiful to listen to a brook running murmuring through life, it is nevertheless comical that a sum of rational creatures is transformed into a perpetual muttering without meaning. Whether philosophy can use this *plebs* [multitude] as a category by making it a substratum for the greater, just as vegetative sludge gradually becomes solid earth, first peat and so on, I do not know. . . .

Spiritlessness can say exactly the same thing that the richest spirit has said, but it does not say it by virtue of spirit. Man qualified as spiritless has become a talking machine, and there is nothing to prevent him from repeating by rote a philosophical rigmarole, a confession of faith, or a political recitative.

> *The Concept of Anxiety* 94–95 (KW 8)
> [Voice: Vigilius Haufniensis]

ARBITRARINESS   SELECTING FROM THE
                     COSTUME CLOSET

What does the bored playwright spend his time doing?
                     What takes the ironist's time . . . is
the solicitude he employs in dressing himself in the costume proper to the poetic character he has poetically composed for himself. Here the ironist is very well informed and consequently has a considerable selection of masquerade costumes from which to choose. At times he walks around with the proud air of a Roman patrician wrapped in a bordered toga, or he sits in the *sella curulis* with imposing Roman earnestness; at times he conceals himself in the humble costume of a penitent pilgrim. Then again he sits with his legs crossed like a Turkish pasha in his harem; at times he flutters about as light and free as a bird in the role of an amorous zither player. . . . For him, life is a drama, and what absorbs him is the ingenious complication of this drama. He himself is a spectator, even when he himself is the one acting. . . . He is inspired by self-sacrificing virtue the way a spectator is inspired by it in a theater; he is a severe critic who knows very well when this virtue becomes insipid and inauthentic. . . .

But since there is no continuity in the ironist, the most contrasting moods succeed one another. At times he is a god, at times a grain of sand. His moods are just as occasional as the incarnations of Brahma. . . . At times he is on the way to the monastery, and along the way he visits Venusberg; at times he is on the way to Venusberg, and along the way he prays at a monastery. . . .

Boredom is the only continuity the ironist has. Boredom, this eternity devoid of content, this salvation devoid of joy, this superficial profundity, this hungry glut. But boredom is precisely the negative unity admitted into a personal consciousness, wherein the opposites vanish. That both Germany and France at this time have far too many such ironists and no longer need to be initiated into the secrets of boredom by some English lord, a traveling member of a spleen club, and that a few of the young breed in Young Germany and Young France would long ago have been dead of boredom if their respective governments had not been paternal enough to give them something to think about by having them arrested—surely no one will deny. . . .

Now the play speeds ahead, then it stands still; now it stagnates in an episode, then it goes backward; now we are in Peder Madsen's Alley, then in heaven; now something so improbable takes place that the writer knows very well that it is improbable. Now there is a jingling in the distance—it is the pious procession of the three wise men. Then comes a solo for the French horn; now something is asserted in all earnestness and is immediately turned inside out, and the unity of laughter is supposed to reconcile the contrasts, but this laughter is accompanied by the distant flute tones of a deep sadness etc. etc.

*The Concept of Irony, with Continual
Reference to Socrates* 282–85, 305–6
(KW 2)

What color is your life?

My life achievement amounts to nothing at all, a mood, a single color. My achievement resembles the painting by that artist who was supposed to paint the Israelites' crossing of the Red Sea and to that end painted the entire wall red and explained that the Israelites had walked across and that the Egyptians were drowned.

—*Either:* "Diapsalmata"
Either/Or 1:28 (KW 3) [Voice: "A"]

EARNESTNESS   FAME

For what do I [the humorist, Johannes Climacus] want to be known?

I ask for nothing more than to be singled out as the only person who is *unable* to instruct didactically, and thereby also as the only person who does not understand the demands of the times. . . . I ask for nothing better than to be known for being the only one who in our *earnest* times was not earnest.

Concluding Unscientific Postscript to
Philosophical Fragments 1:280–82 (KW
12) [Voice: Johannes Climacus]

NOSTALGIA   AN INADVERTENT
                           BACKWARD GLANCE

How do you learn of what you have left behind?

Justinus Kerner tells somewhere of a man who became bored with his home; he had his horse saddled so he could ride out into the wide, wide world. When he had ridden a little way, the horse threw him off. This turn of events became crucial for him, because as he turned to mount his horse, his eyes fell once again on the home he wanted to forsake. He gazed at it, and behold, it was so beautiful that he promptly turned back.

—*Repetition*
Fear and Trembling; Repetition 171 (KW 6) [Voice: Constantin Constantius]

BOREDOM   THE ENGLISH GENIUS
                           FOR INDIFFERENCE

How is boredom epitomized in language?

At times one meets an English tourist who is an incarnation of this genius, a heavy, inert woodchuck whose total resource of language consists of a single monosyllable, an interjection with which he indicates his highest admiration and his deepest indifference, for admiration and indifference have become undifferentiated in the unity of boredom.

—*Either:* "The Rotation of Crops"
Either/Or 1:290 (KW 3) [Voice: "A"]

CONTRADICTIONS
WITHIN ACADEMIA

Education and the Universities

ADAPTING TO MEDIOCRITY
The Incredible Shrinking
Moral Yardstick

Just how far has the criterion for integrity been deflated within modernity?

Imagine a school, let it have—after all, we can imagine it—a class of one hundred pupils, all of the same age, who are supposed to learn the same thing and have the same criterion. To be number seventy and below is to be far down in the class. Now, what if the other thirty pupils from number seventy had the idea that they might be allowed to form a class by themselves. If so, then number seventy would become number one in the class. That would be an advancement, yes, well, it might be put that way, but according to my conception that would be sinking even lower, sinking into a contemptible false self-satisfaction, because it is still much higher to put up willingly with being number seventy according to an honest criterion. So it is in the actuality of life. What is bourgeois-philistinism [*Spidsborgerlighed*]? What is spiritlessness? It is to have changed the criterion by leaving out the ideals. . . .

See, the reason that there has been retrogression in Christendom is that imitation [following of Christ] has been abolished. . . .

Let us imagine a Christian city. Christianly speaking, the criterion is the disciple, the imitator. But in that place there is, to be sure, no one who can stand up under the criterion. There is, however, Pastor Jensen, for example. He is a gifted, a sagacious man, and there is much good to be said of him. So let us make him number one and adapt ourselves accordingly; it is the sensible thing to do, for then one can still become something in the world. "Yes, but according to the criterion of the ideal, Mr. Jensen (not to forget the illustration) is

285

only number seventy in the class." Blast the ideals! If we have to take them along, no one can feel like enjoying life. And what does Mr. Jensen think? He thinks—and by this we realize that he is not even number seventy—he thinks that he can appropriately provide the criterion and model [Mynster], that these exaggerated requirements are fantasies. And so the game of Christianity is played in that city: Pastor Jensen, a gregarious man about town, almost as if created for this social game, becomes the "true Christian" in the game, even an apostle, is lauded as an apostle in the newspapers. In the character of an apostle—superb!—he is overwhelmed with all of life's amenities, which he—in the character of an apostle?—also knows how to appreciate.

> —*Judge for Yourself!*
> *For Self-Examination; Judge for Yourself!*
> 199–200 (KW 21)*

SUSPENDED JUDGMENT   PROFESSORIAL CHRISTIANITY AS A
NEW SOCIOLOGICAL TYPE

What has modern "Christendom" substituted for the Christian call for decision?

If the Christianity of the Middle Ages is called monastic-ascetic Christianity, then the Christianity of today could be called professorial-scholarly Christianity. Not everyone could become a professor, of course, but everyone took on a tinge of a professor of sorts and of the scholarly. Just as in the beginning not all became martyrs, but all stood in relation to the martyr, and just as in the Middle Ages not all entered the monastery, but all stood in relation to the monastery and saw the true Christian in one who entered it, so in our day all stand in relation to the professor—the professor is the true Christian. And with the professor came scientific scholarship, and with scholarship came doubts, and with scholarship and doubts came the scholarly public, and then came reasons *pro* and *contra*, and *pro und contra* were Germanized, "*denn* [because] *pro und contra* allow *sich* [themselves] to say very much in the matter."

The professor! This man is not mentioned in the New Testament,

286

from which one sees in the first place that Christianity came into the world without professors. Anyone with any eye for Christianity will certainly see that no one is as qualified to smuggle Christianity out of the world as "the professor" is, because the professor shifts the whole viewpoint of Christianity. . . . When the "professor" stands at his highest level and Christianity perceives itself in the professor as it once perceived itself in the monastery, the condition in Christendom will be—Christianity does not really exist, *adhuc sub judice lis est* [the case is still before the courts], the conclusion with regard to what Christianity is, or what is Christianity, is awaited. Faith does not exist; at most it is a mood that vacillates between recalling Christianity as a vanished something and waiting for it as a future something. Imitation [of Christ as prototype] is an impossibility, because inasmuch as everything is put in abeyance, one cannot possibly begin anything decisive, but one's existence drifts with the current and one utilizes natural self-love to make life as cosy as possible for oneself. The "professor" cannot fasten down anything; what he can do is to put everything in abeyance. At times the professor seems to propound something utterly trustworthy. This, however, is an illusion and is due more to his demeanor and assurances; looked at more closely, his firmest point is still in the realm of scientific-scholarly doubt and consequently in abeyance. Only imitation can tie the knot at the end. But just as the king blanched when an invisible hand wrote upon the wall, "You have been weighed and found wanting," so the professor blanches before imitation—it, too, expresses: you, with the weight of all your objective scholarship, your folios and systems, have been weighed and found wanting. No wonder, since Christianly it is precisely the objective scholarship that weighs least on the scales.—When the "monastery" is the deviation, faith must be affirmed; when the "professor" is the deviation, imitation must be affirmed.

> —*Judge for Yourself!*
> *For Self-Examination; Judge for Yourself!*
> 194–96 (KW 21)*

MISUNDERSTANDING   STUDYING FOR THE WRONG EXAM

Can infinite preparation get the self ready to be a self?

To myself I seem like a person who wanted to take his *examen artium* [final comprehensive examination] and had studied beyond measure for seven others but had not studied what was prescribed and therefore failed.

Stages on Life's Way 223 (KW 11)
[Voice: Quidam]

THE LIFELONG SCHOOL   THE ANGELIC MESSENGER WHO
GREW YOUNGER WITH EACH VISION

Why does it take human beings longer than any species in the animal kingdom to learn rightly to be what they already are? How long must one train to be educated for eternity?

The lowest forms of animals are born in one moment and die almost in the same moment. The lower animals grow very rapidly. The human being grows the slowest of all created beings, and thereby he confirms the well-informed man in believing that man is the noblest creation. And we also speak in the same way about education. He who is merely destined to serve in a humble capacity goes to school only a short time. But the one who is destined for something higher, must go to school for a long time. Consequently, the length of the educational period has a direct relationship to the significance of that which one is to become. If, therefore, the school of suffering lasts through an entire lifetime, then this simply proves that this school must train for the highest, moreover, that it is the only one which does train for eternity, for no other time of schooling lasts so long. . . . As a teacher usually says to the youthful student, who is even now finding the time of schooling too long, "Now, just don't get impatient, you have a long life before you"—so eternity speaks with more reason and more reliability to the sufferer:

"Just wait, do not become impatient, there is indeed plenty of time, there is, you know, eternity." . . .

The *joy* in the thought that the school of suffering trains for eternity . . . [calls] to mind what one of the oldest teachers of the Church, one of the Apostolic Fathers, has so beautifully expounded. He relates in the part of his book (Hermas, *The Shepherd*), which is called "The Visions," how God favored him with three visions. These had, in addition to their significant content, also the remarkable feature that the one who showed them to him and explained them, was the first time a very old woman, the second time she was younger and more agreeable to look at, although she still had the hair and the wrinkled skin of an old woman; but the third time she was young, joyous, yet earnest as the youth of eternity is. He now goes on to explain this more particularly, but adds among other things also this: "They who sincerely do penance shall become younger."

—*The Gospel of Suffering*
The Gospel of Suffering and the Lilies of
the Field 60–63*

Philosophical Systems

MISUNDERSTANDING   The Last Words of Hegel

Who has understood Hegel?

Hegel also is supposed to have died with the words that no one understood him except one person, who misunderstood him. . . . Hegel's communication in the seventeen whole volumes is direct communication, so that if he has not found anyone who has understood him, it is all the worse for Hegel. It would be a different matter with Socrates, for instance, who artistically arranged his entire mode of communication so as to be misunderstood. Regarded as a dramatic utterance at the moment of death, Hegel's statement is best regarded as delirium, as thoughtlessness on the part of one who, now in death, wants to take paths he had never taken in life.

> *Concluding Unscientific Postscript to*
> Philosophical Fragments 1:70n (KW 12)
> [Voice: Johannes Climacus]

SYSTEM   The Colossal Plan to Publish a
Final, Sweeping System

When the absolutely definitive philosophic system is written, would there then be any further need in future generations for someone to write still another?

I swear: as soon as possible to realize a plan contemplated for thirty years to publish a logical System, as soon as possible to honor my vow taken ten years ago concerning an esthetic System; furthermore I promise an ethical and dogmatic System, and finally *the* System. As soon as this has been published, future generations will not even need to learn to write, for there will be nothing further to write, but only to read—the System.

—*Prefaces: Light Reading for Certain Classes as the Occasion May Require* 31 [Voice: Nicolaus Notabene]

EVASION   THE PRINTER'S ERROR

What is the cornerstone of the Hegelian philosophical system?

By means of "Everything will become clear at the end" and the category "This is not the place to go into this further," the cornerstone of the system, a category often used as ludicrously as if under the rubric of printers' errors someone were to cite one and then add: "There presumably are more [errors] in the book, but this is not the place to go into them further."

Concluding Unscientific Postscript to Philosophical Fragments 1:327–28 (KW 12) [Voice: Johannes Climacus]*

SYSTEMATIC INCOMPLETENESS
                    THE NOT QUITE FINISHED SYSTEM

If a system of thought remains in some small detail incomplete, is it rightly called a system?

I am as willing as anyone to fall down in worship before the system if I could only catch a glimpse of it. So far I have not succeeded, and although I do have young legs, I am almost worn out by running from Herod to Pilate. A few times I have been very close to worshiping, but behold, at the very moment I had already spread my handkerchief on the ground, so as to avoid dirtying my trousers by kneeling, when I for the last time very innocently said to one of the initiates, "Now, tell me honestly, is it indeed completely finished, because if that is the case, I will prostrate myself, even if I should ruin a pair of trousers" (on account of the heavy traffic to and from the system, the road was rather muddy)—I would invariably receive the answer, "No, it is not entirely finished yet." And so the system and the kneeling were postponed once again. . . .

When commission agent Behrend had lost a silk umbrella, he advertised for a cotton umbrella, because he thought this way: If I say that it is a silk umbrella, the finder will be more easily tempted to keep it. Perhaps the systematician thinks this way: If on the title page or in the newspaper I call my production a continued striving for the truth, alas, who will buy it or admire me; but if I call it the system, the absolute system, everyone will buy the system—if only the difficulty did not remain that what the systematician is selling is not the system.

Concluding Unscientific Postscript to
Philosophical Fragments 1:107–8
(KW 12) [Voice: Johannes Climacus]

APHORISM   THE JOY OF BECOMING A FOOTNOTE
                            IN THE SYSTEM

By what means can one avoid living in vain?

I perhaps did right in submitting my aphorism to a systematic appraiser. Perhaps something may come of it, a footnote in the system—great idea! Then I would not have lived in vain!

—*Repetition*
Fear and Trembling; Repetition 149–50
(KW 6) [Voice: Constantin
Constantius]

HEGEL'S SYSTEM   THE NEED FOR PLENTY OF TIME TO
                     FORGET A LOGICAL MISTAKE

Can actual existence be reduced to an afterthought in the system?

When an author [Hegel] entitles the last section of the *Logic* "Actuality," he thereby gains the advantage of making it appear that in logic the highest has already been achieved, or if one prefers, the lowest. In the meantime, the loss is obvious, for neither logic nor actuality is served by placing actuality in the *Logic*. Actuality is not served thereby, for contingency, which is an essential part of the actual, cannot be admitted within the realm of logic. Logic is not served thereby, for if logic has thought actuality, it has included something that it cannot assimilate, it has appropriated at the beginning what it should only presuppose. The penalty is obvious. Every deliberation about the nature of actuality is rendered difficult, and for a long time perhaps made impossible, since the word "actuality" must first have time to collect itself, time to forget the mistake. . . . And now what will be the result? Presumably language will celebrate a great sabbatical year in which speech and thought may be at rest so that we can begin at the beginning.

The Concept of Anxiety [9]–10, 12
(KW 8) [Voice: Vigilius Haufniensis]*

CIVIL DISCOURSE   THE RUCKUS AT THE
                      ACADEMIC SOCIETY

How is order maintained in civil academic discourse?

The President. Since holding such long monologues violates our rules as well as the dramatic decorum we have hitherto observed in our society, I must, by virtue of my office, interrupt you.

von Jumping Jack. . . . Indeed, Mr. President, I will wager that it does not last more than one-and-a-half minutes, because I have prepared it precisely with regard to our society's requirements.

293

President. I am obliged once again to call you to order and call for silence.

v.J. It was Descartes who said *cogito ergo sum* and *de omnibus dubitandum* [everything must be doubted].

President. Silentium. [Silence].

v.J. Spinoza now carried through this standpoint purely objectively, so that all existence [*Tilværelse*] became undulations of the absolute.

President. Beadles, step forward!

v.J. This objectivity, however, was entirely distilled out in the critical development, and whereas Kant carried through this skepticism only to a certain extent, it was reserved for Fichte to look this Medusa in the face in the night of criticism and abstraction.

President. Arrest him and take him away.

v.J. Since I see that force will be used, I cannot do the piece on Schleiermacher, but it was Hegel who speculatively drew together the previous systems, and therefore with him knowledge has reached its proper dogmatic peak.

[The beadles make as if to seize him]

Now I have finished, and with Hegel world history is over; you can just as well take me away, for now there is nothing but mythology left, and I shall myself become a mythological figure.

Phrase. This is a totally one-sided standpoint [*clears his throat*]. Gentlemen, I have gone beyond Hegel; where to, I cannot yet say very precisely, but I have gone beyond him. . . .

Hurrison. I demand that there be a vote.

President. Is it to be by ballot or by show of hands?

v.J. I demand to speak. It seems to me unreasonable to want to decide such a question by voting, and it is my humble opinion that the finitude of discussion achieved by voting is actually no finitude but rather the spurious infinity.

[Several speaking at once]

A. It is a matter of utmost importance.

B. It is a question of life.

C. It is a question of principle.

D. It is a principle of life.

A Polytechnic Student. The state is a galvanic apparatus.

v.J. The state is an organism.

Phrase. Mr. President, I call upon you to declare whether I am the one speaking; otherwise I demand to be given the floor.

Hurrison. I demand that there be a vote on whether there is to be a vote. I am fighting for freedom. We will no longer let ourselves be oppressed by these tyrannical philosophers. . . .

President. The difficulty is whether our rules permit voting in such a case.

A Philologist. I request that a committee of people expert in the study of the past be appointed in order to find out through sound criticism the meaning of the rules.

President. The honorable speaker's proposal seems to be superfluous, because the rules are only one year old.

> —"The Battle between the Old and the
> New Soap-Cellars"
> *Early Polemical Writings* 118–19, 122–23
> (KW 1)

Pure Thought

EPISTEMIC CONSTIPATION
ON SEEKING WHAT ONE KNOWS

Can I seek what I do not know?

A person cannot possibly seek what he knows, and, just as impossibly, he cannot seek what he does not know, for what he knows he cannot seek, since he knows it, and what he does not know he cannot seek because, after all, he does not even know what he is supposed to seek.

—Philosophical Fragments
Philosophical Fragments; Johannes
Climacus 9 (KW 7) [Voice: Johannes
Climacus]

CONCEALING ABSENTMINDEDNESS
THE HAND IN THE SPINACH

When absentmindedness is exposed, how does it conceal its error?

If one knows that a man is absentminded, one becomes used to it and does not reflect upon the contradiction until it occasionally doubles, and the contradiction is that what is supposed to serve to conceal the first absentmindedness reveals it even more. For example, an absentminded person reaches his hand into a spinach casserole, becomes aware of his absentminded-

296

ness, and in order to conceal it says, "Oh, I thought it was caviar"—
for one does not take caviar with the fingers either.

Concluding Unscientific Postscript to
Philosophical Fragments 1:516n
(KW 12) [Voice: Johannes Climacus]

JUSTIFICATION   THE COMPULSIVE NEED TO FIND AT
                       LEAST THREE REASONS FOR
                       DOING ANYTHING

**Suppose one is seeking reasons for acts of charity, love, and
prayer—do all those reasons add anything substantive to that
which is reasoned about?**
                                Suppose that someone has a ware-
house full of gold, and suppose he is willing to give every ducat to the
poor—but in addition, suppose he is stupid enough to begin this
charitable enterprise of his with a defense in which he justifies it on
three grounds: people will almost come to doubt that he is doing any
good. . . .
    Imagine a lover. Is it not true that he would be capable of speaking
about his beloved all day long and all night, too, day in and day out?
But do you believe it could ever occur to him, do you believe it
would be possible for him, do you not think he would find it loath-
some to speak in such a manner that he would try to demonstrate by
means of three reasons that there is something to being in love—
somewhat as the pastor proves by means of three reasons that praying
is beneficial, because praying has become so cheap that in order to
raise its prestige the three little reasons have to be adduced. Or the
way the pastor—and this is the same, only even more ridiculous—
proves with three reasons that to pray is a bliss that "passes all understanding." What a priceless anticlimax—that something that passes
all understanding—is proved by three reasons, which, if they do anything at all, presumably do not pass all understanding and, quite the
contrary, inevitably make it obvious to the understanding that this
bliss by no means passes all understanding, for "reasons," after all, lie
in the realm of the understanding. No, for that which passes all un-

297

derstanding—and for him who believes in it—three reasons mean no more than three bottles or three deer!

The Sickness unto Death 87, 103–4
(KW 19) [Voice: Anti-Climacus]*

SPECULATING ON TRAVEL WITHOUT A MEANS OF CONVEYANCE   RIDING TO DEER PARK ON A COFFEE GRINDER

How does human freedom acquire a beginning point from which to speculate?

I remember once having heard a speculator say that one must not give undue thought to the difficulties beforehand, because then one never arrives at the point where he can speculate. If the important thing is to get to the point where one can begin to speculate, and not that one's speculation in fact becomes true speculation, it is indeed resolutely said that the important thing is to get to the point of speculating, just as it is praiseworthy for a man who has no means of riding to Deer Park in his own carriage to say: One must not trouble himself about such things, because he can just as well ride a coffee grinder. This, of course, is the case. Both riders hope to arrive at Deer Park. On the other hand, the man who firmly resolves not to trouble himself about the means of conveyance, just as long as he can get to the point where he can speculate, will hardly reach speculation.

The Concept of Anxiety 83–85 (KW 8)
[Voice: Vigilius Haufniensis]*

LOGICAL INFERENCE   TOTTERING WITH A TALL STACK OF BREAKABLES

With what shall we compare the attempt to keep one's balance in philosophy without any non sequiturs or logical discrepancies?

When we see a person carrying a load of breakable articles stacked one upon the other, we are not surprised that he walks warily, and is all the time trying to keep his balance. But if we do not see the pile, we smile. Thus many people smiled at J.C. [Johannes Climacus], not suspecting that he was carrying a far higher pile than would normally cause surprise, and that his soul was anxious lest a single one of the logical inferences should drop out, and the whole pile fall to pieces.

—*Johannes Climacus, or De Omnibus*
  Dubitandum Est
  Johannes Climacus, or De Omnibus
  Dubitandum Est; and a Sermon, 104
  [Voice: Johannes Climacus]*

Doubt

THE IMPRESSION OF PROBITY
Maintaining a Fixed Point Amid Doubt

Amid infinite doubt how does one discover any fixed point?

Mr. von Jumping-Jack is a little un-impressive man, whose one leg is a good six inches shorter than the other, and, in order to illustrate his philosophical ideas, after first having raised himself on the longer leg, he used to desert this illusory standpoint, as he usually expressed it, to win the deeper reality. . . . When von Jumping-Jack was really expounding his skepticism, he used to lay his finger significantly on his nose in order, as Hurrison observed, to have at least one fixed point amid the infinite doubt.

> —"The Battle between the Old and the
> New Soap-Cellars"
> *Early Polemical Writings* 114–15 (KW 1)

PURE THINKING AND PURE DOUBTING
The Novice Doubter

What comes from falling in love with doubt?

When J.C. [Johannes Climacus] grew older he had no toys to lay aside; for he had learnt to play with that which was to be the seriousness of his life. And this never lost its attraction. A little girl plays with her doll so long that at last it is metamorphosed into her lover; for woman's whole life is love. J.C.'s life had a similar continuity; for his whole life was thinking.

300

J.C. entered the University, passed his second examination, reached the age of twenty, and still there was no change in him. . . . His love [for thinking, not for a girl] . . . was as if he must blush if he talked about it, and he feared to get to know too much or too little. On the other hand, he always took notice of what others said. Just as a young girl deeply in love does not readily talk about her love, but with an almost painful tension listens hard when other young girls talk about theirs (for she wants to test in silence whether she is as fortunate, or even more fortunate than they, and will snatch at any little hint that will guide her), so did J.C. take notice of everything; and when he got home he pondered what the philosophers had said. . . .

The purer and so to say more virgin-like his problem was, the more he loved it. The less others had helped him forward with his thoughts, the happier he was, and the better everything went for him. I suppose he felt it an imperfection that he could best think a thought when it came to him like newly fallen snow, without having gone through others' hands. . . .

By listening to others his attention became specially drawn to a phrase which came up again and again. It passed from mouth to mouth and was always eulogized, always revered. Innumerable times he heard it repeated, *De omnibus dubitandum est*: "Everything must be doubted." He clung to this phrase and it came to play a decisive role in his life. It became to his soul what a name often is in the story of any person's life. By mentioning this name you sum up everything. . . .

"The sentence 'Philosophy begins with doubt' does not pertain to any particular philosophy. It is a statement about Eternal Philosophy, to which everyone who wants to partake in philosophy must ally himself." J.C. noticed that these words patently moved the audience. . . .

The words seemed to him so beautiful that he could not help dwelling on them, as one sadly gazing on a flight of wild geese in the sky. Anyone who wants to belong to that upper world, must ally himself to these words, and yet J.C. had never seen anybody who had partaken in such a flight. . . .

"Philosophy begins with doubt" was a frequent general theme for discussion. J.C. now heard that the beginning of philosophy is a threefold affair. There is (1) the *absolute* beginning, i.e., the concept of Absolute Spirit or Mind, which is also the goal and end of the System. (2) The *objective* beginning, i.e., the absolute undefined concept of Pure Being, the simplest definition that exists. (3) The *subjective* beginning, i.e., the work of consciousness; a work by which consciousness is elevated to thinking or to postulating abstraction.

This statement made a salutary impression on J.C. It seemed to him reliable and trustworthy, and even though it lacked the intoxicating power of enthusiasm, yet it seemed to him to possess clarity and coolness. The remarkable thing to J.C., however, was that this statement which set out to elucidate the proposition about philosophy's beginning with doubt, in the end declared that the beginning of philosophy was a threefold affair. Each of the three constituents was mentioned, but none of these beginnings was described as philosophy's beginning with doubt. If J.C. was to explain this by saying that philosophy had four beginnings, and the fourth was doubt, then he was in the awkward position of having to suppose that the proposed explanation explained everything except the very thing he wanted explaining.

—*Johannes Climacus, or De Omnibus
Dubitandum Est*
*Johannes Climacus, or De Omnibus
Dubitandum Est; and a Sermon* 108–9,
115, 130–33 [Voice: Johannes
Climacus]*

THE VOLATILITY OF DOUBT

More than Difficult

What is the special hazard of beginning all thinking with doubt?

[Johannes Climacus] had read a story in an old saga about a knight who received from a gnome a rare sword, which, besides its other characteristics had also this, that as soon as one drew it forth, it claimed blood. When the gnome handed it to him, the knight's desire to see it was so great that he drew it forth from its scabbard, and lo! the gnome had to fall victim. Such it seemed . . . must be the case with our proposition [the commitment to doubt everything]. When one said it to a second person, it became in the latter's hand a sword which must murder the first. . . .

Aller Anfang ist schwer, "all beginning is difficult," was a German saying J.C. [Johannes Climacus] had always thought correct; but this beginning seemed to him to be more than difficult; and to call this a beginning and merely dub it "difficult," seemed to J.C. like as if a fox had classed "being flayed" under the category of "transition."

> —*Johannes Climacus, or De Omnibus*
> *Dubitandum Est*
> *Johannes Climacus, or De Omnibus*
> *Dubitandum Est; and a Sermon* 138–39
> [Voice: Johannes Climacus]*

FIRSTHAND EXPERIENCE IN DOUBTING
RIGHT, LEFT, LEFT, RIGHT

Is it the case that those who commend doubting everything as the premise of truth-seeking often find it impossible to do just this?

In the world of the intellect one cannot indicate particular points as precisely [as on a sailor's chart]. Rather it may well be as simple as when a yokel says, "First to the right, then to the left, then again to the left, and then to the right . . . . ."

Now when J.C. [Johannes Climacus, a youthful truth-seeker] had racked his memory, he found himself in a curious position. For it became clear to him that there had hardly fallen a single word in the conversations of the philosophers about all the experiences and adventures in which a man must be tried when setting out to doubt everything. And yet you would have expected to hear something about this. Indeed you might have thought they would talk about this more than everything else, just as seafarers absolutely love to talk about experiences they have been through; being specially incited thereto when they meet people who have traversed the same seas. . . .

[He] therefore, said good-bye to these philosophizers for ever. . . . He followed now the method he had hitherto been wont to follow, i.e., to make everything as simple as possible.

> —*Johannes Climacus, or De Omnibus*
> *Dubitandum Est*
> *Johannes Climacus, or De Omnibus*
> *Dubitandum Est; and a Sermon* 144–45
> [Voice: Johannes Climacus]*

THE VOCATION TO DOUBT
A Modest Project of Suspending Judgment

Have philosophers understood what they themselves have said?

It is gratifying to see philosophy spread itself all around the country, so that soon there is no longer found any person who is not touched by its breath, initiated into its blessings. Yet for me this gratification has not been able to conquer the doubt about whether really all the many *qui nomen philosophiae dederunt* [who have given their names to philosophy] understood what was said and what they said themselves. This doubt is very natural to me, since it has often gone thus with me, even though my ἐποχή [suspension of judgment] has prevented me from posing as a philosopher. . . . When I was not able, in spite of every effort, to raise myself to the dizzying thought to doubt everything, I decided— in order to doubt at least something—to gather my mind for the more human task of doubting whether all those philosophizing understood what they said.

> —*Prefaces: Light Reading for Certain Classes*
> *as the Occasion May Require* 79–80
> [Voice: Nicolaus Notabene]

Speculation and Idealism

SPECULATIVE THOUGHT   The Dancer Who Insisted He
Could Fly

**How high does the speculative thinker think he can leap
existentially?**

If a dancer could leap very high, we
would admire him, but if he wanted to give the impression that he
could fly—even though he could leap higher than any dancer had
ever leapt before—let laughter overtake him. Leaping means to belong essentially to the earth and to respect the law of gravity so that
the leap is merely the momentary, but flying means to be set free
from telluric conditions, something that is reserved exclusively for
winged creatures, perhaps also for inhabitants of the moon, perhaps—and perhaps that is also where the system will at long last find
its true readers. To be a human being has been abolished, and every
speculative thinker confuses himself with humankind, whereby he
becomes something infinitely great and nothing at all.

> *Concluding Unscientific Postscript to*
> Philosophical Fragments 1:124 (KW 12)
> [Voice: Johannes Climacus]

THE ETHICS OF PRINCIPLE
         Sewing On a Coat Button
         "on Principle"

**What can be said of one who has an idealistic compulsion to act
"on principle"?**

A good-natured nobody suddenly be-
comes a hero "on principle," and the situation is just as comical as a

man would be—or everyone if it became the style—if he were to go around wearing a cap with a thirty-foot visor. If a man were to have a little button sewed on the breast pocket of his coat "on principle," that trivial and really expedient precautionary measure would suddenly take on tremendous import—it is not improbable that a society would be founded as a consequence.

> Two Ages: The Age of Revolution and the
> Present Age, a Literary Review 101
> (KW 14)

MAKING PROMISES　　　The Expansive Promise of a
　　　　　　　　　　　Complete System of Thought

What advantages accrue to allowing the complete system of thought to remain in the realm of promise rather than enter into actuality?

　　　　　　　　　　　A promise has the admirable quality that, like politeness, it costs the one who issues it nothing, and yet unconstrainedly he can let it denote a work that is more remarkable than any wonder of the world. With respect to the recipient (the reading public) it exercises a mollifying and calming influence, acts as a resolvent for dispelling every more anxious worry about grasping some subject. . . . A promise is highly portable, and therefore there is nothing that express messengers would rather run with up the garden path than promises. . . .

Let us dwell yet a moment with this thought with which presumably we have all been familiar for several years: the thought of the prospect of hope about the System. Thus, to be quite brief, *posito*, I posit that the System appeared here in Copenhagen, what then? Then of course one must read it, unless Mr. C.C. forthwith should be so good and philanthropic as to promise an overview of the System and to position us at the right standpoint—for then again we would be saved by the promise. If this did not happen, then of course one must read it. What an inconvenience. . . . Furthermore, if the System were read, perhaps the reading would serve to distinguish between those who were regarded as understanding it and those who were regarded as not understanding it. Discord and factions would arise, whereas now the whole generation lives in concord and equality before the promise, to which everyone is equally close.

—*Prefaces: Light Reading for Certain Classes as the Occasion May Require* 67–69
[Voice: Nicolaus Notabene]

ASPIRATIONS HOLDING A DINNER PARTY ON THE IDEA OF A MENU

What characterizes the consciousness of the idealist who construes his own fantasies with absolute seriousness?

To regard every time's breeze as a hint by Governance that has significance for what he should do, just as it had for the journeyman tailor—for the puff of wind was strong enough to blow him off the table; to want to ride summer into town on a stalk of chives one has raised in a flowerpot; to want to conquer the Holy Land without even knowing where it lies on the map; to raise an outcry in the whole congregation because one has been mistaken oneself and taken a cow for a windmill; to summon all tailors to explain to them that one must tie a knot in the thread; to walk the whole day through the streets like a postman and ring people from their work to offer them a prospectus; to hold a dinner party on the idea of a menu and feed the hungry with the thought of a Society whose purpose is to promote the prosperity of all the needy—it is either a joke, and as such sometimes rather funny, or it is in earnest, and as such a preposterous joke, and the more preposterous, the more radical the lunacy is.

—*Prefaces: Light Reading for Certain Classes as the Occasion May Require* 73–74
[Voice: Nicolaus Notabene]

Socrates

SOCRATES' DEATH · WHEN IT IS LESS EXPENSIVE TO DIE THAN PAY THE FINE

By what reasoning did Socrates conclude that death would be his most fitting punishment—the remedy most congruent with his relation with the state?

Hegel gives a detailed account in this connection of what was reprehensible in the behavior of Socrates. He shows that Socrates was deservedly condemned to death, and that his crime lay in refusing to acknowledge the sovereignty of the people, in asserting his own subjective conviction in opposition to the objective judgment of the state. . . . So much for Hegel. . . . One would think that the opportunity to determine his punishment should have been desperately welcomed by Socrates, for as his conduct had shown itself to be incommensurable with ordinary determinations, so also must be the punishment. Now Socrates is rigorously consistent when maintaining that the only punishment he can impose upon himself is a fine, since if he had any money it would be no loss for him to forfeit it, in other words, because the punishment in this case canceled itself. . . . What gives this situation such extraordinary ironic elasticity is the prodigious opposition: the sword of the law is suspended above Socrates' head by a hair, a human life hangs in the balance, the people are grave and circumspect, the horizon dark and overcast—and then Socrates as absorbed as an old geometer in trying to solve the problem of making his life congrue with the conception of the state, a problem as difficult as trying to square the circle inasmuch as Socrates and the state exhibit themselves as absolutely incongruous figures. It would indeed be comical to see Socrates attempt to conjugate his life according to the paradigm of the state, since his life was wholly irregular; but the situation becomes

308

still more comical by the *dira necessitas* which under pain of death bids him find a similarity in this dissimilarity. It is always comical when one conjoins two things which can have no possible agreement. But it becomes even more comical when it is said: make no mistake about it, unless you discover an agreement you must die. The life of Socrates in its complete isolation must appear wholly incongruous with every determination of the state. Similarly, the movement of thought, the dialectic by which Socrates seeks to bring about a relationship, must also exhibit the most extreme oppositions. He is pronounced guilty by the state, the question concerns what punishment he deserves. But as Socrates feels his life can in no wise be comprehended by the state, it would appear that he might just as well merit a reward. He proposes therefore meals in the prytaneum at public expense. Should the state not feel called upon to reward him in this fashion, he will then concentrate harder and consider what punishment he might deserve. In order to escape the death penalty demanded by Meletus he could choose either a fine or banishment. But he is unable to arrive at any decision in the matter, for what could induce him to choose one of these two alternatives? Could it be the fear of death? This would surely be irrational, for he does not know whether death be a good or an evil. Hence it would appear that Socrates himself was of the opinion that death was the most fitting punishment, and this because no one knows that it is an evil, that is to say, because the punishment here again, as previously in the case of the fine, cancels itself. . . .

We have an irony carried through to its utmost limit, an irony that allows the objective power of the state to crush itself against the rock-like negativity of irony.

The Concept of Irony, with Constant
Reference to Socrates 218–21

What is the most preposterous thing that ever happened to Socrates?

The most ludicrous situation preserved about him (see *Antoninus philosophus—ad se ipsum*, XI, 28)—in which Socrates, because Xanthippe [his wife] had put on his clothes and gone out, had to throw [an animal] hide around himself and to the great amusement of his friends appeared in the marketplace dressed like that—nevertheless he still remained a human being and even in his hide was not nearly as ludicrous as he later became in the [Hegelian] system, where he shows up fantastically wrapped in the rich systematic drapery of a paragraph. Did Socrates talk about what the times demanded, did he understand the ethical as something that a prophet with a world-historical gaze was supposed to discover or had discovered, or as something to be decided by voting? No, he was occupied solely with himself, did not even know how to count to five when it was a matter of counting votes (see Xenophon).

Concluding Unscientific Postscript to
Philosophical Fragments 1:147n
(KW 12) [Voice: Johannes Climacus]*

UGLINESS   THE DISTINCT ADVANTAGE OF
                                 BUMPS ON THE FOREHEAD

Why did Socrates find himself especially favored by his exceptional ugliness?

He was very ugly, had clumsy feet, and more than that, a number of bumps on his forehead and other places, which were bound to convince everyone that he was a depraved character. This, you see, was what Socrates understood by his advantageous appearance, and he was so pleased as Punch about it that he would have considered it chicanery on the part of the god if, in order to keep him from being a teacher of morals, he had been given the pleasing appearance of a sentimental zither player, the languishing look of a *Schäfer* [amorous swain], the small feet of a dance director in the Friendship Society, and *in toto* as advantageous an appearance as a job seeker in *Adresseavisen* or a theological graduate, who had set his hopes on a patronage appointment, could possibly wish for himself. Now, then, why was that old teacher so pleased with his advantageous appearance, unless it was because he perceived that it might help to place the learner at a distance so that he would not be caught in a direct relation to the teacher, perhaps would admire him, perhaps would have his clothes made in the same way, but might understand through the repulsion of opposition, which in turn was his irony in a higher sphere, that the learner essentially has himself to deal with and that the inwardness of truth is not the chummy inwardness with which two bosom friends walk arm in arm with each other but is the separation in which each person for himself is existing in what is true.

> *Concluding Unscientific Postscript to*
> Philosophical Fragments 1:248–49
> (KW 12) [Voice: Johannes Climacus]

HOMELINESS   ON NOT MENTIONING "ROPE" IN
                          THE HOUSE OF A HANGED MAN

Did Socrates' ugliness inhibit him in attesting beauty?

See, that simple wise man of ancient times [Socrates], who of all people knew how to speak most beautifully of the love that loves beauty and the beautiful, he was, yes, he was the ugliest man in the whole nation, the ugliest man among the most beautiful nation. One would think that this would have deterred him from speaking about the love that loves the beautiful—after all, one does avoid speaking of rope in the house of a man who has been hanged, and even beautiful people avoid speaking about beauty in the presence of the strikingly ugly, to say nothing of the ugly person himself. But no, he was eccentric and strange enough to find just this appealing and inspiring, that is, eccentric and strange enough to place himself in the most disadvantageous position possible. When he spoke about the beautiful, when in the longing of his thought and discourse for the beautiful he transported the listener, who now inadvertently happened to look at him, he became even twice as ugly as he already was, he who already was the ugliest man in the nation. The more he spoke, the more beautifully he spoke about the beautiful, the more ugly he himself became by contrast.

Works of Love 371–72 (KW 16)*

Teaching

PROFICIENCY   SEEKING EMPLOYMENT WITH A
                               TRAVELING THEATER

Why not quit teaching and become an actor?

For some time now, I have been
speculating about what really was the reason that moved me to resign
as a schoolteacher. When I think about it now, it seems to me that
such an appointment was just the thing for me. Today it dawned on
me that the reason was precisely this—that I had to consider myself
completely qualified for this post. If I had continued in my job, I
would have had everything to lose, nothing to gain. For that reason, I
considered it proper to resign my post and seek employment with a
traveling theater company, because I had no talent and consequently
had everything to gain.

—*Either:* "Diapsalmata"
Either/Or 1:33 (KW 3) [Voice: "A"]

GRAMMAR   THE LATIN MASTER'S
                               ALTERED VOICE

How is the indicative mood distinguishable from the subjunctive?

When I attended grammar school as
a boy I had a Latin teacher whom I frequently recall. He was very
capable, and by no means was it the case that we learned nothing
from him, but at times he was somewhat strange or, if you choose to
look at it that way, somewhat absentminded. Yet his absentmindedness was a matter not of losing himself in thought, falling silent, etc.,

313

but of occasionally speaking suddenly in a completely different voice and from a completely different world. One of the books we read with him was Terence's *Phormio*. It tells of Phaedria, who fell in love with a cither player and was reduced to following her to and from school. The poet then says:

> *ex advorsum ei loco*
> *Tonstrina erat quaedam; hic solebamus fere*
> *plerumque eam opperiri, dum inde rediret domum*
> [right opposite
> was a barber's shop; that's where we used
> generally for the most part to wait for her to
> come out and go home].

With pedagogic gravity the teacher asked the pupil why *dum* in this instance takes the subjunctive. The pupil answered: Because it means the same as *dummodo* [if only]. Correct, replied the teacher, but thereupon began to explain that we were not to regard the subjunctive mood in an external way as if it were the particle as such that took the subjunctive. It was the internal and the psychical that determined the mood, and in the case at hand it was the optative passion, the impatient longing, the soul's emotion of expectancy. Thereupon his voice changed completely, and he went on to say: The person sitting and waiting there in that barber shop as if it were a café or a public place such as that is not an indifferent man but a man in love waiting for his beloved. In fact, if he had been a porter, a chair carrier, a messenger, or a cabdriver who was waiting there, then the waiting could be thought of as occupying the time while the girl was at her music and singing lesson, which is not to be considered subjunctive but indicative, unless it was the case that these gentlemen were waiting to be paid, which is a very mediocre passion. Language really ought not to be allowed to express that kind of expectation in the subjunctive mood. But it is Phaedria who is waiting, and he is waiting in a mood of: If only she, if she would only, would that she might only soon, soon come back; and all this is appropriately the subjunctive mood. There was a solemnity and a passion in his voice that made his pupils sit as if they were listening to a spectral voice. He fell silent, then cleared his throat, and said with the usual pedagogical gravity: Next. This was a recollection from my school days. Now it is clear to me that my unforgettable Latin teacher, although he concerned himself only with Latin, could have taken on other subjects as well as Latin.

Stages on Life's Way 204–5 (KW 11)
[Voice: Quidam]

TRUTH-TELLING   SPEAKING TRUTH WHILE STANDING
                     ON ONE LEG

What is the relation of the truth to how it is told?

If a man were to stand on one leg in a droll dancing posture, swing his hat, and in this pose recite something true, his few listeners would fall into two classes, and he would not have many, since most of them would promptly abandon him. The one class would say: How can what he says be true when he gesticulates that way? The other class would say: Well, it makes no difference whether he performs an entrechat or stands on his head or turns somersaults; what he says is true, and I will appropriate it . . .

Concluding Unscientific Postscript to
Philosophical Fragments 1:264 (KW 12)
[Voice: Johannes Climacus]

THE INTEGRITY OF THE TEACHER
                     THE COST OF SOCRATIC HONESTY

Why was Socrates unbribable?

[Socrates] refused to accept honor or honorific appointments or money for his teaching, because he formed his judgments with the unbribability of one who is dead. What rare contentment—how rare today, when no amount of money can be large enough and no laurels splendid enough to be sufficient reward for the gloriousness of teaching.

—*Philosophical Fragments*
Philosophical Fragments; Johannes
Climacus 23 (KW 7) [Voice: Johannes
Climacus]*

How Comic Episodes Correlate
with the Stages

            Kierkegaard's comic voices are located at various points in the stages along life's way. Remember that in any narrative the correlation is proximate and inexact, since a narrative does not yield easily to systematization. Nonetheless it is not difficult to show that comic episodes correlate with the existential stages. These affinities may be seen cursorily in the outline visualization that follows, and explored further for validation. Each stage has voices, some overlapping. With each persona we fine portrayed various comic episodes appearing within the order of existential stages. (Here "SK" indicates Kierkegaard's own voice.)

FROM AESTHETIC EXISTENCE: THE
VOICES OF PURE IMMEDIACY

The Young Man, "A":
- Immortal Mozart!
- The Cure for Denmark's Debt Crisis
- What's Wrong with Throwing Money Out of the Window?
- The Leap of the Hare
- On Keeping the Other Foot Out of the Fox Trap

Constantin Constantius:
- On Settling Everything with a Ballet Pose
- How Did I Get Here and Why Was I Not Asked if I Wanted to Come?

Victor Eremita:
- The Impeccable Banquet

The Fashion Designer:
- The Ladies' Tailor Speaks

SK (Two Ages):
- The Pre-Exam Vacation

Anti-Climacus:
- Procure Possibility!

FROM AESTHETIC EXISTENCE:
VOICES SUGGESTING IMMEDIACY
WITH REFLECTION

Constantin Constantius:
- The Joy of Becoming a Footnote in the System
- Xanthippe Surprised *in Flagranti* by Socrates
- The Interminable Vacillator
- The Speck of Dust
- The High Diver's Challenge

Victor Eremita:
- A Little of Everything

Vigilius Haufniensis:
- The Need for Plenty of Time to Forget a Logical Mistake
- Riding to Deer Park on a Coffee Grinder
- Why the Battle Command Waited until June 14

SK (Two Ages):
- Inventing Excuses for Staying in Bed

Johannes Climacus:
- Hegel's Last Words
- The Dancer Who Insisted He Could Fly
- The Philosophy Astride a Wild Horse

FROM ETHICAL EXISTENCE: VOICES
INTERPRETING DECISION AND ITS
AVOIDANCE (IRONIC EXAMPLES)

SK (The Concept of Irony):
- A Management Exercise
- Selecting from the Costume Closet

Judge William:
- The Blessing of Children—at a Distance
- What the Bachelor Cannot Celebrate
- The Vague Hankering for a Divining Rod
- The Personal Identity of a Jellyfish

318

Johannes Climacus:
- Tottering with a Tall Stack of Breakables
- The Committee to Beautify the Path of Virtue

Quidam:
- Explaining Hegel to God
- The Second Rap of the Nightstick

FROM ETHICAL EXISTENCE: VOICES
INTERPRETING COMMITMENT AND THE
BINDING OF TIME

Judge William:
- Why Woman Is Stronger than Man
- Admonition to an Impoverished Aesthete

SK (For Self-Examination):
- Saved by Commentaries

SK (The Concept of Irony):
- Why It Is Less Expensive to Die than Pay the Fine

FROM COMIC EXISTENCE: VOICES
REVEALING CONTRADICTION

Vigilius Haufniensis:
- The Freeze of the Mime
- The Bowlegged Dancing Master

Quidam:
- The Latin Master's Altered Voice
- It Hurts Everywhere
- The Inflationary Trend in Ardent Language

Johannes Climacus:
- Explain Eternal Happiness While I Shave
- Dr. Hjortespring's Hegelian Miracle
- The Comic Scythe in the World of Spirit
- So Few Chinese—So Many Germans
- The Exponential Increase of Assistant Professors
- The Mediocre Pupil Who Finished Early

Anti-Climacus:
- The Unexpected Coincidence of Comic and Pathetic

SK (Two Ages):
- Sewing a Button on One's Coat "on Principle"
- Suicide by Discussion

FROM THE AWAKENING OF THE
RELIGIOUS EXISTENCE: VOICES POINTING
TOWARD FAITH

Eighteen Upbuilding Discourses (SK):
- On Running a Foot Race with Heavy Armor

Quidam:
- Unlike Other Saloonkeepers
- Seventy Years

Anti-Climacus:
- The Bewildering Speed of Guilt

Johannes Climacus:
- Whether God Could Have Incarnated as a Large Green Bird
- The Hide of Socrates
- The Emperor Who Became a Meddlesome Part-Time Waiter

FROM CHRISTIAN EXISTENCE:
VOICES OF FAITH

Anti-Climacus:
- Ignoring His Majesty's Visit

SK (Practice in Christianity):
- How Long Did It Take Not to Invent Gunpowder?

SK (Christian Discourses):
- Wings to Be Used Only in Extremities

SK (The Point of View):
- The Authority of the Riot Police
- The Ordeal of Being an Author in Denmark

This list is not complete, but its sequence generally follows the order of existence-modes from esthetic to ethical to religious consciousness. The purpose of this list is to indicate in a preliminary way that various types of comic perception correlate approximately with the sequence of stages. This work is not a discursive dissertation on how each one works, but an ordered presentation of examples.

BIBLIOGRAPHY

PRIMARY SOURCES EXCERPTED

The Book on Adler. Ed. and trans. Howard V. Hong and Edna H. Hong. Kierkegaard's Writing 24. Princeton: Princeton University Press, 1998. [*Bogen om Adler, Papirer VII*^{2} *B 235*, 1846–47.].

Christian Discourses (with *The Crisis and a Crisis in the Life of an Actress*). Ed. and trans. Howard V. Hong and Edna H. Hong. Kierkegaard's Writings 8. Princeton: Princeton University Press, 1997. [*Christelige Taler*, 1848].

Christian Discourses (with *The Lilies of the Field and the Birds of the Air*, and *Three Discourses at the Communion on Fridays*). Trans. Walter Lowrie. London: Oxford University Press, 1940. [*Christelige Taler*, 1848].

The Concept of Anxiety. Ed. and trans. Reidar Thomte and Albert B. Anderson. Princeton: Princeton University Press, 1980. (Kierkegaard's Writings 8) [*Om Begrebet Angest*, 1844].

The Concept of Irony, with Continual Reference to Socrates. Ed. and trans. Howard V. Hong and Edna H. Hong. Kierkegaard's Writings 2. Princeton: Princeton University Press, 1989. [*Om Begrebet Ironi*, 1841].

The Concept of Irony, with Constant Reference to Socrates. Trans. Lee M. Capel. 1965. Reprint, Bloomington: Indiana University Press, 1968. [*Om Begrebet Ironi*, 1841].

Concluding Unscientific Postscript to Philosophical Fragments. Ed. and trans. Howard V. Hong and Edna H. Hong. Kierkegaard's Writings 12, vols. 1–2. Princeton: Princeton University Press, 1992. [*Afsluttende uvidenskabelig Efterskrift*, 1846].

The Corsair Affair and Articles Related to the Writings. Ed. and trans. Howard V. Hong and Edna H. Hong. Kierkegaard's Writings 13. Princeton: Princeton University Press, 1982.

Early Polemical Writings. Ed. and trans. Julia Watkin. Kierkegaard's Writings 1. Princeton: Princeton University Press, 1990. [*Endnu levendes papirer*, 1838].

Eighteen Upbuilding Discourses. Ed. and trans. Howard V. Hong and Edna H.

Hong. Kierkegaard's Writings 5. Princeton: Princeton University Press, 1990. [*Atten opbyggelige taler*, 1843–44].

Either/Or. Ed. and trans. Howard V. Hong and Edna H. Hong. Kierkegaard's Writings 3–4. Princeton: Princeton University Press, 1987. [*Enten-Eller*, I–II, 1843].

For Self-Examination (with *Judge for Yourself!*). Ed. and trans. Howard V. Hong and Edna H. Hong. Kierkegaard's Writings 11. Princeton: Princeton University Press, 1990. [*Til Selvprøvelse*, 1851].

The Gospel of Suffering (with *The Lilies of the Field*). Trans. David F. Swenson and Lillian Marvin Swenson. Minneapolis: Augsburg Publishing House, 1948. [*Opbyggelige Taler i forskjellig Aand*, pt. 2, 1847].

Johannes Climacus, or De Omnibus Dubitandum Est and A Sermon. Trans. T. H. Croxall. Stanford: Stanford University Press, 1958. [*Johannes Climacus eller De Omnibus Dubitandum Est*, 1842–43].

Judge for Yourself! (with *For Self-Examination*). Ed. and trans. Howard V. Hong and Edna H. Hong. Kierkegaard's Writings 11. Princeton: Princeton University Press, 1990. [*Dommer Selv!*, 1852].

Kierkegaard's "Attack upon "'Christendom'"" 1854–1855. Trans. Walter Lowrie. 1944. Reprint, Boston: Beacon Press, 1956. [*Bladartikler*, 1854–55; *Øieblikket*, 1855; *Hvad Christus dømmer om officiel Christendom*, 1855].

The Moment and Late Writings. Ed. and trans. Howard V. Hong and Edna H. Hong. Kierkegaard's Writings 23. Princeton: Princeton University Press, 1998. [*Øieblikket*, 1855; *Bladartikler*, 1854–55; *Dette skal siges, saa være det da sagt*, 1855; *Hvad Christus Dømmer om Officiel Christendom*, 1855; *Guds Uforanderlighed*, 1855].

On Authority and Revelation: The Book on Adler, or a Cycle of Ethico-Religious Essays. Trans. Walter Lowrie. Princeton: Princeton University Press, 1955. [*Bogen om Adler, Papirer VII^2 B 235*, 1846–47].

Philosophical Fragments (with *Johannes Climacus*). Ed. and trans. by Howard V. Hong and Edna H. Hong. Kierkegaard's Writings 7. Princeton: Princeton University Press, 1998. [*Philosophiske Smuler*, 1844].

The Point of View for My Work as an Author: A Report to History, and Related Writings. Trans. Walter Lowrie. New York: Harper and Row, 1962. [*Synspunktet for min Forfatter-Virksomhed*, 1859; *Om min Forfatter-Virksomhed*, 1851].

Practice in Christianity. Ed. and trans. Howard V. Hong and Edna H. Hong. Kierkegaard's Writings 20. Princeton: Princeton University Press, 1991. [*Indøvelse I Christendom*, 1850].

Prefaces (with *Writing Sampler*). Ed. and trans. Todd W. Nichol. Kierkegaard's Writings 9. Princeton: Princeton University Press, 1997. [*Forord*, 1844].

Prefaces: Light Reading for Certain Classes as the Occasion May Require. Trans. William McDonald. Tallahassee: Florida State University Press, 1989. [*Forord*, 1844].

Repetition (with *Fear and Trembling*). Ed. and trans. Howard V. Hong and Edna H. Hong. Kierkegaard's Writings 6. Princeton: Princeton University Press, 1983. [*Gientagelsen*, 1843].

The Sickness unto Death. Ed. and trans. Howard V. Hong and Edna H. Hong. Kierkegaard's Writings 19. Princeton: Princeton University Press, 1980. [*Sygdommen Til Døden*, 1849].

Stages on Life's Way. Ed. and trans. Howard V. Hong and Edna H. Hong. Kierkegaard's Writings 11. Princeton: Princeton University Press, 1988. [*Stadier paa Livets Vej*, 1845].

Two Ages: The Age of Revolution and the Present Age, a Literary Review. Ed. and trans. Howard V. Hong and Edna H. Hong. Kierkegaard's Writings 14. Princeton: Princeton University Press, 1978. [*En literair Anmeldelse*, 1846].

Works of Love. Ed. and trans. Howard V. Hong and Edna H. Hong. Kierkegaard's Writings 16. Princeton: Princeton University Press, 1995. [*Kjærlighedens Gjerninger*, 1847].

Works of Love: Some Christian Reflections in the Form of Discourses. Trans. Howard and Edna Hong. New York: Harper, 1962. [*Kjærlighedens Gjerninger*, 1847].

Writing Sampler (with *Prefaces*). Ed. and trans. Todd W. Nichol. Kierkegaard's Writings 9. Princeton: Princeton University Press, 1997. [*Skriftprøver*, 1914–16].

KIERKEGAARD'S THEORY OF HUMOR

Allison, Henry E. "Christianity and Nonsense." *Review of Metaphysics* 20 (March 1967): 432–60. Reprinted in *Essays on Kierkegaard*, ed. Jerry H. Gill. Minneapolis: Burgess, 1969. Pp. 127–49.

Auden, W. H. "Knight of Doleful Countenance." *New Yorker* 44 (25 May 1968): 141–58.

Carnell, Edward John. "Boundaries between the Stages." *The Burden of Søren Kierkegaard.* Grand Rapids: Eerdmans, 1965. Pp. 57–60.

Christensen, Arild. "Der junge Kierkegaard als Schriftstellerpersönlichkeit." *Orbis Litterarum* 18.1–2 (1963): 26–47.

Daab, Annelise. "Ironie und Humor bei Kierkegaard." Diss., Heidelberg University, 1926.

Diem, Hermann. "The Dialectician's Irony and Humour." *Kierkegaard's Dia-*

lectic of Existence. Trans. Harold Knight. Edinburgh: Oliver and Boyd, 1959. Pp. 41–46.

Fenger, Henning. *Kierkegaard, The Myths and Their Origins: Studies in the Kierkegaardian Papers and Letters*. Trans. George C. Schoolfield. New Haven and London: Yale University Press, 1980.

Glenn, John D. "Kierkegaard on the Unity of Comedy and Tragedy." *Tulane Studies in Philosophy* 19 (1970):41–53.

Grimault, Marguerite. *La mélancolie de Kierkegaard*. Paris: Aubier-Montagne, 1965.

Heinecken, Martin J. "The Border Line of the Humorist." *The Moment Before God: An Interpretation of Kierkegaard*. Philadelphia: Muhlenberg, 1956. Pp. 311–314.

———. "Irony and Humor." *The Moment before God: An Interpretation of Kierkegaard*. Philadelphia: Muhlenberg, 1956. Pp. 309–11.

Hirsch, Emanuel. *Kierkegaard-Studien*. 2 vols. Gütersloh: C. Bertelsmann, 1933. 2:759ff.

Holm, Søren. *Humor; en Æsthetisk Studie*. Copenhagen: Graabrødre torvs antikvariat, 1964.

Holmer, Paul. "Something about What Makes It Funny." *Soundings* 57.2 (1974): 157–74.

Jolivet, Régis. "L'ironie et l'humour." *Aux sources de L'existentialisme chrétien: Kierkegaard*. Paris: A. Fayard, 1958. Pp. 180–83.

Kierkegaard, Søren. "Humor, Irony, The Comic." *Søren Kierkegaard's Journals and Papers*. Ed. and trans. Howard V. Hong and Edna H. Hong. 4 vols. Bloomington: Indiana University Press, 1967–75. 2:248–79, 585–89.

———. *The Laughter Is on My Side: An Imaginative Introduction to Kierkegaard*. Ed. Roger Poole and Henrik Stangerup. Princeton: Princeton University Press, 1989.

Mackey, Louis. "Almost in Earnest." *Kierkegaard: A Kind of Poet*. Philadelphia: University of Pennsylvania Press, 1971. Pp. 133–95.

Malantschuk, Gregor. *Kierkegaard's Thought*. Ed. and trans. Howard V. Hong and Edna H. Hong. Princeton: Princeton University Press, 1971. Pp. 41–60, 150–52, 211–16, 274–80.

Martin, Harold Victor. *Kierkegaard, the Melancholy Dane*. New York: Philosophical Library, 1950.

Niebuhr, H. Richard. "Søren Kierkegaard." *Christianity and the Existentialists*. Ed. Carl Michalson. New York: Scribner, 1956. Pp. 23–42.

Nissen, Lowell Allen. *Kierkegaard on Humor*. M.A. thesis, University of Minnesota, 1958.

Parrill, Lloyd Ellison. "The Concept of Humor in the Pseudonymous Works of Søren Kierkegaard." Diss., Drew University, 1975.

Percy, Walker. "The Message in the Bottle." *Thought* 34 (Fall 1959): 405–33.

Pivcevic, Edo. *Ironie als Daseinsform bei Sören Kierkegaard.* Gütersloh: Gütersloher, 1960.

Rougemont, Denis de. "Kierkegaard's Irony." *Arizona Quarterly* 1 (Summer 1945): 4–6.

Schousboe, Julius. "Om Begrebete Humor hos Søren Kierkegaard. En filosofisk afhandling." Diss., University of Copenhagen, 1925.

Shmuëli, Adi. *Kierkegaard and Consciousness.* Princeton: Princeton University Press, 1971.

Sontag, Frederick. "Melancholy/Humor." *A Kierkegaard Handbook.* Atlanta: John Knox Press, 1979. Pp. 81–91.

Stendal, Brita K. "Climacus-S. Kierkegaard-Anti-Climacus." *Søren Kierkegaard.* Boston: Twayne, 1976. Pp. 162–94.

Theunissen, Michael. "Die ernste Ironie und der ernste Humor." *Der Begriff ernst bei Søren Kierkegaard.* Freiburg: Karl Alber, 1958. Pp. 66–73.

Thomte, Reidar. *Kierkegaard's Philosophy of Religion.* Princeton: Princeton University Press, 1949. Pp. 99–102.

GENERAL THEORY OF HUMOR

Aristotle. *The Basic Works of Aristotle.* Ed. R. McKeon. New York: Random House, 1941.

Bergson, Henri Louis. *Laughter: An Essay on the Meaning of the Comic.* New York: Macmillan, 1912.

Freud, Sigmund. "The Relation of Wit to Dreams and to the Unconscious." *Basic Writings of Sigmund Freud.* Ed. and trans. A. A. Brill. New York: Modern Library, 1938. Pp. 745–61.

———. "Wit and the Various Forms of the Comic." *Basic Writings of Sigmund Freud.* Ed. and trans. A. A. Brill. New York: Modern Library, 1938. Pp. 762–803.

Huizinga, Johan. *Homo Ludens: A Study of the Play-Element in Culture.* Boston: Beacon, 1950.

Hyers, Conrad, ed. *Holy Laughter: Essays on Religion in the Comic Perspective.* New York: Seabury, 1969.

Moltmann, Jürgen. *Theology of Play.* New York: Harper and Row, 1972.

Nevo, Ruth. "Toward a Theory of Comedy." *Journal of Aesthetics and Art Criticism* 21 (Spring 1963): 327–32.

Polanyi, Michael. *The Tacit Dimension.* Garden City, N.J.: Doubleday, 1966.

Scott, Nathan A., Jr. "The Bias of Comedy and the Narrow Escape into Faith." *Christian Scholar* 44 (Spring 1961): 9–39.

Shaw, Esther B. "Comedy, a Very Serious Matter." *Philosophy of Education: Proceedings* 22 (1966): 125–28.

Villiers, Andre. "The Comic and Its Uses." *Diogenes* 75 (Fall 1971): 58–84.

Zucker, Wolfgang. "The Clown as the Lord of Disorder." *Theology Today* 24 (October 1967): 3.

INDEX

Holberg, Ludvig, 89–90, 121, 214
Holophernes, 224
homeliness, 311–12
Hong, Edna, 6–7
Hong, Howard, 6–7
hope, 82–83
horseflies, 10
horses, 26, 49, 61, 77
human classification, 47
humiliation, 65–66
hypotheses, 226–27

idealism, 305–7
identity diffusion, 139–40
illusion(s), 96, 221
imagination, 47
immediate, immediacy, 13, 101–2, 117, 199, 274, 317–18
immobility, 81–82
immortality, 88–90, 124–26
impatience, 81–82
impracticality, 265–66
impression management, 251–53
Incarnation, the, 12, 35–37, 99–102, 105
incommensurability, 12, 137, 228
incompleteness, 291–92
incomprehensibility, 104–5
incongruities, 10–12, 77–79. See also contradiction
indecision, 52. See also decision
indictment, 71–72
indifference, 282
inference, 108, 298–99
information overload, 223–25
innkeepers, 231. See also tavern keepers
innocence, 187
insecurity, 79
insurance, erotic, 174
integrity, 285–86, 315–16
interruption, 205
inventors, inventions, 227–28, 269–70
inwardness, 70, 137, 207, 223, 246, 311

ironists, irony, 13, 17–20, 22–26, 205–6, 243, 279–80, 309

jellyfish, 85
jest, 310
Jesuits, 167
Jesus Christ. See Christ
Jews, 49
Johannes Climacus: about, 28–30, 208–10, 299–304; selections in the voice of, 46, 51, 55, 63, 65, 67–68, 73, 77, 85, 87, 90, 92, 95, 98, 100–103, 107, 115–16, 118, 120, 125, 129, 133, 135–37, 140–43, 160, 199–201, 203–6, 215, 223–24, 227–28, 231–33, 254, 281, 290–92, 296–97, 299, 302–5, 310–11, 315–16
Johannes Climacus, or De Omnibus Dubitandum Est, 299, 302–4
John Climacus, Saint, 23, 28–29
journalism, 41, 241–47
Judge for Yourself!, 96–97, 106, 123, 144, 173, 286–87
Judge William: about, 8, 14–16, 20; selections in the voice of, 52, 62, 66, 81, 84, 88–89, 110, 131, 151, 167–68, 170, 173, 178, 183, 186–87, 220, 274
Judgment Day, 117–18
justice, 122
justification, 297–98

Kerner, Justinus, 281
Kierkegaard, Søren: editorial apparatus of selections and, 6–7; melancholia/despair of, 2, 5; modern standards of humor and, 2–3; pseudonymous voices of, 8, 14, 18, 28–30; theory of comedy and, 3, 8–35; translation of, 6–7
kings, emperors, monarchs, 9, 46–47, 72, 99, 104, 113, 140, 156, 260
Knights, The (Aristophanes), 243–44
knowledge, 222–25, 296

333

laughter, laughing, 173, 197–98, 203–7
Laughter Is on My Side, The (ed. Poole and Stangerup), 8
leadership, 230, 250
leap of faith, 50–51
legitimacy, 231
lifeboats, 80
lifelong tasks, 63, 85, 288–89
listening, hearing, 78, 157
literary criticism, 193–96
living in vain, 292
living off nothing, 148–49
longing, 81
loss, 80–81, 84, 91, 132–33, 184–85
love, 69, 91–92, 97, 156–57, 163–69, 175–76, 188–89, 223
Lowrie, Walter, 7
lust, 274
Luther, Martin, 14, 104, 141, 238

majors, 230
male vulnerability, 174–78, 182–85
marriage, marital duty, 15–17, 134–35, 164–68, 170–73, 175, 177–78, 183, 186
Martin, W.B.J., 9
martyrs, martyrdom, 72–73, 80, 286
Master Erik, 168
Mathews, Joseph, 9
meaning, 51–52, 59, 64, 97–98, 123
mediation, 253
medicine, 226–28
mediocrity, 285–86
men of distinction, 264–65
mentors, 83
merchants, 80, 82, 241, 268
miracles, 120
miscommunication, 200–201
mistakes. *See* errors
misunderstanding, 205, 288, 290, 304
modernity, modern age, 96–97, 118, 138–42, 220, 248, 251–52, 285–86. *See also* present age, the

Moment, The, 49, 139, 147, 149, 160
monarchs. *See* kings, emperors, monarchs
money, 22, 65–66, 72–73, 105, 175, 206–7
morality, 83
mourning, 91
movements, 239–40, 250, 257
Mozart, Wolfgang Amadeus, 195–96
mundane, the, 150–51, 214–15
mutterers, 278–79
Myson, 173

names, 85
Nebuchadnezzar, 130
"Newspaper Articles 1854–1855" (in The Moment *and Late Writings*), 96, 141, 268
New Testament, 139, 141
Nicolaus Notabene, 49, 119, 121, 159, 166, 194–95, 212, 214, 253, 259, 291, 304, 307
Niebuhr, H. Richard, 9
Niebuhr, Reinhold, 9
nightsticks, 199–200
nostalgia, 281–82
Notebene, Nicolaus. *See* Nicolaus Notabene
numerical ratios, 237–38

Oehlen Schläger, A. G., 171
offence, 104
Olson, Regina, 29
On Authority and Revelation, 80, 146, 150, 159, 213, 222, 240, 246, 250, 255, 257, 264
"Open Letter, An" (in *The* Corsair *Affair*), 237–38
opulence, 83
ordination, 149–50
others, 249
owners, 118

suffering, 11–12, 13, 17, 31–32, 39–41, 80–83, 109–10, 199–200, 226, 263, 288–89
suicide, 10, 15, 176, 247
suspicion, 122
Swenson, David F., 7
swimmers, swimming, 52–53

Taciturnus. *See* Frater Taciturnus
tailors, 307
talent, 131, 229
talkativeness, 77–78, 246
talking machines, 278–79
taste, 229
tavern keepers, 21. *See also* innkeepers
taxonomy, 47
teachers, teaching, 117, 155, 313–16
temperance societies, 258–59
tennis balls, 131–32
Terence, 314
thanksgiving, 136
theater, the, 147, 313
theologians, theology, 119–23
thieves, 188–89
thinkers, thinking, 65, 89–90, 118, 141, 160, 300–303
thought, 296–99
three-cornered hats, 79
Tieck, Ludwig, 183
time, 12, 17–19, 100–101, 108–9, 188
tipping one's hat, 194–95
titles, 229–30
toll clerks, 255
Tornacensis, Simon, 113
Town Hall, marketing of, 267
toys, 132–33
tragedy, tragic, 32–33, 177, 220
trains, 84
traitors, 177
transformation, 85

travelers, traveling, 78, 82, 105, 116, 298
trousers, 134–35
truth, truth-telling, 69, 96, 100, 203–7, 241, 244–46, 268–69, 315
turtles, 171
Two Ages, 207, 219, 221, 244, 247, 249, 252, 260, 306

ugliness, 176, 310–12
uncertainty, 55, 113, 211–12
understanding, 77, 89, 131–32. *See also* misunderstanding
uneasiness, 108
unexpected, the, 22, 45–46, 200
universities, 285–89

vaccination, certificate of, 140–41
vacillation, 50–52
value, 72–73, 228, 251
veracity, 147
Victor Eremita, 60, 171, 184–85
Vigilius Haufniensis, 62, 64, 78, 113, 126, 131–32, 156, 231, 234, 251, 255, 275–77, 279, 293, 298
virtue, 67, 131

waiters, 120–21, 140
walking on all fours, 251
warning signs, 163–64
water inspectors, acting, 194
wealth, 122
wedding anniversaries, 170
whoremongers, whorehouses, 138
William. *See* Judge William
William Afham, 78, 92, 164, 174, 177
winged pen, 69–71
wings, 82
wishes, wishing, 107, 135–36, 187
wit, witticisms, 47, 207
women, 174, 179–85
words, 72, 97–98, 200–201
work, 65–66, 88–89, 123